A Matter of Basic Principles

Bill Gothard and the Christian Life

Foreword by Ron Rhodes

Don Veinot
Joy Veinot
Ron Henzel

A Matter of Basic Principles

Bill Gothard and the Christian Life

Copyright © 2002 by Midwest Christian Outreach, Inc.
Lombard, Illinois

Published by 21st Century Press
2131 W. Republic Rd.
PMB 41
Springfield, MO 65807

ISBN 0-9717009-2-3

Cover: Mark Fredrickson
Book Design: Lee Fredrickson and Terry White

Dedication

In Mark 10:13, children were brought directly to our Lord. There was no "chain of command" or other mediators. The disciples rebuked those who brought them. What was our Lord's response? Jesus said, "Suffer the little children to come unto me, and forbid them not: for of such is the kingdom of God." (Mark 10:14)

With this in mind, we dedicate this volume to the Lord Jesus Christ and the children, families, and churches who have suffered under the bondage of the teachings of Bill Gothard and his *Institute in Basic Life Principles.*

What Leaders Are Saying About This Book

This book truly surprised me! I knew that Gothard's exegesis was wooden, that he was trying to introduce a Romanist view of divorce into the Bible-believing churches and that he had sundry other strange views. But, bad as those things are, what I read on the pages you hold in your hand goes far beyond them. Unless you are one of the few who are on the "inside" of the movement, I suspect that you too will be astounded and dismayed exactly as I was. This is a must read for all thinking believers who wish to protect their churches.

—Dr. Jay Adams
Author of Competent to Counsel
Professor of Practical Theology
Westminster Theological Seminary
Philadelphia, PA

The Veinots and Henzel have taken on an important task in responding to Bill Gothard. A Matter of Basic Principles: Bill Gothard and the Christian Life is a much-needed book that should be read by virtually all evangelical pastors—and all supporters of Bill Gothard. Their book is provocative, well-researched, easy to read and understand. Through it all they are fair and demonstrate a genuine concern for the state of the 21st century Church. I recommend A Matter of Basic Principles to anyone who has attended a Gothard seminar, is considering attending one, or just wants to know more about the ministry of Bill Gothard.

—Dr. Robert B. Stewart
Assistant Professor of Philosophy and Theology
New Orleans Baptist Theological Seminary
New Orleans, LA

The Institute in Basic Youth Conflicts (now known as the IBLP) began in 1964 under the leadership of Bill Gothard and enjoyed unprecedented expansion during the '70s. As board members we recognized that God was at work in this ministry.

In May 1980 we were shocked to learn of gross immorality that had prevailed for years among the staff under Bill's supervision as president. Bill failed to share this information with the board nor did he seek their counsel. By the end of that year it became apparent that Bill continued his authoritarian style of leadership, dismissing those on the board as well as staff who disagreed with him. Consequently I found it necessary to resign.

As early as 1973 questions were raised about IBYC/IBLP by various individuals such as Dr. Ronald B. Allen, Dr. Earl Radmacher, Wilfred Bockelman and others. In the pages of this volume — which everyone who is involved with IBYC/IBLP should seriously evaluate —the reader will find that repeated attempts have been made to dialogue with Bill Gothard about his lack of submission to authority, his lack of accountability, and his failure to apply biblical principles to his own life. Bill's teaching on legalism, law, and grace deserves careful examination. The authors are to be commended for their concern in publishing this helpful volume.

—Dr. Samuel J. Schultz.
Professor Emeritus of Old Testament
Wheaton College
Wheaton, IL

Early in the 1970's, I attended my first of four or five Basic Youth Conflicts seminars. Later, with men from the church where I was, I attended the Advanced Seminar in Los Angeles and later several of the Ministers' One-Day Conferences. There were areas of concern each time I attended, but they did not seem to be a major issue and I did not want to cause division in the work of God.

It did concern me that Bill Gothard's entire approach was based on stories and experience more than the Word of God. This was presented to him numerous times by others. In recent years, however, I have cautioned others about the cultic tendencies that

I have observed.

This volume is a well-documented and carefully studied evaluation of, and warning concerning, Bill Gothard and the IBLP. Therefore, because of its findings, it needs to be read by every person who has ever attended the seminars. My prayer is for all those in Christian leadership to walk in truth.

—Dr. Elwood H. Chipchase, President
Calvary Bible College & Theological Seminary
Belton, MO

This book is needed in many of our Evangelical Christian churches because

1. It's a challenge to churches and Christians to test those teachers that are in our churches and the Christian community. This doesn't only apply to Bill Gothard and his Institute of Basic Life Principles (IBLP), but to many other ministries.

2. It's balanced by going into the positive ends like giving a history of the problems that Christians were facing in their Christian living and in their own faith, how IBLP came into existence, and what attracted Christians to IBLP.

3. It's a demonstration on how the principles of a Berean are to be carried out in testing what Bill Gothard teaches. When you read about the problems relating to Bill Gothard, the problems are logically expressed by properly applying the Scriptures and using Gothard's own IBLP teachings. In addition cases are documented which make us question the foundation of IBLP.

4. The book starts off by challenging us as Christians and concludes in the same way. It's not just about

questioning a false teacher; it's about waking us up. Does it take tragedies like Jonestown, Waco, and events related to doomsday cults to wake us up?

Adjunct Professor at Golden GateTheological Seminary
Host of Contending for the Faith on
KFAX AM
Pastor of Tiburon Christian Fellowship
Tiburon, CA

The authors of this carefully documented book have not written an angry polemic against Bill Gothard and his ministry. Instead, they have carefully laid out the scriptural reasons for grave concern over the teachings and methods of this man and his organization. This book serves not only to reveal what is being taught at IBLP, but issues a clear warning to all Christians about the dangers of scriptural distortion, however subtle.

—*Ingrid J. Schlueter*
Producer and Co-Host
Crosstalk Radio Talk Show
Milwaukee, WI

I have followed the teachings of the Institute of Basic Youth Conflicts (now IBLP) from its inception over 35 years ago. From the beginning I have been deeply concerned about the misuse and distortion of the teachings of God's Word in their interpretation and application. I have had numerous occasions to voice my concerns in person and by telephone to Bill Gothard, his father, and other of his siblings. I have listened to the complaints of such scriptural abuse from many former administrators and staff of the Institute. I believe that Don and Joy Veinot and Ron Henzel of Midwest Christian Outreach have done the Christian public a tremendous service in their careful analysis and consequent warnings about the teachings that are promulgated by

IBLP. The terrible hurt to so many staff and others that became public in the early '80s need never have happened if there had been the humility to be corrected by numerous pastors and teachers. My prayer is that God will be pleased to use this work to bring the correction that is needed to bring the IBLP teachings into compliance with the Apostle Paul's admonition of 2 Timothy 2:15.

—*Earl D. Radmacher, Th.D.*
Distinguished Professor of Systematic Theology and
President Emeritus of Western Seminary
Portland, OR

Sometimes a book is described as "a page-turner," or "something I simply could not put down." But I found in my reading of this book that I put it down often. I found I could only read a chapter or two at a time; more would be too much. Feelings of incredulity, sorrow, even tears, and at times anger—such were responses that impeded a fast or leisurely reading of this book.

William Gothard has many followers. His organization claims that more than two-and-one-half million people have taken part in one or more of his seminars over a period of more than three decades. This is an amazing statistic! Countless people have made decisions for Christ, have found ways of renewal in their marriages, and have been strengthened in their families through the principles they have learned in week-long seminars, pastors' conferences, home-school curricula, and a wide variety of published materials coming from the Gothard organization. Well-respected pastors across the nation have encouraged congregations to attend seminars en masse, even by arranging for chartered busses and group discounts. Massive funds have been raised to build retreat centers to further the work of Bill Gothard.

Bill Gothard! He is a living Christian institution!

So why, one would well ask, why would anyone wish to write a book (much less *read* a book) that brings a critical eye on such a successful ministry, or on such a revered figure as Bill Gothard?

Pastor after pastor has told me over the years something along this line:

> Well, sure, there are some problems here and there in Gothard's use of Scripture, in his confusion of his own personal, even quirky, ideas with those that are taught in the Word of God, and in the curious dogmatism with which he presents his idiosyncratic views. But, with all the supporters he has, he must be doing something right.

Finally, here is a book-length treatment of the Bill Gothard ministry that I can hold out to such pastors and other devoted Christian persons and say, "Oh really? Read this book and see if you still believe that the issues are only some problems here and there."

In *A Matter of Basic Principles*, the authors have sifted through an amazing amount of material, have sorted through many issues, and have presented a powerful indictment of many serious errors in Gothard's teaching, the alarming level of hypocrisy in his personal behavior, and his decades-long resistance to consider correction and improvement of biblical understanding by people who once really wished to be a help to him. The book is marked by grace, logic, wit, and common sense. It is also focused on Scripture *sans* twisting.

At one point in this book the authors evaluate Gothard's peculiar teaching on the subject of courtship in this manner:

> We find Gothard's courtship teaching to be unbiblical, unfair, unreasonable, unworkable, and ultimately unwise. Other than these few considerations, we have no major problem with it.

After reading this book, it is likely that you will conclude this is a proper summary not only of Gothard's views on courtship, but on a great deal of his entire ministry.

The authors have not just dealt with ideas; they have interacted with people. It is in the records of damaged lives that this book is so difficult to read as a "page turner." When a person presents distortions of Scripture as though these ideas are the true teaching of Scripture, it is not just that the person has erred. This is not just a "goof." These errors impact people's lives; sometimes the results are horrendous. It is for these reasons that the Apostle Paul spoke so strongly against false teachers in the first century. Paul had occasion even to speak directly against Peter when Peter moved slightly from grace. Bill Gothard has not moved slightly; this book demonstrates that he misunderstands grace as much as he confuses the function biblical dietary laws had in ancient Israel with principles for "good eating" among Christians today.

One more note: The writers score strongly in their many witty analogies from film, fiction, television, and other elements of popular culture. This makes a solid book more enjoyable for the teachable person to read. My suspicion is that when Mr. Gothard reads this book, not only will he continue to resist its intended correction in his personal life and public ministry; he is also rarely to "get" the wonderful jokes in these allusions, as they come from a world (the world in which real people live) in which he has had so very little experience.

–Dr. *Ronald B. Allen*
Professor of Biblical Exposition
Dallas Theological Seminary
Dallas, TX

Contents

Acknowledgements

This work really has been a team effort, and we want to thank those who have so greatly encouraged and assisted us each step of the way. The former IBLP staff members and "alumni" who were willing to share their stories and pray for us. The group which included pastors, former and current IBLP staff and "alumni" who read through each chapter as we went along to suggest corrections and clarifications as well as to point out if we were getting mean-spirited and help us to refocus. We also want to thank Rev. G. Richard Fisher, Dr. Harry Adams, Dr. Norman Geisler, Dr. Earl Radmacher, and Dr. Ronald B. Allen for their assistance in assuring doctrinal integrity and supplementary information. We want to extend our deepest appreciation to Mr. Robin Phillips for his research and participation in writing the chapter on courtship. He made invaluable contributions to this subject. We thank the editors Paul Carden, Corkey McGehee, and David Penny for their diligence, patience and professionalism.

We also want to thank our families for their sacrifice of our time to this project as well as for their love, prayers and encouragement. We thank all of the above for keeping us accountable through this process. And finally, we thank our Lord and Savior Who delivered us from the bondage of sin and the bondage of legalism.

Foreword

I became a Christian when I was a teenager. Though that was a long time ago (*too* long), I can still vividly remember the announcements our church youth leader made regarding Bill Gothard's Institute in Basic Youth Conflicts, scheduled for our area the following month. He urged everyone to go. He said Gothard had lots of great principles engineered to help young people live more effectively and deal with some of the problems unique to kids our age. It sounded relevant.

For whatever reason, I didn't go. But lots of my friends did. One of my closer buddies let me look at a Gothard manual the following week, and as I flipped through it, I carefully digested some of the principles and looked up some of the accompanying Bible verses Gothard cited. In some cases, I remember thinking to myself, "Where did he get *that* principle from *that* Bible verse?" As a young Christian, I had no great skill at interpreting Scripture. In fact, at that time I definitely fit into the category of "biblically challenged." I didn't know much. But still, even as a young Christian, I distinctly remember coming across a number of principles where I felt that Gothard was reading something into a particular verse that simply was not there. I wondered at the time if anyone else felt this way, or if perhaps I was just missing something.

Today, some thirty years later, I have the *same* opinion – only now, my convictions run much deeper. After reading this new book, it is clear that the problems with Gothard's Bible interpretations go deeper than I ever imagined.

One reason this is a concern for me personally is that what a person comes to believe doctrinally will inevitably mold or at least influence his or her worldview, attitudes, and behavior – whether in a positive, wholesome way, or in a negative, destructive way. By way of example, a person dying of cancer may turn on the television at night and hear a Word-Faith televangelist say that if you are sick, it shows you have a lack of faith are out of tune with God, and perhaps a demon is residing in you.

15

Upon hearing and believing such damaging doctrines, you may suffer immense guilt and even despair. (*Believe me, this has happened to some people.*)

By contrast, *correct* doctrinal belief has a positive, beneficial effect on people. Biblical doctrine (based on a correct and balanced interpretation of Scripture) enables us to develop a realistic worldview, without which we are doomed to ineffectual living (Matthew 22:23-33; Romans 12:3; Timothy 4:3-4). Moreover, biblical doctrine can protect us from false beliefs that can lead to destructive behavior (1 Timothy 4:1-6; 2 Timothy 2:18; Titus 1:11). The person who thoroughly understands God's grace, for example, will be insulated from the debilitating guilt and bondage to legalism that many Christians suffer who do not understand God's grace. The person who understands the biblical teaching that we cannot set dates for Christ's return will not succumb to unwise decisions based on a belief that the Lord is coming in the next few years - like not saving for retirement, or putting off a college education (*as some have done in the past*).

It is in view of such practical factors that the present book takes on importance — for this book puts the doctrinal teachings of the popular Bill Gothard under the scrutiny of the Bible and seeks to demonstrate how some of his teachings and principles can have a detrimental effect on people. The authors do not presume to judge Mr. Gothard's heart. They do not seek to personally attack Mr. Gothard. Rather, in the name of truth, they focus primary attention on his *teachings* and the *effect* of those teachings on people. Among other things, they demonstrate quite convincingly that Gothard wrongly defines grace and falls prey to legalism. They also take him to task for often citing biblical passages to argue points and principles that they do not prove. They *insist* on being biblical.

I commend this book to Christians everywhere who, like the Bereans of old, seek to insure that *all* they believe is thoroughly biblical (Acts 17:11).

—*Dr. Ron Rhodes*
Reasoning from the Scriptures Ministries
Rancho Santa Margarita, CA

Prologue

The Birth of a Movement

Where does one begin analyzing a movement such as Bill Gothard's IBLP?[1] According to the Institute, there are more than 2.5 million "alumni."[2] In addition to the Basic Seminar, there are the Advanced Seminar, Pastor's Seminars, home-schooling curriculum, Medical Institute of America, a correspondence law school, and the *Character First!* curriculum for cities, towns, schools, and even nations. Bill Gothard has managed to create a cradle-to-grave system for his followers. It would seem reasonable to start with the beginning of the ministry, but that wouldn't really tell the whole story. After all, movements don't start in a vacuum; they spring forth from the soil in which they were planted. The same is true with IBLP. To examine the soil that germinated this particular seed, we need to look back a few hundred years.

How Secular Humanism Took Over America

Dr. Norman L. Geisler has an excellent message titled, "How Secular Humanism Took Over America."[3] In it he chronicles the birth of our nation and certain events which have led us to today's culture. An element that Dr. Geisler does not address in this message, which is pertinent to our study, is: Where was the church through all of this? With his permission, I will use that outline and add in the other side of the equation to establish the setting in which IBLP was born and developed by Bill Gothard.

In 1776, the United States of America's *Declaration of Independence* was ratified and signed. In the second paragraph it reads, "We hold these truths to be self-evident, that all men are created equal, that they are endowed by their Creator with certain unalienable Rights, that among these are Life, Liberty, and the pursuit of happiness." With these important 35 words,

America's birth certificate affirmed that we are all created beings, which assumes a Creator, and acknowledges that the rights we have come from Him.

It should come as no surprise that reasoning and faith were intimately woven together in the lives of America's founding fathers. Traditionally Christians have been the great thinkers, artists, musicians, poets, scientists, etc., down through history, and the influence of this tradition was felt in the late 1700s as well. Intellectual and spiritual pursuits went hand in hand. Public and private prayer were as important as public and private debate.

The Age of Reason

But this doesn't mean that the United States of America was necessarily founded as a "Christian" nation. Christianity had a strong influence among the founders, even though some of them were deists who denied the miracles of Scripture. While they believed that God created everything that exists, and that we would ultimately stand before him to account for our actions, a few early Americans went so far as to speak out against the Bible (e.g., Thomas Paine's book *The Age of Reason*). The new government secured and protected freedom of worship partially because of the oppressiveness of the European state church system, but also because voices were already being raised questioning whether Christianity was the only true faith.

Despite the propaganda of recent mythmakers, the period extending from the American Revolution to the beginning of the 19th century was, in reality, a period of steep decline for the church in both North America and Europe. Church attendance was at an all-time low, and many churches that survived were in the process of abandoning their commitment to the Scriptures. The corrosive influence of Enlightenment philosophy pervaded America's institutions of higher learning, turning thousands of young minds against the Gospel. Public morals had reached low-ebb, and some even wondered out loud whether Christianity itself would survive much longer.

Spiritually speaking, this new nation started down a very unsteady and uncertain course that would require divine intervention and correction. Fortunately, God remembered the spiritual faithfulness of the early colonial settlers and sent the Second Great Awakening in the early 1800s. If He had not intervened, today's America would look very different indeed from the one with which we're familiar.

We can be thankful that God's mercy and the Christian roots of American culture helped her weather these early storms. But seeds of secular humanism were sown in that period that would bear bitter fruit in our times.

If the concept of freedom of religion had taken firmer root in a society where the Christian church was strong, the spiritual history of late 18th and early 19th century America might read very differently today. We might read of men and women of God who fully utilized their freedom on behalf of the Gospel — who cooperated with each other to spread the truth of Jesus Christ and lovingly confronted, in a unified way, the enemies of Christianity. Things like this did eventually happen, but they were late in coming, and the delay gave ample opportunity for spiritual chaos to take root and spread.

History has taught us to expect that a great revival such as the Second Great Awakening would be followed by a period of spiritual chaos, as Satan vigorously countered the move of God with a move of his own. Hence the 19th century gave birth to many false "Christian" movements propagating many newly minted false Gospels.

Cult Explosion

It was a period marked by the "democratization" of religious belief — a time of folks doing spiritually what was right in their own eyes and following whatever spiritual fads and gurus

19

appealed to them. Indisputably, there was much "spiritual" fervor during this period, but "spirituality" does not necessarily have anything to do with the Christian faith. The schools of the higher critics had begun "demythologizing" the Scriptures, separating the faith from "the book" that had acted as its anchor throughout the centuries. Mystical pied pipers were more than willing to fill the void left by a gradual abandonment of the fundamentals of the faith.

In 1830 a young occultist, treasure seeker, and teller of tall tales by the name of Joseph Smith published a book now known as *The Book of Mormon*. Spiritism, although biblically condemned, had become popularly accepted, so Smith's claims of visits by "Heavenly Father" and Jesus were received without difficulty by some.

A few years later, in 1843, a Baptist minister by the name of William Miller believed that he had discerned the actual date for the return of Christ. Many of Miller's followers (known as Adventists) sold their possessions and awaited His arrival at the predicted time. It didn't happen. Miller then "realized" that his calculations had been "off" by a year, so he and most of his followers geared up for the new date of His arrival, which passed without incident. This false prophecy became known as "The Great Disappointment" for obvious reasons.

Out of ashes of "The Great Disappointment" came yet another new sect. A young Adventist woman by the name of Ellen Harmon, later to become Ellen G. White, claimed that she received a revelation from God to the effect that Miller's date had been correct after all — instead the expected event was wrong. 1844 was the date that Christ entered and cleansed the sanctuary. Though she offered no proof for her assertion, many of the "greatly disappointed" attached themselves to her, and the movement became known as the Seventh-day Adventist Church. The church had its formal beginning in 1863. Ellen White had "received revelation" that Sunday worship was the "mark of the beast" and that true Christians must keep the Sabbath and worship on Saturday.

The Adventist movement started by William Miller in the 1840's continued to split into numerous competing sects. Charles Taze Russell founded one of these Adventist "cousins" in the 1870's. He broke with his Second Adventist mentor, Nelson Barbour, and began publishing *Zion's Watchtower* in 1879. He had already rejected much of the Christian faith and claimed, as Joseph Smith and Ellen G. White had claimed before him, that he was "restoring" the true Christian faith. He was a religious eclectic, borrowing doctrines from various occult thinkers of his day and mixing them all together with run-of-the-mill Adventism to create his new "Bible Student" movement. He adopted such occult/pagan ideas as pyramidology, phrenology (purporting to prove a man's character by the shape of his head), and various other mystical and occult teachings. He also predicted the date of Christ's return, 1914, which of course failed, proving Russell to be a false prophet. Russell believed and taught that *he* was God's channel, and that it was necessary to study his books to gain a true understanding of spiritual things. Today the group Russell founded has been splintered into hundreds of different sects. Of these, the largest is the Watchtower Bible and Tract Society, popularly known as Jehovah's Witnesses.

A New Age of Age-old Mysticism

In 1875, Madame Helena Petrovna Blavatsky founded a metaphysical movement called the Theosophical Society. This mystic taught that God's wisdom is found in all religions — with the possible exception of biblical Christianity. Her disdain of Christianity is very apparent in this statement:

> The name has been used in a manner so intolerant and dogmatic, especially in our day, that Christianity is now the religion of arrogance, par excellence, a stepping-stone for ambition, a sinecure for wealth, sham, and power; a convenient screen for hypocrisy.[4]

21

Science and Health by Mary Baker Eddy, another religious mystic, was also published in 1875. Eight years later, in 1883, the *Key to the Scriptures* was added. Essentially, Eddy taught Hinduism using Christian terminology. She taught that life is an illusion, that there is no physical world and therefore no such thing as sickness. Any symptoms of illness that one experienced were merely a problem in thinking. It was claimed, of course, that this teaching came from God, that Eddy was merely a channel of the information to mankind. The Church of Christ Scientist (a.k.a. Christian Science) was founded in 1879 in Charlestown, Massachusetts.

Another "mind science" group began in 1889. Called simply Modern Thought, it was started under Charles and Myrtle Fillmore and borrowed heavily from New Thought and Christian Science. In 1890 the name was changed to Christian Science Thought, then simply to Thought in 1891, and renamed in 1895 as *Unity*, and is now known as the Unity School of Christianity. Hence, there is good evidence that they gave a lot of thought to their name, if nothing else.

These were just several among scores of strange new religious movements, aberrations, and cults that either sprang from America's own spiritual soil or opportunistically invaded it from overseas during the 19th century. Christians were not the only ones concerned about some of these movements. Samuel Clemens (a.k.a. Mark Twain), for example, expressed alarm at the growing financial and political clout of Christian Science. And early Illinois residents rose up against the misdeeds[5] of their Mormon neighbors. Joseph Smith was jailed and eventually killed in an exchange of gunfire with an enraged mob.

Atheism Goes Mainstream

On the philosophical front, in 1848 the Communist Manifesto, by Karl Marx and Fredrich Engels was published. These individuals took an essentially materialistic view of life. In their view, man was really in control of his own destiny and had made remarkable progress in controlling the forces of nature and growing toward his creative potential. It was a well-constructed view, and Marx, a formidable polemicist, argued his points with vigor.

In 1859, eleven years later, Charles Darwin published his work, *On the Origin of Species*. The first printing sold out the first day of publication. At this juncture, the religious and scientific communities began to part ways. Naturalistic materialism was displacing the biblical account of origins. Faith and reason seemed to be mutually exclusive ideas. Darwin applied his view to humans in 1871, and Darwinian evolution rocked the world. It utterly changed, for many, the view of our place in the world, and indeed our place in the universe and the hereafter.

Friedrich Neitzche, although an atheist himself, realized the moral implications inherent in a universe without God. In his work *The Gay Science* (sec. 125), he penned the words:

> God is dead! God remains dead! And we have killed him! How shall we console ourselves, the most murderous of all murderers? The holiest and the mightiest that the world has hitherto possessed, has bled to death under our knife – who will wipe away the blood from us?

Neitzche realized that if there is no God to Whom we are accountable and to Whom we owe obedience, then all things are permissible. There really is no right or wrong, good or evil in such a universe – there are just predator and prey.

Dis-harmonic Convergence

As we have already pointed out, this was also a period when theological liberalism and spiritistic occultism were competing with Christianity for the allegiance of mankind. The Scriptures had been under attack by the schools of higher critics for some time and were increasingly viewed as myth and fable to be believed only by the uneducated and fearful.

Perhaps if it had been atheism alone, or occultism alone, or liberalism alone, or the explosion of religious cults alone, that the church had to face, it may have put up a better fight. But with the convergence of all of these at the same point in time, vast inroads were made against the truth of the gospel. When the light of the gospel grows dim in any society, darkness takes over. Little could anyone have imagined, however, that these 19th century religious and secular philosophies would leave their bloody footprints all over the twentieth century.

Christians occasionally defended their faith against these new religious movements and atheistic philosophical ideas that were proliferating, but the response of the church was largely haphazard and uncoordinated. By the end of the 19th century, Christians had managed to forge many interdenominational alliances in such important areas as evangelism (e.g., D.L. Moody's ministry) and youth work (e.g., the YMCA). But any major united efforts among Christians to "earnestly contend for the faith which was once delivered unto the saints" (Jude 3) were perhaps 50 to 60 years away from being realized. Meanwhile, major historical events were on the horizon — events that many Christians would misinterpret as a signal to withdraw from interaction with society and culture altogether and complacently await the Second Coming.

Ushering in the Kingdom

As the 19th century came to a close, times were good. Many people both inside and outside the church believed that the world was witnessing the dawn of a Golden Age. They could point to marvelous technological advances — railroads, steamboats, electric motors, the telegraph and telephone, refrigeration, the light bulb — and a host of other inventions that were beginning to greatly raise the standard of living. Everyone became convinced that even greater marvels were right around the corner. The 1800s had given birth to mass communication, rapid transit, and the domestication of electricity for human use. It gave us break-throughs in astronomy, medicine, physics, and just about every science you can name. Why would anyone doubt that soon cures for every disease would be found, along with solutions for the age-old problems of poverty and war?

The general optimism of the age fueled the popularity of "postmillennialism" – the belief held by many Christians that the church would soon usher in the long-awaited Millennium, fol-lowed by Christ's return to accept His Kingdom. Liberal Christians carried aloft by that same optimism believed the 20th century would be "the Christian century," one in which their "gospel" of the "universal fatherhood of God and brotherhood of man" would spread throughout the world, resulting in global peace and harmony. They even began publishing a magazine named *The Christian Century*, which has somehow survived the 20th century's global wars and holocausts and is published by that same name today. The "Christian century" produced atroc-ities on a scale never imagined by these hopeful humanists – to say that their optimism about human nature was misplaced would be an understatement indeed.

Christians in Retreat

But beneath the surface of all this burgeoning and near-delirious optimism, there was ample reason for concern among Bible-believing Christians. Far from a global embracing of the Christian Gospel, the world was rapidly turning to mysticism and occultism to fill its spiritual need. The Scriptures were being further undermined by the higher critics. The Christian doctrine of origins was under attack by the scientific community. Atheistic philosophers had become the intellectual elite. Schools of higher learning, such as Harvard, Yale, and others originally founded to train ministers had long since abandoned the Christian faith, and indeed, seemed set to destroy it. Christians generally had no well-developed intellectual response to defend their faith against these challenges and so gradually began retreating from culture.

In 1893, the first Parliament of the World's Religions was held in Chicago. It was predominantly a Christian event, but a very articulate individual from India by the name of Swami Vivikananda made quite a favorable impression upon the assembly. East met West as Hinduism had now officially made its way to America. Vivikananda captured the minds and hearts of those attending. Hinduism and Darwinian evolution (which was being more commonly accepted) are very compatible belief systems. Darwinism asserts physical evolution through change and adaptation from lower forms of life to higher forms of life — Hinduism asserts spiritual evolution from lower forms of life to higher forms of life through reincarnation.

In an effort to address these attacks on the faith, Dickson, Torrey and Meyer edited a twelve-volume work, published between 1910 and 1915 and titled simply, *The Fundamentals*.

Christians who rejected theological liberalism and affirmed the cardinal truths delineated in these books came to be known as "fundamentalists." In its early days, fundamentalism was a broadbased movement which included some well-educated pastors, theologians, and lay people from a variety of denominational backgrounds. They disagreed over many things, but shared a high view of the Bible as God's inerrant Word, and a willingness to engage secular culture on issues essential to the Christian faith.

While *The Fundamentals* contains some flawed essays, it also preserves evidence that at the dawn of the 20th century there were still conservative Christians who could think deeply and articulate clearly on intellectual matters important to the Gospel. It was also a hopeful sign that Christians could unite to carry out the biblically mandated defense of the faith.

Postmillennialists may have taken this as yet another hopeful sign that the Millennium was imminent — error was now being refuted! However, with the incredible destruction, carnage, and human suffering brought about by the Great War (known today as World War I) only a few years later (1914-18), the postmillennial hopes of both conservative and liberal Christians were dashed. Europe — the continent with the world's most concentrated assortment of "Christian nations"— had slaughtered 10 million of its own in a four-year bloodbath in which every invention that supposedly heralded the Millennium had been pressed into murderous service. Plowshares had been beaten into swords pruning hooks into spears. By the time the U.S. entered the fray, "atrocity," "trench warfare," and even "genocide" had already become familiar words in the American vocabulary.

The Ascension of Dispensationalism

By 1920, the optimistic, classic theological liberalism of the 19th century was dead. But so was optimistic conservative Christianity. While dejected liberals turned to such fresh theological develop- ments as Karl Barth's "Neo-Orthodoxy," many conservative Christians (by now sometimes called fundamentalists) turned away from postmillennialism and toward a premillennial belief which denied that the church would ever usher in the Millennium. Sobered by the lessons learned of the depths of human evil, many now believed that things would only get worse and worse until Christ Himself came to intervene in a global Armageddon. Most who held this view called themselves "dispensationalists." Prior to the catastrophe of World War I, postmillennialists had scoffed at dispensational premillennialists for their pessimistic outlook. Not anymore — the tables had turned.

One of the things postmillennialists feared would happen if dispensationalism spread throughout the church was that Christians would give up trying to improve the world around them and withdraw from society in general. Such isolationism was by no means an essential feature of dispensationalism, but some of the more extreme elements in that movement displayed those tendencies and justified the fears of the postmillennialists to an unfortunate extent.

A considerable number of dispensationalists and others

reasoned that if society was only going to deteriorate until Christ returned, why waste time, energy, and resources to effect only limited, short-term betterment? Why get involved in civic affairs, such as the public school system? Why dirty our hands in the political arena or run for public office? Why debate with atheists or try to reach out to cultists with an apologetic for the faith? The ship was going down. So, as far as some were concerned, dispensationalism had provided a theological basis for complete withdrawal from "this present evil age."

Of course, not all conservative Christians, dispensational or otherwise, were convinced that this was the right path to take, but in the mid-1920s a media event would cause most fundamentalists to beat a hasty retreat from engagement with society in the cause of the Gospel.

A Pivotal Event

Darwinian evolution by this juncture had made great strides in science and education and was moving quickly into every aspect of cultural thinking. To stem the tide and protect its young people from this anti-Christian notion, the state of Tennessee passed a law forbidding the teaching of evolution in school. The ACLU, ever the self-appointed champion of the "oppressed," advertised to find a teacher that would be willing to step up and challenge the law in court. A part-time teacher, John Scopes, took the step. Looking back, the 1925 trial was probably more hype than anything else and served primarily to get the town of Dayton, Tennessee, on the map. The textbook that John Scopes was using would be an extreme embarrassment to enlightened humanists of our day, teaching as it did that blacks are the lowest form of evolved humans while caucasian Europeans were the highest form of humanity.

The theatre of the event was the main attraction to the masses — it was billed as a clash of titans. William Jennings Bryan came to town to defend the law — Clarence Darrow to argue that the law was unconstitutional. In reality, of course, this battle was not really fought over science or law. It was fought over competing faiths — the Darwinist's faith in the theory of evolution versus the Christian's faith in God and the Bible — and the stakes were high. The ultimate winner would set the moral boundaries (or upset them) for the nation and the world. For approximately 1700 years, Christianity had been the predominant worldview in the west, but the world was about to witness "the changing of the guard."

Ironically, in the Scopes trial Clarence Darrow argued that it would be sheer bigotry to teach only one view of origins — ironic in light of the fact that Darwinists today demand that we only teach one view of origins: theirs. But that's another subject for another day.

The Christian "side" prevailed in the trial, but the battle for the minds of the succeeding generations was only beginning, and the church was ill prepared for the fight. The young would be the target; "intellectual acceptance" would be the bait. In the course of time, many young people who were raised in Christian or nominally Christian homes were sent to the universities, where they were taught to *abandon* the faith in which they were raised and embrace the "thinking man's" faith of secular humanism and Darwinian evolution.

Phillip Johnson in his excellent book, *The Wedge of Truth*, tells of one such individual, Philip Wentworth, who entered Harvard in 1924. Johnson points out that in 1932 the *Atlantic Monthly* published Wentworth's essay *What College Did to My Religion*. Johnson himself entered Harvard in 1957 and writes, "We both encountered an institution that had long ago abandoned its origins as a seminary for Christian ministers and was pursuing its current naturalistic faith with at least as much confidence as the seventeenth-century Puritans had once had in the providence of God. Wentworth says he came to Harvard with a strong Christian faith, which was then (to his surprise) undermined by the education he received there."[6]

Christians Leave Academia

Despite the fact that old-line theological liberalism was in disarray and decline after World War I, it retained its hold on American institutions of higher learning, effectively shutting conservative views out of higher education. Fundamentalists responded in kind to protect their flock, differing only in technique. What liberals had accomplished through the political manipulation of the academy, fundamentalists accomplished through sheer authoritarianism. Christian young people would be kept "safe," not by training Christian youth to respond intellectually to the liberal arguments, but by keeping them out of liberal universities. Thus, liberal views would simply not be heard, except as they were filtered through fundamentalist polemics. Certainly no dialogue between the two camps would be encouraged.

As a result, the 1930s witnessed the isolation, intellectual stagnation, and ideological hardening of the "fundamentalist movement." What began as an attempt to bring Christians back to the fundamentals of the faith and stem the tide of apostasy now forsook altogether the notion of challenging culture and answering the attacks on the faith. Christians, having abandoned the institutions of higher learning, started a sort of "Christians Only" college and university system called the Bible College Movement. Over the next 10-15 years hundreds of Bible colleges were founded. Often, these schools indoctrinated Christian young people, teaching them *what* to think instead of *how* to think. By and large they did not stress scholarship, replacing intellectual pursuit with a more authoritarian approach to higher education.

And Then Along Came John

Just as many fundamentalists were climbing down into their cultural manholes and pulling the covers over their heads, seeds of radical social change were being sown. In 1933 John Dewey authored the Humanist Manifesto. In it he argued that there is no creator, no creation, and no moral absolutes. This was a sharp departure from the birth certificate of the nation, the Declaration of Independence, which affirmed belief in all three. In 1934 Dewey authored a book titled *A Common Faith*, in which he further argued for abortion, euthanasia, and for the aggressive teaching of these views.

Also in1934, the Teacher's College of Columbia University took up the same banner as John Dewey in using education to accomplish social engineering:

> The first issue of *The Social Frontier*, produced by Teacher's College of Columbia University, urges the remaking of American society through the schools. The journal's first editorial says that "for the American people the age of individualism in economy is closing and the age of collectivism is beginning." This journal describes not "teachers" but "educational workers." It says these must join "into a mighty instrument of group consensus, harmonious expression, and collective action." Overtly urging teachers (sorry, educational workers) to indoctrinate students, the journal soon calls for a "united front" between progressives and Marxists, as the brief Popular Front Era begins.[7]

Social Darwinism was flourishing, largely unchecked by the Christian community. Many social Darwinists believed that the human race could be perfected through genetics and selective breeding. Adolph Hitler was a social Darwinist who loathed Christianity as a religion of the weak and hoped to help evolution produce the ideal man through "purifying the gene pool," murdering both physical and racial "inferiors" to allow the superior Aryan "superman" to evolve. Many Americans do not realize that eugenics, as this "selective breeding" program is called, was not really a new idea in the 1930's, nor was it confined to evil Nazis in Germany. The Nazis had the ruthless leaders with the power to turn these ugly and evil ideas into legally sanctioned murder, but the German eugenicists borrowed the theory from America and England, where these ideas were born.

American feminist leader, Victoria Woodhull, who in 1872 became the first woman to be nominated for president by a political party, stated:

> Thus society, while expending millions in the care of incurables and imbeciles, takes little heed of or utterly ignores those laws by the study and obedience of which such human abortions might have been prevented from cumbering society with their useless and unwelcome presence. Grecian and Roman civilizations were, it is true, deficient in the gentler virtues, the excess of which in our day is hindering the progress of the race rather than helping or ennobling it. They, by crushing out the diseased and imperfect plants in the garden of humanity, attained to a vigor and physical development which has never been equated since. And in so doing they were entirely in accord with nature, whose mandate is inexorable, that the "fittest" only shall be permitted to live and propagate. She is a very prodigal in her waste of individual life, in order that the species be without spot of blemish.
>
> Not so our modern civilization, which rather pets its abortions and weaklings, and complacently permits them to procreate another race of fools and pygmies as inane and useless as themselves.[8]

Margaret Sanger, greatly honored today as the founder of Planned Parenthood, pushed the eugenics idea even further than past adherents had. As a devout humanist and evolutionist, she advocated the elimination of such "inferior" human beings, as the poor and minorities. Their problems, in her view, weighed down society and held back the superior human stock — the wealthier and supposedly more highly evolved white race.

She bluntly defined "birth control," a term she coined, as "the process of weeding out the unfit" aimed at "the creation of superman." She often opined that "the most merciful thing that the large family does to one of its infant members is to kill it," and that "all our problems are the result of overbreeding among the working class."

Sanger frequently featured racists and eugenicists in her magazine, the *Birth Control Review*. Contributor Lothrop Stoddard, who also served on Sanger's board of directors, wrote in "The Rising Tide of Color Against White World-Supremacy" that "[w]e must resolutely oppose both Asiatic permeation of white race-areas and Asiatic inundation of those non-white, but equally Asiatic regions inhabited by really inferior races."[9]

"Roots" of Black Liberal Theology

It would be wonderful to report that racial discrimination and segregation were not a problem within the church — that God's people would never have allowed such obviously (to us) unchristian and patently unfair thinking and practices to hold uncontested sway in their midst, but sadly, they did. It is always easy, and usually unfair, to judge the ignorance of the past by present day enlightenment. It was, it would seem for the most part, a blind spot rather than a consciously malicious way of thinking. We dare not harshly judge those who were of another time, for the reason that we may be judging people who were, in many ways, better persons than we are. But we can judge what took place. The ignorant and virulent racism that stains our past was cruel and immoral, a dark seed sown that has reaped the whirlwind, both socially and within the church, doing terrible damage to the wonderful Christian unity that might have been, should have been, but may never be. How tragic — what a waste! Blacks were excluded from the "Christian Only" Bible colleges and universities which had shamefully turned out to be for "White Christians Only." A few years later, blacks were to be trained for the ministry went to the schools which *would* accept and even provide scholarships to them: the liberal institutions which had been utterly abandoned by the Church and which were in the business of destroying the true faith. This gave birth in the 1960s to a new black liberal theology, or as Dr. Jerry Buckner puts it, "The Cult of Black Liberal Theology." This development has not turned out to be any better for society or the church than the racial segregation of old, since it has become another seemingly insurmountable wall of division among those who should be working in harmony to preach the gospel to a lost world.

The Neo Harold

By the late 1940s several Christians came to realize that the previous two decades of an increasingly narrow brand of fundamentalism had produced a very rigid, inflexible, and academically poor church. They realized that not only hadn't they reached the world for Christ, the Church was steadily losing influence. Eventually, as many fundamentalists publicly identified themselves with such questionable issues as opposition to new Bible translations, or became vocal supporters of racial segregation, tensions began to rise within fundamentalism. Many who originally identified with the movement either abandoned it or kept very quiet about their affiliation. The promising start fundamentalism exhibited at the beginning of the 20th century was now becoming intellectually backward and academically ingrown as the movement steadily marginalized itself within society.

Many conservative Christians felt there were only two choices: stay where they were and endure parochialism and even paranoia, or compromise their convictions on Scripture by joining a liberal church.

In 1947 Harold Ockenga, pastor of Park Street Church in

Boston, preached a sermon titled A *New Evangelicalism*. His desire was to bring the Church out of the fortress mentality in which they were now trapped by recovering the spiritual dynamic of the evangelical movements of the eighteenth and nineteenth centuries. Even though these new evangelicals still considered themselves conservative, fundamentalist hard-liners almost immediately began accusing this new group of compromise and disdainfully labeled them "neo-evangelicals."

Keepers of rules

By 1950, fundamentalist Christians had become more defined by a particular set of do's and don'ts than by answering the "whats" and "whys" of their beliefs. Their world had become neatly divided into "the black hats" and "the white hats," the good folks and the bad. The anti-intellectual faith of the Christian community had reduced its practical distinctives into a set of dress and behavioral codes. "The rules" stated clearly that Christian men must have short hair — women must always wear dresses. No one could listen to music with a "jungle beat" or go to movies. And of course, no good Christian would "drink, smoke, or chew or date girls that do." These issues are primarily external and represent a very sub-cultural, Americanized form of Christianity. The biblical teaching that a Christian should be salt and light in a dark world had largely been eroded from the faith.

The Times, They Are a-Changin'

Little did these Christians know that they were riding the cusp of a huge societal rebellion, a rebellion that would shake their isolated world. Their moral, ethical and behavioral rules, often respected and somewhat emulated by even the secular society of the 1950's, came to represent "the establishment" that had to be toppled, and the rules that had to be broken, in a quest to create "the perfect world."

To say that fundamentalists mounted no serious, concerted response to these cultural paradigm shifts is an understatement. Many were too busy fighting the bogey of encroaching modernism to notice the vast changes that were about to burst on the scene, that their children and grandchildren would be facing when they came of age. They would not, however, be able to keep their heads in the sand much longer. Along with the skyrocketing birthrate of the Baby Boom came mounting fears about a generation that was being raised in a "permissive society" and that seemed to be getting out of control.

At this point Darwinism and secular humanism had dominated the education in the universities for nearly 30 years. The educators graduated attorneys, judges, and politicians, not to mention teachers and university professors, who were fairly well schooled in socialism and intent on creating a new utopia for mankind. Over the previous 30 years the country had lived on the borrowed capital of Christian morals, or what has been called a Christian hangover. The "hangover" was about to wear off.

In 1961, the Supreme Court referred to secular humanism a religion. Indeed, it is a religion, one that is in direct conflict with the founding document of the United States. In 1962, after a 300-year tradition, the Supreme Court banned Bible reading and prayer from the public classroom[10]. In 1968, the Supreme Court ruled that the teaching of evolution *could not* be banned from school. These decisions rocked the Christian community – the world that they had wanted to ignore was invading their sanctuary, forcing them to pay attention. From the Christian perspective, all went downhill from there. The explosive Roe v. Wade decision legalizing abortion would be handed another five years later.

The early 1960s brought The Beatles from England. After becoming the most successful rock musicians in the western world, they went east in search of spiritual enlightenment. They were quite instrumental in popularizing Hinduism and eastern thought with the current crop of college students. And there were a lot of college students — by 1967 fully one-half of the U.S. population was less than 21 years old, and by 1968 it had become frighteningly obvious in the anti-war protests how much damage these youths could do! The assassinations of President John F. Kennedy, Martin Luther King, and Robert F. Kennedy, as well as notorious crimes like the "hippie" Manson murders, added to the social turmoil and to the fears of traditional and law-abiding Americans. The 1960s became the crossroad intersection with no stop signs where the competing worldviews and philosophies were about to collide.

Generational Conflict

It would be unfair to caricature the whole of the '60s as one long hippie love-in. In the early '60s, youth rebellion had pretty much been limited to the occasional street and motorcycle gang. With a president who mirrored their own youthful idealism, this generation exchanged their Mickey Mouse ears for membership in the Peace Corps, and the future was full of hope. Young people believed they were able to isolate American political demons and send Freedom Riders to exorcise them. But with the JFK assassination, youthful idealism began to fade, and with the troop buildup in Vietnam, it seemed ready to disappear altogether.

It helps to remember that the discovery of the German concentration camps and the Jewish Holocaust was only about 20 years old back then. And the post-World War II Nuremberg war-crimes trials had left the world to ponder the haunting refrain that was used to justify more than ten million, savage murders: "We were only following orders." In light of this monumental horror, it was only natural that the next generation should recoil from the dangers of unquestioned authority.

Added to this was the rediscovery of America's own heritage of civil disobedience for the cause of liberty and justice — which re-established a place of honor for protest and the confrontation of seemingly abusive authority in American life. The previous decades of cultivation in the institutions of higher learning were able to witness the maturing of their views. By all accounts, the "Free Speech Movement" on the campus of the University of California at Berkeley in 1964 (a symbol of student protest in the '60s) was almost a religious experience for those in attendance. The violence that later came to characterize the '60s can be seen as youthful idealism turned angry.

The vast majority of these young people of the '60s were among "the best and brightest" of their time and would have been so in any generation before or since. But, their parents reasoned, if tomorrow's leaders were brawling with the local "fuzz" in Chicago, blowing up college buildings, burning draft cards, inciting to riot, taking drugs, challenging traditional sexual morality, listening to raucous music, and making a general nuisance of themselves, what hope was there for the future? Shaking off the vestiges of society's "Christian hangover," all traditional moral values were questioned by the young and summarily discarded, in favor of the new moral values spurred on by youthful idealism and Marxist philosophy. While the World War II generation was thrown completely off guard and didn't know what to think about their offspring's radical bent, the younger generation judged the older generation's "morality" by their new "enlightened" moral system. How could the older generation make a claim to morality, the thinking went, when they allowed materialism, racism, sexism, and all those other evil "isms" to flourish without protest under their watch? New "sins" rapidly replaced the old. Sex before marriage, for example, couldn't be a sin, since it "didn't hurt anybody." But war, for whatever "good" reason was obviously a SIN!

The older generation's problem in defending their culture was similar to the churches' problem of the past century, when their Christian faith began to be challenged by emerging philosophies. Even though the Bible commands believers to be prepared to give a reasoned defense for their faith, they had little idea of how to defend it, because never in their wildest dreams did they imagine that they would *have* to. The walls were high, the fortress seemingly impenetrable. In the same way, the World War II generation felt that American culture and values were safe — they had only recently rescued the world from Nazi Germany, and life was good. In their minds, the superiority of American culture, morals, and worldview was self-evident. Certainly they never expected to have been confronted and condemned by their own children, for whom they had sacrificed and to whom they had handed the world on a platter.

Poised at the brink of this social tidal wave was a man who promised order in the midst of chaos, peace in the midst of conflict, sanity in the midst of psychedelia. To the cynical, politically correct unbelievers of today, he would have been considered merely a spiritual pied piper offering to bring the children back from darkness. To the church-going, God-fearing, and terrified parents and grandparents of the '60s and '70s, he appeared to be a godsend armed with overheads and three-ring binders. His name was Bill Gothard.

Small Beginnings

Bill Gothard began his career as a youth minister. The 1950's were an ideal time to build a career in the fledgling youth ministry movement. World War II had resulted in millions of absentee fathers, and society, in this far more orderly era, became alarmed as the violence of youth gangs began to rival the tales of Al Capone and John Dillinger. In response to this problem, youth ministries went forth and multiplied. Youth for Christ was formed in 1945 and Torrey Johnson was elected as the first president, Billy Graham was hired as the first full time employee that same year. Bill and Vonette Bright started Campus Crusade for Christ at UCLA in 1951 and developed the "Four Spiritual Laws" tract as an evangelistic tool in 1952.

Youth ministry was not a totally new concept. The late nineteenth century had given birth to InterVarsity Christian

Fellowship and the Young Men's Christian Association (YMCA). But what made the second half of the 20th century so unusual was a phenomenon unparalleled in American history: the fabled Baby Boom. Following World War II, the rate of live births in the U.S. accelerated sharply until, between 1954 (just after the Korean War) and 1964, it exceeded 10 million annually. (This is the period officially designated by the U.S. Census Bureau as the Baby Boom, although most people use that phrase to roughly denote the two decades following World War II, 1946-1965.)

Bill Gothard's brand of Christianity had incubated in the isolated, ingrown, and even somewhat paranoid world of 1930s, '40s, and '50s fundamentalism. Much of American society in the 1950s pretty much accepted Christian morals as being "right" and, to a good extent, even followed their "rules." But up until the social upheaval of the 1960s, there wasn't a very big market for this brand of extremely authoritarian faith in American culture at large. Disorientation and fear were the key cultural ingredients that suddenly made that reactionary culture palatable to the masses.

Where Did We Go Wrong?

A symbol of what seemed to have gone wrong in many people's minds was the arrest of "The Baby Book Doctor," Dr. Benjamin Spock, for assisting in the destruction of draft cards. Millions of well-intentioned mothers and fathers in the '50s and '60s had raised their children on the instruction Dr. Spock had given — which included the advice that children should not be spanked. Now here was the same baby doctor aiding and abetting many of those same children in breaking the law. Could it be the whole essence of the '60s youth problem was that an entire generation had been turned into a bunch of spoiled, narcissistic brats because their parents had listened to the wrong "experts?" Maybe we needed new experts! Bill Gothard presented himself and his teachings as the solution to the problems of youth conflict.

A Man With a Plan

Thanks to cold-war politics, not only were we losing thousands of young people to a war in southeast Asia, but we were also spending billions to beat the Soviets to the moon. America was on the cutting edge of space, the economy was buzzing along smoothly, and it seemed as if science had discovered just about everything short of the meaning of life. So, millions left the church in search of answers elsewhere. And yet, a man came on the scene quoting verses from the Bible that predated the scientific method in order to prove something many people were actively rejecting: that authority was their friend.

It was a case of being at the right place at the right time. In the middle of all the upheaval and rapid change that characterized the '60s and early '70s, fearful parents just trying to raise decent and successful children were desperate for direction. Right on time, a man with a plan came along. There Gothard stood – confidently holding out one simple word as the center of his world view: *authority*. It was not a message designed to appeal to those youths who were at the forefront of society's problems at the time, but that in itself did not make Gothard's message wrong.

Taking a Stand

A large part of his appeal was his willingness to stand fast for his convictions at a time when convictions everywhere were giving way to confusion. One of the more popular youth slogans in the '60s was, "Never trust anyone over 30." For the first time anyone could remember, kids stood right in the face of their elders and shouted, "Hell, no! We won't go!" it seemed as though no one – not parents, not teachers, not government – seemed willing or able to effectively stand up to the young rebels. It was downright scary, even to the young people who were not radicalized, to see their elders so cowed. Another popular notion among the radical young was "rejection of the establishment." Again, the "establishment" seemed completely disoriented by the fury of these attacks and largely incapable of defending itself. And yet, there Gothard stood: a thirty-something (born November 2, 1934), ordained, evangelical Christian minister when he founded what was originally called The Institute in Basic Youth Conflicts.[11] Who *dared* to tell young people their basic problem was a failure to submit to authority. It was impressively courageous in an era of retreat, and it bought him the admiration of many.

Who Was That Masked Man?

Bill Gothard, who was at the time, closely associated with Samuel Schultz, professor of Old Testament at Wheaton College, graduated from the same institution with a B.A. in 1957 and an M.A. in 1961. His master's thesis was titled, *A Proposed Program for Hi-Crusaders Clubs.* According to those who remember him, he was reclusive throughout his college career, seeming to shun the limelight; his picture appearing in only one college yearbook, atypical of the students at that time. Some were impressed by the amount of time he spent in solitary prayer. At one point he devoted 35 hours per week to youth work with a Chicago missionary society while still a full-time student at Wheaton, 25 miles away.

Gothard also seemed to have a tender conscience. According to Bill Gothard, one day some of his fellow youth workers confronted him, saying they detected "spiritual pride" in him, perhaps due to his success in youth ministry. He said he became convicted this was true and confessed it to one of his fellow workers. That person dealt harshly with him and advised him to confess the sin to several others, including the head of the missionary society for which Gothard worked. Gothard's boss fired him shortly after he made this confession.

Many people have been discouraged right out of the ministry by incidents such as this. But despite this negative experience, Gothard pressed on. He would later counsel thousands of young people to follow his example and confess such sins to others.

Sometime around 1964, Gothard was invited to teach a course on youth ministry at Wheaton. Forty-five students attended, including pastors, youth workers, and educators. The materials he presented at the time became the foundation for his seminars.

In 1966, Gothard presented a seminar to 1,000 people in the Chicago area. He repeated the performance in 1967 and held his first out-of-town seminar in Seattle for 42 in 1968. Gothard's new organization, the IBYC, was born.

The Ministry Takes Off

From such small beginnings, it was difficult to see the great popularity he would enjoy down the road. His combined attendance for all his seminars in 1968 was actually around 2,000. But then things really took off! As Wilfred Bockelman later would report in his book, *Gothard — The Man and His Ministry: An Evaluation*, "In 1969 there were around 4,000; 1971, 12,000; 1972 over 128,000 including 13,000 in the Seattle Coliseum; in 1973 more than 200,000."[12] Before you could say, "post-Watergate social malaise," Gothard's public career had outlasted that of most major rock-and-roll stars, including the Beatles (as a group), and his live audiences were at least as huge as those at rock concerts. Churches in every city, town, and hamlet in America were taking their young people to his seminars by the busload. Little bands of three-ring-binder-toting Gothard disciples sprang up on college and university campuses across the country.

Meanwhile, Back at the Ranch

In the early '70s the "revolutionary" fervor that had gripped so many of the youth began to cool. Toga parties began to replace campus sit-ins. Why? "The Establishment" had had enough of this "fun and frivolity" and things began to get, well, scary. In the shadow of the Kent State massacre, the Woodstock generation woke up to the fact that radicalism could cost some of them their lives. This was definitely not cool. Revolution was not supposed to be *dangerous!* And commitment to a cause was soooooooooo 1950s. The '60s "radicals" who wreaked such havoc was comprised of a small percentage of true Marxists bent on destroying "Amerika" and the capitalist system through revolution, and a much larger percentage of kids who were just trying to save their skin while having the time of their lives. The self-righteousness earned from protesting society's evils was a plus. Rebellion could be fun, but seeing as how the prospect of being killed was a big reason why this second group was protesting Vietnam in the first place, getting shot on campus seemed to defeat the purpose. When the Vietnam War finally ended, there seemed little to care about for many young people, aside from where to take their next toke on a joint, or where to have their next sexual encounter. So, while the older generation was relieved that its children were no longer about the business of tearing down "the Establishment," new fears dawned of a directionless generation with declining scholastic aptitude, addicted to gratification and sexual freedom.

It must here be said that it was the violent and worst behaved of the '60s generation who got all the press. There were innumerable young people in the 1960s who never protested the war, or were involved in radicalism in any way. Countless young people of that generation didn't "do drugs" beyond the occasional aspirin. But since so many of the former '60s "radicals" are the present-day establishment — the academic elite of our universities and those who dominate the culture and the media — they *still* get all the press! They have been able to self-righteously frame the period as they wished, propagandizing the succeeding generations with tales of the pristine purity of their motives and incontestable rightness of their cause, while ignoring the disastrous fall-out of their rebellion. Rather than coming to terms with the damage done, they have been able to romanticize the era as one of America's best. On the contrary, the Psychedelic '60s had taken a massive toll on our nation's moral and ethical health — Humpty Dumpty has not to this day been put back together again.

Going to the Other Extreme

In the aftermath of the Age of Aquarius, Gothard could be assured that hundreds of thousands of parents would continue to attend and bring their kids to his seminars. IBYC soon grew to be a multi-million-dollar organization. In 1976 alone, Gothard held 32 seminars at $45 per attendee ($35 if part of a church group, $55 per married couple). It was not unusual for Gothard to pack out auditoriums with capacities of 8,000 to 20,000 people. Society's continuing problems with its youth virtually assured IBYC's growth for the foreseeable future.

Just What Was in Those Three-Ring Binders?

When your home is on fire, you don't ask the fireman to what denomination he belongs. During the '60s and '70s, many Americans thought their home was on fire, and it was their children who were burning. Maybe that's why so many parents and pastors did not exercise a great deal of discernment with respect to the actual content of Gothard's seminars. They seemed satisfied knowing that he professed to be an evangelical Christian and held to "the essentials" of the faith — short hair and no beards for men, only dresses for women, no contemporary music. In addition, he had the confidence and the endorsement of Christian leaders whom they knew. Besides, what they *did* hear sounded good: Obey the authority figures God has ordained! Follow biblical principles in making every decision! Why should parents worry about Gothard when the Timothy Learys and Abbie Hoffmans of the world were advising kids to "turn on, tune in, and drop out?" Bill Gothard, whatever he taught, was one of the good guys.

A Talmud for Christians?

Were Gothard's teachings actually biblical — or was he creating an Evangelical Talmud for Christians? You may ask, "What is a Talmud?" The Talmud is the body of Jewish oral traditions extending back at least to the Babylonian Captivity which were written down and completed by the fifth century A.D.[13] and considered authoritative by the Jews. These were the same oral traditions that Jesus opposed in his rebuke of the Pharisees (e.g., Matt. 23). Now is the time to critically examine and discern whether Gothard's teachings are truly based upon the Bible or largely Christian oral traditions which, like the opinions and oral traditions of the Pharisees, have been given by many a level of authority nearly equal to that of Scripture.

Chapter 1

Citizen Kane and a History of Inconsistency

C harles Foster Kane was the main character of Citizen Kane, the 1941 film, which was partially written and directed by Orson Wells. Wells also starred in the film, which opens with multiple views of Xanadu,the mammoth estate which Kane had built. The scene changes to a view of a bed where we see a hand, the hand of Charles Foster Kane, holding a glass ball, which falls out of his hand as he dies, alone except for hired staff, without the comfort of family and friends. With his last breath he whispers one word, "Rosebud."

The next scenes catalogue the holdings in Kane's empire with a narrator saying of Kane's residence, "Since the pyramids, Xanadu is the costliest monument a man has built to himself." In a moment we find out that what we have been watching is a soon-to-be-released newsreel announcing Kane's death. In order to learn more about the man behind the legend, the news department head dispatches a reporter to track down the meaning of "Rosebud."

The film then shows us a few short glimpses of Kane's childhood, but the real introduction to the main character comes when he turns twenty-five and acquires a failing newspaper with a view to running it himself. Charles arrives with his two best friends, Mr. Jedediah Leland and Mr. Bernstein, to assume control. The first edition of the paper contains Kane's idealistic "Declaration of Principles:"

1. I'll provide the people of this city with a daily paper that will tell all the news honestly.

2. I'll also provide them with a fighting and tireless champion of their rights as citizens and as human beings.

This was Kane's public persona, the way he wanted people to see him. Almost immediately, however, Kane's idealism gives way, and we see him distort, invent, and twist the news in his drive for personal power and recognition. His towering personal ambition masks the illusion that everything Kane does is to protect the common people. His vaunted love of "the people" cannot hold a candle to his all-consuming love for Charles Foster Kane. His onetime business associate and personal friend, Mr. Leland, says of him after his death:

> I was his oldest and dearest friend, and as far as I was concerned he behaved like a swine. Not that Charlie was ever brutal; he just did brutal things.

What made Kane tick? What motivated the man? On the one hand, he seemed genuinely concerned for those who were struggling and lacked hope and protection. On the other, he brutalized anyone who got in his way and eventually lost everyone who had cared for him.

Kane was a thoroughgoing hypocrite, having two sets of standards — one for himself and one for others. When he ran for governor on a platform of honesty, integrity, and morality, he railed against the immorality of his opponent — yet all the while he was carrying on an affair in his personal life. When the affair was uncovered, Kane simply launched even more vicious attacks on those who exposed him. As a result, he lost the election and his marriage, but he stubbornly refused to accept responsibility for his own downfall. Charles Foster Kane was not the righteous man he claimed to be.

Citizen Gothard

Of course, we are not suggesting that Kane's life in every way parallels Gothard's. But comparisons can be made. For example, like Charles Foster Kane, Bill Gothard seeks to help people, yet he tramples over anyone who stands up to him and opposes his will. He is a "principled man" who seems quite willing to suspend his principles when necessary to hold onto power.

We do not doubt Gothard's sincerity — he seems to truly believe that his seven principles, applied diligently, will insure that God's desires are carried out in the lives of those who follow them and that the adherents will be the better for it. These "principles," rather than a relationship with God, are the focus of Gothard's teaching.

Bill Gothard's seminar ministry grew in the 1970s. Gothard was not only packing out churches but stadiums. The small handful of detractors went relatively unnoticed and unheeded. Like Charles Foster Kane, Bill Gothard was loved by "the people," but behind closed doors at the institute some of "the people," whoever challenged Gothard's rule, were being mistreated. The authoritarianism that had become Gothard's trademark is exemplified by his firing of a female staff person in 1971 because she did not obey his order to forego dating.[1] The prideful spirit which cost him his youth ministry years earlier[2] began showing itself as he gained popularity, and in practice Gothard's *opinions* began to be equated with Scripture, both in his own mind and the minds of his followers.

Scandal Hits the Institute

On May 14, 1980, we as board members were shocked to learn of the gross immorality that had prevailed for some time among the staff under Bill's supervision as president.[3]

What was the nature of the "gross immorality" which shocked Samuel Schultz, former professor at Wheaton College and Institute board member since 1965, as well as the other board members? Bill's brother, Steve Gothard, Institute employee and a vice-president, had been involved in sexual affairs with seven of the Institute secretaries. In fact, a total of 15 people were involved in sexual immorality — a very bad (and sad) situation in any Christian organization and particularly so for one whose primary emphasis is high moral character.

The scandal that rocked the ministry in the early 1980s is not new news. It is a matter of record, having been reported in such Christian periodicals as *Christianity Today* and such secular media as the *Los Angeles Times* (some of which will be referenced in this chapter). So why bring it up now? Our concern here is not so much with the "sex angle." It seems that Steve has long since repented of his immoral behavior.[4] Our concern is with the cover-up that Bill engaged in, and with his blatant disregard for his own vaunted "principles" when they conflicted with his will.

Lack of Accountability to Authority

We disagree heartily with Gothard's "chain of command" authority structure, in which each individual is basically under the lordship of the person directly up the chain from him. Not only does this type of system tend to be abusive, but it sets up a mediatorial role between the individual believer and his God — a position which has already been filled by the Savior of us all! But despite our objections to the teaching, we would still expect Gothard to practice what he preaches to others and submit himself to his authority — the board of directors of the Institute.

Bill Gothard, though, seems to regard his board of directors as mere figureheads whose input is not needed. This is, of course, in *direct opposition* to his public teachings on the "Chain of Command/Umbrella of Protection." He has held others within the organization to this teaching to the point that, as pointed out earlier, he fired one of the young women in 1971 because "she did not respond favorably to his order not to date."[5] Yet Gothard himself seems to have had no patience for being called to account, even by those whose job it was to do just that.

Edwin Brown was on the board from 1967-1977.[6] Dr. Brown was a medical staff physician at Indiana University. Bill Gothard asked him to resign in 1977 when he went to Saudi Arabia to start a medical school. Brown was disappointed at Bill's request, but he complied. He believes he was asked to step down because "he started questioning the Institute's finances during several board meetings in 1977."[7] Steve Gothard had purchased 350 acres of land in Michigan. The Institute paid to improve this land, which they used for retreats, etc. According to former staff members, Steve was able to purchase this property because the Institute paid for most of his living expenses,[8] allowing him to save most of his $30,000 per year salary. This came to the board's attention when the Institute attorney proposed that the ministry reimburse Steve for the use of his property. Edwin Brown confessed that the board knew nothing about the ministry's finances for the ten years he was on the board. He is also quoted as saying:

> All we did was rubber-stamp the recommendations of the president.[9]

Interestingly enough, during this time when Brown says that the board merely rubber-stamped Bill's recommendations, the ministry brochure stated, "All funds are carefully controlled by the board of directors."

Another ex-board member concurred with Brown: former IBYC board chairman Sam Schultz, who remarked at a board meeting in 1980:

> Bill has not demonstrated that he is under the authority of the Board.[10]

In a damage-control meeting with the entire staff that was held soon after the sex-scandal story came to public attention, one of the board members stood up and "admitted that the Board had never functioned as a decision- making group, only as a figurehead. The Board began to realize during this time that they had not been told what they needed to be told over the years by the Gothards."[11] More on this later...

Is Gothard Under Pastoral Authority?

Since Gothard essentially rejects the authority of the IBLP board, to whom is he accountable? Anyone with an acquaintance with the teachings of Bill Gothard knows the role of the pastor in his chain-of-command ladder. So it is more than reasonable to ask if Gothard is under the authority of *his* pastor and church. It appears as though he is not. The pastor of Gothard's home church, the church which ordained him and of which he was a member, declined to get involved in calling Gothard to account at the time of the scandal, even though IBLP (then IBYC) staff had pleaded with him to do so. Pastor E. Hovey of the LaGrange Bible Church opted not to get involved because "Bill Gothard has never been under the authority of the local church either as a member or as a Christian leader."[12] It is a serious matter to hold others to a standard that you refuse to subject yourself to.

Over time, many staff members of IBLP began to take note of this double standard, especially as it touched on his handling of the sex scandal. Sam Schultz writes that the members of the board "were soon made aware of the almost total loss of confidence by the staff in Bill as an administrator and teacher in the seminars. The basic charge: *"Bill does not practice what he teaches."*[13]

The Cover-up

When the scandal broke in 1980, the public spin was that Steve's sexual escapades were a recent development and that no one had been aware of the problem. Bill Gothard was quoted as saying:

> I must report to you that there has been serious failure within our staff. My brother, who was in a leadership position, has confessed to deception and fornication with several women. Those involved have acknowledged their personal responsibility, have submitted to scriptural discipline, and have been dismissed from the staff as a step toward restoration.[14]

By all accounts, however, Bill Gothard who is a bachelor had known for over four years that Steve who was a bachelor at the time was having affairs with his secretaries, but he misused his power "at the top" to silence witnesses within the ministry. Instead of dealing with this crisis openly, with the hope of a resultant repentance and restoration, Gothard moved Steve and his "problem" to a remote location — and, only when the secretaries publicly brought charges did Gothard remove them from their positions at the Institute. We realize the seriousness of this claim, but the documentation which follows will bear this out.

This is the story as it unfolded: In January of 1976 one of the secretaries had "informed Ed Martin [an Institute executive] of Steve's immoral actions with her which had been over a period of time. She couldn't get him to leave her alone and she was seeking help."[15] This was relayed to Bill, who in that same month interviewed the young woman personally. During the interview "Bill became angry that she had not come to him first about it. Bill indicated no resolve to deal with Steve, and showed no grief, shock, comfort or help to her and quickly ended the conversation."[16]

Yet something had to be done to put the matter to rest. At the singles retreat on Valentine's Day a confession meeting was held. At this meeting as well as another staff meeting on Sunday, February 22, 1976 Bill and Steve *both* confessed to what they called "defrauding" staff secretaries. This is a somewhat ambiguous term Bill uses which could mean anything from sexual relations to unwanted advances.[17] Former staff members have told us that Bill Gothard engaged in inappropriate sexual contact with some of the staff women, but to our knowledge he did not have sexual intercourse with them. Neither man stepped down from leadership, even though that would be expected and demanded by Bill of anyone else who might engage in such conduct.

The same month (February 1976) another secretary confessed to Norma Smalley[18] (Gary Smalley's wife) that she had engaged in immoral relations with Steve. Bill's solution, as we mentioned earlier, was to send Steve to their Northwoods retreat facilities even though witnesses tell us Steve wanted help and restoration. Within a fairly short period of time Bill announced that Steve was healed and began assembling a staff at the Northwoods facility which included a number of young women. Ed Martin and Gary Smalley made a special trip to the

Northwoods retreat to confront Bill and Steve about dealing with the immorality in a biblical way. This would certainly seem appropriate in light of the ministry's emphasis on morality and biblical conflict resolution. Bill, however, was firm that Steve would stay at the Northwoods site and "continue his writing and work on Character Sketch books in the area of 'becoming a servant' because that is what he needs most."[19] He was resolute in this decision.

Never Give an Evil Report

As might be expected, these events stirred up talk amongst the staff — talk that threatened to spill out into the public arena and hurt the Institute. According to former staff, on Wednesday, March 25, 1976 Bill introduced a brand-new teaching on Matthew 18. He passed around a large poster-like contract for all to sign promising never to "give an evil report but only say good things about other people."[20] According to former staff members, this teaching was meant to intimidate the staff and squelch any critical talk about what was going on within the organization. Any discussion of perceived problems was to be considered "gossip." This tactic of staff intimidation was strongly reiterated in the fall of 1980 after the sex scandal became public.[21]

The Scandal "Hits the Fan"

Eventually, of course, despite Gothard's best efforts at containment, the scandal did go public — very public. The story was reported in the *Los Angelos Times*, and it was not just Steve's sexual improprieties that were brought into the light of day. Russell Chandler reported in the *Times* that "Bill Gothard was seen by staff members patting and fondling women employees. Later, he admitted in staff meetings that these actions were 'moral failures' on his part."[22]

Again, our aim in bringing up this ancient scandal is not to titillate the reader. Our emphasis here is to show that many of Gothard's *teachings* are false and to demonstrate how people are being hurt by Bill's extreme authoritarianism, *not* to embarrass Gothard *personally* by showing him to be a fallen human being like all of mankind. We believe, however, that this issue exemplifies Bill's unwillingness to live by the rules that he dictates to others. "Other people" would be expected, under similar circumstances, to submit and meekly accept, without question, any discipline that their authority meted out to them. "Other people," such as single young men and women staffers, would be booted out of the organization for breaking Gothard's rule against *dating*, yet Gothard heads the organization today after engaging in serious wrongdoing. (Bill relinquished control of the organization when the heat was on, but his "resignation" lasted less than a month, after which he took power again.) We shall present situations in which "other people" were excoriated and blacklisted by Bill Gothard for committing *no sin at all*, yet Gothard, caught in sin, forgives himself and moves on.

The Institute's Problem

As time went on and things went from bad to worse, several of the board members began to perceive the real problem at the Institute. Former IBYC board chairman Sam Schultz wrote:

> So Bill is our problem. He is our basic problem. We dismissed the staff involved in immorality and gross pornography with pornographic films ordered by IBYC personnel under Bill's jurisdiction. Dozens of staff members have left with deep-seated grievances against Bill not only since May but during the last five years because of Bill's failure to apply the biblical principles he taught in public. Over four years ago, many tried to communicate to Bill and his father the concerns they had about Steve but like Eli in biblical times, these warnings were ignored.[23]

The example Schultz used was a very accurate comparison. Eli was the priest in 1 Samuel to whom Hannah gave her first-born, Samuel. Eli's sons, Hophni and Phineas, worked as priests alongside Eli (1 Samual 1:4). It was a "family business," you might say. Hophni and Phineas abused the offerings which were brought by the people for the Lord's work (2:12-17) and committed fornication (2:22). Eli heard the reports (2:23) privately talked with his sons (2:24) but did little else. God warned Samuel that Eli would be judged because, although Eli knew of his sons' sins, he allowed them to continue "and he did not rebuke them" (3:10-13).

Bill Gothard knew at least by 1976 through various meetings and confrontations what was going on with his brother but chose not to deal with it. Several high-level leaders in the Institute pressed Bill the rest of that year to act upon the biblical principles he teaches in order to bring Steve to repentance and restoration. Gary Smalley and other disillusioned staff people left the Institute during this time. Bill Gothard was less than honest about their reasons for leaving, which only heightened the disappointment of those who stayed.

The warnings continued over the next four years. One of the staff members recorded in his diary in 1977: "one year after revelation of Steve's sexual immorality nothing is being done."[24] In 1979 Bill met with the family of one of the secretaries and attempted to negotiate a marriage between their daughter and Steve. He did this knowing full well that Steve had not limited his physical relations to this one young lady — making such a union a risky proposition for her. The family did not give permission.[25]

In 1979, staff member and video seminar emcee Tony Guhr verified the facts regarding the sexual immorality by Bill and Steve. Guhr scheduled meetings with Bill on five separate occasions to discuss these facts, all of which Bill Gothard canceled. By this time, Bill had had three years to deal with the problem but had not done so, and tensions were escalating within the organization. Tony, knowing that something had to be done, spent time praying and studying Scripture in order to know the proper steps to biblical discipline in this situation.

On Monday, April 14, 1980, after leading staff members had

attempted for four years to bring this to biblical correction, Gary Smalley, Tony Guhr, and another individual flew to Dallas, Texas, where Bill and Steve Gothard were conducting a minister's seminar. They met with Steve privately for about 10 hours to confront him, and he confessed to most of the affairs (more would come out later). Bill Gothard was unhappy to see them and continued to frustrate the process with delaying tactics.[26]

April 22 through 24 saw a series of meetings with Bill and Steve Gothard, Tony Guhr, and several other individuals who sought to confront the problems and apply biblical solutions. Over the rest of the month the problems were brought to the Gothard family.

The staff distrust of Bill Gothard was reaching an all-time high. Sam Schultz comments:

> Bill's credibility even with the present staff is so low that they feel it necessary to check every statement he makes. Recently he reported a conversation he had with a former staff member and before many hours had passed, at least three telephone calls were made to check on Bill's report. It has been commonly reported that in recent years staff members found it necessary to have pad and pencil in hand to record everything Bill said, lest he deny it later.[27]

Finally, after four and a half years of stonewalling, this situation was brought before the board *against Bill's direct orders* on Tuesday, May 13, 1980. Steve confessed to having affairs with five women (two more would be acknowledged a little later). Tony suggested that there might be more to the story, as yet uncovered, and more women involved. Bill Gothard criticized Tony sharply for suggesting there were more young women involved and demanded that Tony stop checking out any more possibilities.[28] In fact, Bill convinced the board to forbid Tony from talking further with the secretaries involved "because he is unmarried." [29] This reason is, of course, completely bogus, and yet another example of Bill Gothard's double standards in action, since Bill himself is unmarried and felt it was just fine for *him* to interrogate the secretaries. Over the next several days staff confessional meetings were held. On May 16th a sixth secretary came forward, and on the 17th the seventh secretary became known, as well as other male staff and managers, bringing the total to 15 key staff.

Much of this could have been avoided if Bill Gothard had applied the same principles to himself, concerning submission to authority, zero tolerance for sexual sin, etc., four and a half years earlier, that he rigorously applied to those around him. However, even now that it had been revealed to the directors, instead of repenting, he rebelliously dug in his heels. On May 27 the directors presented Gothard with 31 questions regarding financial and legal irregularities. Bill opened the meeting that morning by:

1. Questioning the authority of the directors to ask such questions (financial and legal) of the Institute leadership;

2. Stating that these questions challenged the integrity of Bill Gothard and the IBYC accountant; and

3. Warning the directors by reminding them of the dire consequences that had befallen others who had opposed him, saying that those who have "raised themselves up against Bill Gothard have subsequently experienced financial and family failures."[30]

Some of the financial questions revolved around large payments made to disgruntled former employees without board approval. Sam Schultz points out:

> In an effort to clear his relationship, he even endorsed a $50,000.00 check without board approval or authorization. This kind of action has resulted in almost endless payments of thousands of dollars which in secular language would be called "hush" money or bribes.[31]

Damage Control Begins

The department managers met on Wednesday morning, May 28

to construct a letter which would be sent out to all alumni pastors to explain what was going on at the Institute. At 11:30 Dr. Bob Wood, administrative vice president of Bob Jones University, came in to lead the staff Bible study. After the study, Bill met with Wood and Rev. Van Geldren (board member of Bob Jones University) and somehow convinced them that the Institute staff was rebelling against him. In all likelihood, these men were unaware of the extent and gravity of Gothard's own failures and lack of accountability. But without confirming the truth and accuracy of the information that they received from Bill, they met with the directors and staff that afternoon and rebuked *them* for challenging *Bill's* authority. Bill had successfully twisted his own "umbrella of protection" teaching to place the directors under his authority, leaving him accountable to no one!

Sadly, this ploy seemed to intimidate the board — the decision was made to not send a letter out to the pastors but to keep everything quiet. Bill spent the rest of the month of June canceling commitments for audits and attempting to make sure that no records would be open to the inquiry of the directors.[32]

The Political Fallout

A few short weeks after his dressing-down of the staff and board, Van Geldren, to his credit, apologized to some of the staff for his "blind support of Bill," stating that he now realized that Bill could not be trusted. Van Geldren withdrew his daughter from working at the Institute. Over the next several days, Bill established a no-talk rule within the Institute in an effort to conceal everything that had transpired. And even though Bill had led people to believe that his brother Steve had been fired from the Institute, Bill still had him working at the Northwoods property. When this was discovered and he was confronted with yet another deception, he refused to make any changes, insisting that there was no harm in it, since there would be no public outcry if it were not made public. It seems that correcting wrongdoing was not what mattered to Bill — all that mattered was presenting a clean face to the world.

Tony Guhr had been asked by Bill Gothard earlier to stay in place until solutions were instituted and the problems were resolved. In light of the on-again, off-again nature of things Tony asked Bill on two separate occasions if his job was at risk for working to resolve this situation. He was assured in a meeting with IBLP's board of directors and a meeting with the staff that this was not the case.[33] Nevertheless, after Gothard successfully evaded accountability, Tony was fired in July of 1980.

Facing the Music

The board of directors called a meeting for Saturday, July 5. The meeting began at 10:00 a.m. and lasted until 1:00 a.m. Sunday morning. Bill was confronted on violating the requirements for a minister of the gospel on 12 points. As each point was raised, he first declared his innocence. But each time, as witnesses were brought forth, he was forced to confess to the charge. In light of these distressing findings, the board made the decision to conduct only those seminars that were scheduled for that week, and to cancel the balance of the seminars for the year. The next afternoon (Sunday) at the staff meeting, Van Geldren recommended that Bill resign immediately. Bill agreed, tendered his resignation the same day, and the board accepted. Later the same day the resignation was announced to an all-staff meeting.

Friends of Bill

On Tuesday, John Maclario, an attorney from Milwaukee, who was on the board of Bob Jones University and was recommended by Bob Jones III, was appointed as president of Basic Youth Conflicts and chairman of the IBYC board. It looked like righteousness would prevail in the situation after many false starts. But, unbelievable as it seems, that very same day Dr. Charles Stanley, Dr. Jack Taylor, Rev. Miles Seaborne, Rev. Gordon Dorian, and Mr. Jim Simmons arrived and had a 9:30 p.m. meeting with the staff where they berated them for rebellion because they had forced Bill's resignation. Over the next week, 31 staff members were fired, dismissed, or resigned. (The total grew to 50 out of a staff of 76 by December.)

Sadly, after one week as president and chairman John MacLario himself resigned for reasons that remain unclear. Bill took advantage of the leadership vacuum to simply resume his position, as though he were returning from a brief vacation. How and why the board allowed this to happen is also unclear. After Gothard resumed leadership in the organization, things quickly got back to "business as usual." In light of all that had transpired, the Institute board had committed to the principle of not hold-ing a seminar unless the churches in a particular area wanted them. But Bill, presumably holding the conviction that princi-ples and commitments are made for lesser men, refused to sub-mit to the area committee in Los Angeles that had voted not to hold a seminar until the Institute problems were properly resolved. The committee was simply removed from their place of authority and replaced; the seminar went ahead.

In the end, neither his board nor his church was able to hold Bill Gothard accountable. Rejection of authority, foot-dragging, spiritual intimidation, and cover-up — these, not godly principles, were the tools that Gothard successfully used to "ride out" the crisis.

A Scandal of Another Kind

It is our conviction that Bill's extreme authoritarian control and improper interpretation of Scripture are every bit as scandalous as the sexual immorality that went on behind the scenes at the Institute. We do not believe that the world at large has any idea of the amount of control that Gothard exerts over the everyday lives of his staff and IBLP members.

> Bill Gothard's personal secretary of more than nine years charged in a 10-page account [two class-action lawsuits had been filed against the Institute] of "personal griev-ances" that he twisted Scripture to achieve "total con-trol'"over her mind and emotions. She said he dictated

how to compose letters to her parents; her personal nail care, makeup and dress; which friendships she could develop, whether she could date or marry, and where and with whom she spent her free time.[34]

Think about it: Bill felt that it was his prerogative to dictate to this woman whether she was free to marry — who she could spend time with — how to dress and do her nails! This type of power over other adult human beings is very corrupting. And playing God for other people can have disastrous results. Steve had gone to Bill years earlier to express his desire to marry but was forbidden to do so. We will look at more stories of people who were damaged by Bill Gothard and IBLP in future chapters.

Chapter 2

The Unconfrontable Bill Gothard

Mr. Veinot then concludes that responsible adults and those "who teach the Scriptures for a living" did not pay attention or "exercise a great deal of discernment with respect to the actual content of Gothard's seminars." Correcting this assumed failure of parents and pastors is apparently now the stated mission of the *Midwest Christian Journal*.

— Bill Gothard[1]

One of the questions that arise from time to time is whether we have attempted to confront Bill Gothard on the issues we raise. The answer is, absolutely! Another question occasionally asked is whether other people have seen these problems and attempted to confront Bill Gothard with their concerns. The answer to that is also, absolutely! The above quotation from Bill Gothard's *A Response to the Midwest Christian Journal* gives the illusion that we are the only ones who have addressed these issues. He also asserts that it is the "stated mission" of *Midwest Christian Outreach, Inc.*, to correct this "assumed failure of parents and pastors." These claims are at best misleading and at worst outright falsehoods. We are not out to correct failing pastors and parents or even to persecute Bill Gothard but to bring about repentance on his part, causing him to repudiate the false and harmful teachings that he promotes.

Are we the only ones?

Dr. Ronald B. Allen, former professor of Hebrew Scripture at Western Baptist Seminary in Portland, Oregon (where he taught for 25 years), was very concerned about Bill's erroneous teachings. He attended a seminar with his wife in 1973. He wrote:

> In this seminar I was regularly assaulted by the misuse of the Bible, particularly of the Old Testament, on a level that I have never experienced in a public ministry before that time (or since).[2]

His misgivings about Gothard's teachings were so great that he spoke with the then president of Western Baptist Seminary, Dr. Earl Radmacher. Dr. Radmacher voiced similar concerns and proposed to set up a meeting with Bill Gothard in an attempt to address these concerns. Bill Gothard declined to meet with Dr. Allen. About this futile attempt at resolution, Allen recalls:

> Gothard said his instruction is from God and that he will not be instructed by one of Radmacher's seminary faculty.[3]

For the next *eleven years* Allen made numerous attempts to set up a meeting, but was unsuccessful. In 1984, Dr. Allen came out with his document, *Issues of Concern − Bill Gothard and the Bible, a Report*, in which he enumerated some of the problem areas that he perceived in Gothard's teachings. During this same period of time, Dr. Radmacher did meet with Gothard on numerous occasions, but no resolution was reached.

According to Dr. Radmacher, Bill agreed to make changes but did not follow through in making any substantive alterations of his false and harmful teachings. The changes he did make were purely cosmetic. For example, the picture we alluded to in the last chapter of the "hammer" father beating on the "chisel" wife who in turn chipped away at the children was eliminated. Bill also changed his titles in this section from the "Chain of Authority" to the "Umbrella of Protection." The actual content of the teachings, and the resultant authoritarianism, which were the source of the concerns, remained unchanged.

In an attempt to bring this before the church at large, Dr. Allen produced his aforementioned *Issues of Concern*, in which he wrote:

> I do not raise these issues with any desire to deny that God has been pleased to bring blessing to many thousands of people through the ministry of Bill Gothard. But I do raise these issues to demonstrate that – willful or not – Gothard's use of Scripture is so suspect as to render him a poorly informed and untrustworthy teacher. To cite letters of approval based on success stories is beside the point, unless one wishes to argue that the end justifies the means.[4]

This is an important point. One of Bill Gothard's "proofs" that God has His hand on this ministry is the numbers who have attended the seminars and the anecdotal stories of people who claim to have been helped by the ministry. We are not saying that people haven't been helped, but that in no way proves that his teachings are true. We have pointed out to Bill numerous times that if numbers equal "success" (two and a half million have attended the Basic Seminar according to IBLP), Jehovah's Witnesses (who have more than three times the "alumni" – about six million) would certainly have to be considered as having God's blessing as well. Similarly, the LDS (Mormons) have nearly twelve million adherents. Both of these organizations also claim to have helped people, and they publish anecdotal stories as "proof." There are many other groups that could be cited that use the same fallacious criteria to show that they have God's blessing. Numbers of adherents/followers are simply not the biblical criteria for determining truth.

For a Christian ministry, careful and accurate exposition of the Bible is far more important than attracting crowds. About Bill Gothard's characteristic misuse of Scripture, Dr. Allen commented:

The Book of Job presents a point of view that is dramatically different from Gothard's lists. In fact, Bill Gothard is a splendid modern day example of Eliphaz, Bildad, and Zophar — each of whom approached the problems of Job from a mechanistic, cause-and-effect, point of view. Here was their principle error: while there is a cause-and-effect approach to reality that is found at times in the wisdom literature of Scripture, that is not the only approach to life that the Bible teaches.

The clear teaching of the Book of Job is that a mechanistic, cause-and-effect, approach to life may be way off base! Is it any wonder that Gothard tries to evade the clear teaching of the Bible that Job was a righteous man (the only reading on which the book works!), and finds many sins, neglect of the family, embittered sons, estranged from family, wrong attitudes toward workers? In this way the book is turned inside out and by the strange alchemy Job supports Gothard's lists.[5]

Although Dr. Allen extended to Gothard for over twenty years the offer to meet anywhere at anytime at his own expense if necessary, including lunch or dinner, no meeting was forthcoming. Bill Gothard steadfastly refused to meet with Dr. Allen, while his meetings with Dr. Radmacher over the same period of time were unfruitful. It is difficult to understand why Bill would meet with one and not the other. Bill Gothard finally wrote a response in 1990 to Dr. Allen's 1984 *Report*. In his response, he essentially attempted to make the case that since Dr. Allen disagreed with him, Allen was either a liberal or was trying to justify some hidden sin. Gothard wrote, "Dr. Allen's quarrel is not with me, but with the Word of God itself."[6] He went on:

My experience with those who talk about the "complex questions of life" in which there are no clear biblical answers has been to discover that they do not want clear answers from the Bible because they have adopted practices in their life which the Bible forbids.[7]

With unbridled arrogance, Bill Gothard equates disagreeing with his teaching and methodology to doubting the Word of God. Accordingly, in Gothard's view, the only ones who would call his teaching into question do so in order to comfortably continue in some pet sin.

We reported in the Midwest *Christian Outreach Journal* in 1997[8] that Bill had never met with Dr. Allen. Bill Gothard wrote to inform us that our information was wrong on this point. He stated, "The facts are that I did meet with Dr. Allen and wrote a detailed response to each of his concerns and then asked for a further meeting with him."[9] We contacted Dr. Allen, who immediately and unequivocally responded, in a seven-page "Open Letter," that they had *never* met! Dr. Allen wrote:

Mr. Gothard,

You know that there never was a meeting between you and me. You know that there never has been a phone call between you and me. You know that you have never written me — not me! You have written Dr. Radmacher, and you have met with him many times — something you deny in the same paragraph.

So, Bill, here is the new deal. All bets are off. Twenty-three years (1973-1997) are sufficient. I have had the offer for lunch "on the table" long enough. There will now be no meeting. There will be no lunches. There will be no phone calls. There will be no letters.

Actually, Bill, there is only one letter I wish to receive from you. It is a brief, no-excuses, no-defenses, abject apology for your blatant, outrageous lies about me. I wish this to be mailed to me at my address at the end of this letter. Further, I wish this apology to be distributed at least as far as your lies about me have gone.[10]

Bill Gothard sent a letter to Dr. Allen on November 29, 1997 thanking him, "...for bringing to my attention an inaccuracy in my letter to Don Veinot. I am happy to make the following correction."[11] But no apology was offered.

Drs. Radmacher and Allen are two well respected, credentialed scholars who have attempted to confront Gothard, but they are not the only people who have attempted to correct the problems with Gothard and the IBLP. A number of other pastors, scholars, and others have trodden the path before us to no avail.

Two or Three Witnesses

Well-intentioned people have often encouraged us to meet with Bill Gothard and appeal to Matthew 18:15-20 to make their case. First of all, we do not agree that this passage applies to this situation, because our problem with Gothard is not about private sin, but about the very public teaching of false doctrine. We believe this falls under 1 Timothy 5:20-21:

> Against an elder receive not an accusation, but before two or three witnesses. Them that sin rebuke before all that others also may fear.

Second, however, we *have* met with Bill Gothard in an attempt to work out the issues, only to run into the same wall of obstinacy as did many others who have gone before us. We took the position that there are some good things in the Seminar and that many people claim to have benefited from Gothard's ministry. We made it clear that we only sought correction of false teaching. And so, like those prior to us, we at Midwest Christian Outreach, Inc., have met with Bill, also to no avail. In some cases, Bill made commitments to change his teachings (as with Dr. Radmacher) or to look at other evidence and then simply broke his word when the time came to fulfill his commitments.

Ours is certainly not the first attempt to talk with Mr. Gothard or to deal with the problem of his teachings. Besides those already mentioned, other researchers such as Rev. G. Richard Fisher of Personal Freedom Outreach and David Henke of Watchman Fellowship have attempted to call attention to Gothard's faulty teachings as well. It is important to realize that although Matthew 18 doesn't apply to this situation we have nonetheless followed the steps found there in order to be above reproach in our methodology.

A Blast From the Past

We (Don and Joy Veinot) attended a Basic Seminar in the mid-1970s at the enthusiastic urging of other members of the church we attended who had only good things to say about the program. So we were disappointed to find the teachings very legalistic and a bit of a biblical stretch. But other than when we received the annual birthday cards from the Institute, we didn't think much about Bill Gothard or the Seminar over the ensuing years. In the late 1980s we began reaching out to those in cults and false religions (mostly Jehovah's Witnesses and Mormons) and training others to do the same, which eventually led to our founding of an apologetics ministry, Midwest Christian Outreach, Inc. In 1991 we began receiving phone calls from residents of Oak Brook and Hinsdale who were very concerned over what they perceived as a "communal cult" in their town. These callers alleged that this "cult" was holding young girls against their will on a "compound" in their area. When we asked the name of the group, we were told it was the IBLP. As previously related, we gave Bill Gothard and the Institute little thought prior to that, certainly never with great apprehension, and were quite surprised at the concerns raised. We assured the callers that although they might seem legalistic, to our knowledge they were a fairly mainstream Christian group. Over the next several years we received similar calls and responded in essentially the same fashion.

In 1995 we legally incorporated Midwest Christian Outreach as a 501(c)3, not-for-profit ministry and expanded to general apologetics (defense of the historic Christian faith) as well as cults and false religious movements. The calls for information on Bill Gothard not only continued, but increased.

The Stated Mission?

A large part of dealing with cults and false religious movements is researching their materials, teachings, and group behaviors.

We find many Christians are supportive of exposing and evangelizing groups widely recognized within the church as cults. Within a short period of time, however, we were forced to branch out and deal with other issues involving the defense of the Christian faith, including false doctrine and/or heavy authoritarianism *within* the church. The apostle Paul said that false teachers would arise from both without and within the Christian church, and we soon were able to affirm the truth of his words in our own experience. We are convinced that if we were to expose false teachings and false teachers outside the church we would have to be equally honest and forthright about the false teachings within. To this end, Midwest Christian Outreach began doing the far less popular work of exposing the churches' "homegrown" false teachers and their heretical teachings. By 1996 Midwest Christian Outreach had received a sufficient number of calls that we decided to examine the teachings of IBLP — to either affirm and defend the Institute or, if we found serious problems, to talk with Bill Gothard. Senior researcher Ron Henzel, and Midwest Christian Outreach president Don Veinot, began gathering whatever Seminar material others would donate for this research. By 1997, we were becoming deluged with calls, e-mails, and letters requesting help from "alumni" as well as reports of churches and families that were going through splits over Bill Gothard. At the same time, our own research was giving us cause for serious concern. We present this short history to show that although Mr. Gothard seems to believe that our "mission" is only directed at him, this is patently false. It is but one of many issues that we have researched and written about.

In 1997 Don Veinot attempted to contact Bill Gothard by phone while working on the first of what was planned to be a four-part series of articles on Bill Gothard and IBLP. The phone calls went unreturned. The first article was published in the September/October 1997 issue of the *Midwest Christian Outreach Journal*. In October we were contacted by *The Sandy Rios Show* on WYLL in Chicago and asked to take part in an interview about the Institute. Don Veinot agreed. In the meantime Sandy contacted two other men, Rev. G. Richard Fisher of Personal Freedom Outreach and a psychologist named Lowell Kivley to participate in the program as well. As is her custom, Sandy promoted the show for several days in advance, advertising the topic to be discussed. On the day of the show, Bill Gothard called Sandy Rios and insisted that she cancel the show. She would not agree to that, at which point he insisted that he be allowed to participate as a fourth guest. She felt that was a good compromise and rearranged the show accordingly. As Don was leaving for the interview, Bill called and asked him not to take part in the show. He also asked why he hadn't been contacted about the article we had published in our *Journal*. He was told about our attempts to reach him by phone that were ignored. Bill apologized for not returning the calls and then proceeded to assert that it was unbiblical to print such material. We, of course, could not agree with him on that point. However, we did agree to meet face to face to discuss the issues.

Turn Your Radio On

Bill Gothard writes about that radio interview in a document titled *A Response to the Midwest Christian Journal*, which was written in an effort to refute the information in the aforementioned article in the *Journal*. He writes:

> Mr. Veinot had lined up several of his fellow critics to join the program. They each had a list of "concerns." The host also had questions and concerns. I am sure it sounded like a press conference with each one trying to get their question in and also add their own comments to it. The cacophony was interrupted every few minutes by a commercial, which was actually a relief because it provided an opportunity to think about the questions and the mental frames of reference which prompted them.[12]

As previously noted, *The Sandy Rios Show* — not Don Veinot — set up the participants; hence, Bill is passing out false information. His statement about the "mental frames of reference" is an interesting one. It turns out that his attempt to determine the "mental frames" of the other participants fell almost hilariously wide of the mark. For example, he accused Rev. G. Richard Fisher of being opposed to Bill's teachings in order to justify his desire for alcohol. The interesting aspect of this accusation is that Rev. Fisher practices complete abstinence from alcohol. But as we have seen so often, passing false information about others is not an uncommon thing for Gothard. At the same time, he is very concerned with keeping negative information about himself and the Institute from getting out to the public, for he considers it "unbiblical" to criticize him.

Gothard continues:

> One point became clear in that half-hour of vigorous discussion and further talks with Don Veinot. He has a sharp disagreement with me over the standards of Godly living, which I believe are essential to demonstrate the truth of Christ to our world.[13]

If Gothard means that we disagree that his *opinions* about godly living are the inspired, infallible, and authoritative teaching on this subject, he is correct. If he means that we do not believe in holy living, that is completely false. But as we have found, Bill equates disagreeing with his personal opinions and preferences with doubting the Word of God, wanting to live sinful lives, being "in rebellion," etc. Hence, he sets up a straw man and proceeds to pummel with it those who oppose him. We will be looking at his aberrational teachings beginning with the next chapter.

Let the Meetings Begin

The meeting was scheduled for 7:00 p.m. on November 20, 1997. We mailed Gothard a copy of the *Midwest Christian Outreach Journal*, which contained the first article of what was scheduled to be a four-part series. As is our normal procedure in such meetings, for the sake of accuracy we planned to bring a tape recorder and duplicator in order to record the discussions.

Besides creating a record of our meeting for our own use, we were going to leave copies of the tapes with Bill Gothard. He agreed. Subsequently we received a letter from Gothard dated October 25, 1997. In the first article, we noted that our next article was going to deal with Gothard's legalism, and his letter was primarily written to register his displeasure at being labeled a legalist. His view that questioning his teaching is unchristian is also demonstrated in this portion of his letter:

> Instinctively, I had to look again at your front page which displays the cross of Christ and bold word over it *Christian*. For you to have attended a Basic Seminar about twenty years ago "at the urging of some church members" and now to publicly proclaim your reactions in such a reviling manner does not seem to communicate the message and ministry that you represent.[14]

After attempting to defend his teachings he claimed to have met with Dr. Allen. As we previously pointed out, he has since admitted that this is not true. He also requested a copy of the upcoming article (which, as promised, dealt with the question of whether he should be considered a legalist). We accommodated him and sent the article with our reply on November 3, 1997. We also reminded him that we would be recording the upcoming meeting. On the morning of the scheduled meeting, November 20, 1997, we received a call from his office asking to reschedule as Mr. Gothard had been called out of town suddenly. After consulting with the other participants we agreed to do so. In light of the impending meeting and our hope of bringing resolution to our concerns, we also held up the remaining articles about Bill Gothard and IBLP that were to appear in upcoming *Journals*.

Soon after that, we received a letter dated November 28, 1997 which arrived on the morning of the rescheduled meeting, December 4, 1997. In it, Bill Gothard took exception to a statement we made in the upcoming article that certain Gothard materials are difficult to track down unless you know someone who is willing to lend them to you. He enclosed a catalog to show this was inaccurate. Upon review of the catalog, however, we noted that the material in question (the Seminar books) were *not* available in the catalog and later thanked him for proving our point. In this letter he wrote:

> Don, I need to explain to you that I have scheduled this meeting against the counsel of a very well respected Christian leader who knows you better than I do. He said, "You will be sorry if you have a meeting with Don Veinot, because Veinot does not play by the rules." I am beginning to see what he means.[15]

He then backed out of taping the meeting. Our concerns multiplied at this point. If he was willing to back out of commitments he made in advance and in writing, what would hold him to undocumented commitments? Second, by repeating a vague charge that was allegedly made by some unnamed, purportedly respected Christian leader, he violated his own teaching on listening to and giving "bad reports." We are not saying that we agree with his teaching on this issue, but it is hypocritical to hold others to a standard which you are unwilling to keep. If the alleged accuser were indeed well respected, why not give us a chance to judge that by giving us his name? And if he, this supposedly great leader, has some inside knowledge of wrongdoing on our part, why not come forward publicly with it? It is our general practice to assume that anonymous accusations are unworthy of our attention, but since Mr. Gothard has so much to say about this issue, we felt it best to address it. Our response, which was faxed to him on the afternoon of December 4, 1997, was as follows:

> I am also concerned to learn from your letter of November 28, 1997, that you listened to a bad report that someone else is spreading about me. I am not so much concerned that someone is spreading this bad report, many Jehovah's Witnesses, Mormons, etc., do this as well, but I am concerned that you have listened to it. The reason I am concerned is because you have publicly taught millions of Christians that it is wrong to listen to

such bad reports. For this reason I need to appeal to your conscience before the Lord as a Christian brother.

On page 17 of your 1976 Supplementary Book for Seminar Alumni entitled, "*Rediscovering a Forgotten Truth*," you wrote: "If every Christian were committed to giving only a good report, gossip and slander would cease." On page 21 you wrote, "Each one of us must make a lifelong decision to give only a clear conscience and a desire to restore the offender." I am troubled that the action you describe in your letter — that of listening to a bad report about me — is so obviously inconsistent with your own printed statements.

I do not know who this person is who shared this detrimental information about me with you, but I can assure you that he or she has not followed the steps of Matthew 18 with me, which you insist upon for others. On page 16 of your "*Rediscovering*" book, you wrote: "If a Christian leader gives a bad report about any other brother without having gone to him first in a spirit of love, he becomes a whisperer and damages the wider work of Christ which He prayed for in John 17." Assuming you believe what you wrote is true, I am amazed that you willingly participated with just such a "whisperer" in something that damaged the work of Christ.

In your Supplementary Alumni Book Volume 2, 1976, entitled, "*Instruction for our Most Important Battle*," you spend pages 24 and 25 on the subject of "How to Detect and Respond to a Bad Report." On those pages you ascribe the following eight negative motivations to people who listen to bad reports about others:

1. Pride in having superior wisdom to judge difficult conflicts.

2. Desire for their approval by agreeing with their conclusions.

3. Curiosity for facts about the private lives of others.

4. Desire to know all the facts that may affect one's life and family.

5. Desire to protect and defend one's reputation.

6. Fear of losing something which may be the basis of one's security.

7. Desire to learn about the failures of a spiritual leader to avoid feeling bad about one's own weaknesses.

8. Security of knowing that one is on the "inside" because one has the detailed information that others don't have.

Since these are the only motivations you presented, I assume you do not believe there are any others. Which one of them would you choose to describe your motivation for listening to the bad report about me?

On page 25 you teach that people should take a bad report directly to the person it is about, rather than passing it through someone else, even if that person is a spouse. Why did you not follow your own teaching and advise this person to come directly to me?

Also on page 25, you write of the "Need to Stop a Whisperer." You suggest the following response to one who seeks to give a bad report: "It would be so much better for you to discuss his question with [the person in question] before sharing it with me or anyone else." It is clear from your letter that you did not do this, but rather listened to a bad report.

On page 21 of "Instructions for Our Most Important Battle," you pose the following question: "How can I stop someone from giving a bad report to me?" You answer this question as follows: "As soon as we realize that someone is giving a bad report we should lovingly ask him if he has gone to the person yet. If he has, we could ask, 'Are you telling me so I can go with you to help restore him?'" But instead of following your principle, you violated it.

You further suggest that, "Another response might be to interrupt him with the question, 'Do you feel I am responsible to know about this? I would rather not hear it unless I am directly involved.'" How are you directly involved in the bad report this person has issued against me? Since you are not directly involved, you have no way of knowing whether the bad report is true or false without taking that person's word for it. And since you have taken that person's word for it you have prejudged me.

I could cite many other things you have written, all of which would amply demonstrate this point. Nothing I write here should be taken as a blanket endorsement of all that you teach on the subjects of gossip, slander, giving a bad report, etc. But everything I write here should be taken as my appeal to you to confess that you have not practiced what you have preached.

In light of your listening to a bad report I am doubly surprised that you insist on not recording this meeting. If I thought I was meeting with someone who "...does not play by the rules," I would be more inclined to want to record the meeting.[16]

This experience again illustrates Bill Gothard's trademark refusal to practice what he preaches. His genuine *belief* about how to resolve conflict, as opposed to the conflict resolution method he *teaches*, comes to the fore when his interests are involved. His *personal* method of conflict resolution seems to be as follows: Initiate a meeting, make agreements and nonchalantly break them, and then make *ad hominem* attacks on those who oppose to his teachings. His motive in personal attack may be to provoke the contender to refuse to meet with him, which would allow him to say that he tried to resolve the issues. We discussed this with our board of directors and board of advisors. It was decided that we should proceed with the meeting without recording it since there would be four of us present (Don Veinot, Ron Henzel, Marty Butz and Don's pastor, Fred Greening), to serve as witnesses and to aid in recall.

On December 4, 1997, at 8:15 p.m. we met with Bill Gothard and several IBLP staff (John Stephens, George Mattix, and Nathan O'Brien). The meeting was cordial and at times congenial. We asked Bill about his listening to and passing on what he refers to in his teachings as "a bad report." He was unable to explain why this injunction did not apply in this situation, but simply asserted that it was a different case. We moved on and discussed a number of issues and concerns including legalism, the role of the Law in the life of believers, birth control, circumcision, and rock music. We specifically wanted him to back up some of his dogmatically stated opinions with hard, cold facts. Bill committed to sending us the scientific data to support his claim that "uncircumcised men have, as a group, been more promiscuous than circumcised men."[17] He also committed to providing us with the scientific data that showed that rock music is intrinsically evil and causes evil behavior. To date, the promised data have not been forthcoming. Bill was insistent that Ron Henzel couldn't really understand the Seminar teachings without attending one, and since many of the Seminars are now conducted via videotape, he consented to send us a set for review and comment. A few days later we received written transcripts but no videotapes. We did not accept this substitute, insisting that if we can only understand Bill's teachings via the Seminar itself, they needed to keep their word and send actual videotaped Seminars, which they finally did.

At this point we were quite hopeful that we could work through these issues. Over the next several months we spent time reviewing the Seminar tapes and other materials and had several telephone conversations with Bill Gothard and John Stephens. But as we began pointing out the serious theological flaws that we were finding in the Seminar tapes, Bill had John Stephens demand them back before we could finish our analysis. At that point, communication from IBLP ceased. The next article we published (in the March/April 1998 edition of the *Midwest Outreach Journal*) was an account of the December 4, 1997 meeting which was titled, *An Evening With Bill Gothard*. We also began putting our findings up on our web site, along with other items, such as the *Open Letter* from Dr. Allen.

New Contact

The next communication came in the form of a phone call to Don Veinot from Bill Gothard in early July of 1998. Bill expressed a desire to meet again. During the course of this telephone conversation, Don informed Bill that Midwest Christian Outreach had been contacted numerous times by people who believed the teachings of IBLP to be harmful. Bill said he had no knowledge of any harm coming from his teachings and asserted that if his Seminar were causing problems he wanted to correct them. At that point Don asked him point blank, "Since you have been teaching these same things over the course of thirty years without change and you have so much in print, how willing are you to make changes?" His response was, "Very willing." So, in good faith, Don faxed him a number of e-mails and letters describing the negative and harmful teachings which had been received from broken families, split churches, and concerned family members. We arranged a meeting for July 13, 1998, and Ron Henzel, Don Veinot, Bill Gothard, and John Stevens met at 7:00 p.m. that evening. The meeting lasted until about 1:00 a.m.

The Second Meeting

Some time was spent discussing IBLP's teachings on the "biblical" order of worship and legalism. As for the first issue, Bill expressed surprise that his teaching on the biblical order of worship was still in the pastors manual and instructed John Stephens then and there to remove it from future printings. We were encouraged, as it seemed we were making some headway. Regarding "legalism," Bill continued to insist that the concept was illegitimate because the word cannot be found in Scripture. We argued that this objection is very weak since, there are many good theological terms not found in the pages of Scripture that nonetheless accurately describe biblical teachings. We reminded

Bill that he has himself referred to "legalism" as something to be avoided in his *Instructions for our Most Important Battle*.[18] We finally moved on without reaching resolution on this issue.

The bulk of our time in this second meeting centered on Bill's teaching about the absolute necessity of circumcision for Christians. We made the case that the medical "evidence" he cited in favor of the practice consisted primarily of quotations taken out of their context, which leads to faulty conclusions. In short, his supposed scientific data do not really support his position at all. Having made this point, we made it very clear that our concerns were not of a medical nature; the question of whether to circumcise for medical or even cultural reasons is a matter of Christian liberty. Our concerns were, and continue to be, theological in nature. We pointed out that the entire New Testament book of Galatians devoted to addressing this issue. Never one to beat around the bush, the Apostle Paul bluntly concluded that those who were intent on imposing this practice upon believers *for religious reasons* (as Bill Gothard does in his circumcision booklet) should emasculate themselves (Galatians 5:12). In this context, Paul also unwaveringly asserted that those who eschew their freedom in Christ and submit to compulsory circumcision have put themselves back under the law and have "fallen from grace."

> Stand fast therefore in the liberty wherewith Christ hath made us free, and be not entangled again with the yoke of bondage. Behold, I Paul say unto you that if ye be circumcised, Christ shall profit you nothing. For I testify again to every man that is circumcised, that he is a debtor to do the whole law. Christ is become of no effect unto you, whosoever of you are justified by the law; ye are fallen from grace (Galatians 5:1-4).

These are strong words that convey Paul's strong feelings against such legalistic requirements and against our submission to such supposedly spiritual demands.

The evening ended with Bill asking to review the next article

(on legalism) prior to publication. We agreed to hold the printing for a few more days. He had, as already mentioned, instructed John Stevens to remove the teachings on the biblical order of
worship, and he also agreed to abandon his teachings on circumcision. In fact, John Stevens turned to Bill and said, "The
best that we can say is that circumcision *may* be medically beneficial." Once again, we adjourned somewhat hopeful that real
changes would be forthcoming. Our view at the time was that
even though Bill had not provided the scientific proof that uncircumcised men are more promiscuous than circumcised men, if
he was withdrawing the booklet we would not press that issue
further. Bill had also not yet provided scientific data showing the
causal relationship between rock music and evil behavior, but he
again committed to sending that to us. He also requested that "in
a show of good faith" we remove the *Open Letter* from Dr. Allen
from our web-site, since it was hurting IBLP and some people
were beginning to view IBLP as a cult (something which we had
never stated in our writings). We agreed and accommodated Bill
on this as a good-faith gesture on our part.

Another About-Face

On July 17, 1998 Bill called to say that there were major flaws
in our upcoming article on legalism.[19] He said he was sending a
letter and other information via fax later in the day. At 7:35 p.m.
we received a 20-page fax from Bill Gothard. In response to our
article on legalism he wrote:

> The whole thrust and conclusion of your article is based on
> your definition of "legalism." In support of your definition,
> you cite three evangelical writers and their works, Erwin
> Lutzer, J.I. Packer, and Charles C. Ryrie. To confirm accu-
> racy, I called each of these men to discuss their definition
> of legalism. So far, I have had two conversations with Dr.
> Ryrie, one with Dr. Lutzer and I am waiting a return call
> from Dr. Packer.
>
> These discussions have proven very helpful and the

definitions that they have given to me certainly need to be included in your article if you are going to use them as references.[20]

This new attitude came as a surprise, since he had already agreed to abandon his teachings on circumcision, and we had agreed in good faith to remove the *Open Letter* by Dr. Allen from our web site. Bill had again broken his commitment. For the record, the writers we had cited were referenced in the article's footnotes, including where the citations could be found in their works. Our point was primarily that other respected Christian leaders (including Bill Gothard) have also used the term "legalism" and that there is a commonly accepted definition of the word in Christian circles. However, with some experience now of how Bill Gothard operates, we were concerned about how Bill might have framed the issue in his discussions with Lutzer and Ryrie, so we called and wrote to them. We asked them if he had mentioned his teaching on the need to practice "Christian" circumcision during his discussion with them on their definition of legalism. They were dumbfounded. No, Bill had not mentioned that little detail — and they agreed that they would view such a teaching as legalistic.

Round and Round the Mulberry Bush...

We return now to Bill Gothard's July 17 letter — he writes:

> We also did research on your claim that "the notion that circumcision reduces the risk of cervical cancer in women has been repudiated by the America Cancer Society." The results of this research cannot be ignored if you want to give an honest, truthful, and objective report, and I believe you do.[21]

As we reviewed the information, we noted that it was the *same* material that we reviewed with him on July 14. We had made very clear that we were not concerned with the medical aspects of this procedure but only the theological implications of

Bill's imposition of the practice on believers. Bill called Don Veinot on July 18, 1998. Don again reviewed with Bill the irrelevant (to our case) material that had been faxed to our office. Bill questioned the legitimacy of a letter by Dr. Shingleton and Dr. Heath of the American Cancer Society which is posted on the American Cancer web site. These doctors wrote:

> Research suggesting a pattern in the circumcision status of partners of women with cervical cancer is methodologically flawed, outdated, and has not been taken seriously in the medical community for decades.[22]

Bill suggested that these men were only giving their personal opinion and not the official position of the American Cancer Society. Don countered that the letter is on official American Cancer Society letterhead and is posted on the American Cancer Society web site — it is clearly their official position. Don then went through the other faxed information and pointed out again that the quotes supposedly backing Gothard's position had been taken out of context — and, when read in context, usually said, the *opposite* of what Bill Gothard claimed. Don also questioned if one of Bill's "supporting" studies — comparing uncircumcised men who bathed in the Ganges River to circumcised men who did not bathe in the Ganges — was an example of the "methodologically flawed" studies to which the America Cancer Society was referring. Bill then admitted that he had not actually read the material himself but had a researcher compile the information. Don informed Bill that we would formulate a written response to his faxed information directly. This was completed and mailed on July 20, 1998. We never heard directly from Bill after that discussion.

Ron Henzel followed up with John Stephens by phone to see if they were going to respond to our July 20 material. He replied that he had been told they were formulating a written response which they would have theologians review and send to us prior to printing and distribution. Some time later we were advised by an individual who receives our *Journal* that he had been mailed a copy of a document titled *A Response to Antinomian Rationalism* by Bill Gothard. Ron immediately called John Stephens, who claimed that this document had not been released and was surprised that someone had received a copy. As it turns out, however, several thousand copies had been sent out. As of yet, IBLP has not replied directly to us or sent us a "review" copy. Instead, Bill Gothard created yet another even more regrettable document titled *Definition of Grace*, in which he argues that grace is earned! Furthermore, Bill went back on his word to drop his circumcision booklet and through his assistant, John Stephens, instead sent a proposed revision to Ron Henzel to review. Ron expressed surprise at Bill's breaking this agreement. He also pointed out that the way the proposed revision reads, circumcision has been elevated to a sacrament of the church! We are unsure of the current status of this work. We are now quite certain, however, that Bill regards gestures of good faith and commitment-keeping as applying to lesser men but not to himself.

Arbitration Anyone?

On the morning of October 7, 1999 John Stephens called Ron Henzel and informed him that Bill Gothard had requested an arbitration meeting between himself and the Institute and Don Veinot, Ron Henzel, and Midwest Christian Outreach. Bill Gothard had requested that Dr. Norman Geisler act as the arbitrator of this meeting. We at Midwest Christian Outreach have the utmost respect for Dr. Geisler's integrity and capability to adjudicate fairly, and Don, Ron, and the board of directors were very open to this petition. Don contacted Dr. Geisler, who expressed his willingness to arbitrate. Dr. Geisler stated firmly that ground rules must be established before we could proceed further. Correspondence was sent to John Stephens on October 11, 1999 relaying the acceptance of Midwest Christian Outreach, and Dr. Norman Geisler and defining the questions to be answered regarding the ground rules. Bill Gothard went silent again.

Over a year later, in January 2001, Bill Gothard contacted

Dr. Geisler. Bill advised Dr. Geisler that our material was hurting the ministry of IBLP, and he was writing a response. He asked Dr. Geisler to review it, and Dr. Geisler agreed. Gothard also told Dr. Geisler that it was a shame that Don Veinot wouldn't meet in arbitration, to which Dr. Geisler replied that Don and Midwest Christian Outreach had agreed to meet and that Bill was the one who had "dropped the ball."

During January and February correspondence was faxed back and forth through Dr. Geisler which laid out the subjects to be discussed, which were:

1. Is there a biblical basis for Bill Gothard's teachings on umbrellas of protection?

2. Is there a scriptural foundation for Bill Gothard's teaching on "the iniquities of the father?"

3. Is there a biblical basis for Bill Gothard's teaching on the order of the worship service? (This one surprised us, as when we last met he said he had stopped teaching that and instructed John Stevens to make sure it was taken out of the Pastors Manual.)

4. Is the purpose of the account of the centurion (Matthew 8:5-13) given to teach Bill Gothard's view of authority or to teach who Jesus is and the importance of faith in Him?

5. Do Cabbage Patch dolls prevent the birth of children?

6. Does Bill Gothard's teaching on authority imply that Jesus is a sinner?

7. Does the phrase, "One interpretation, many applications" allow us to have applications that are not based on or even contrary to the one true interpretation?

8. Is it proper to impose Levitical ceremonial restrictions on sexual intercourse within Christian marriages?

9. Is it proper to impose circumcision as a biblical mandate for Christians today?

10. If a Christian leader changes a significant teaching which was shown to be unbiblical, should he not make a public retraction before his followers?

11. Is it biblically proper to say that grace is earned?

All parties agreed to the time allotment for the meeting and the inclusion of an outside observer from a Christian publication who would report on the meeting and results. *World* magazine and *Christianity Today* were suggested as possibilities. Everything was "good to go." The only items yet to be determined were the date and location.

However, the next correspondence from Bill Gothard took a change in course, which we have grown to expect from him. On March 2, 2001, rather than suggesting meeting dates, he sent a thirteen-page fax requesting yet another written response. Two items are of particular interest in his first page.

I reread [Don Veinot's] articles and realized that we have different presuppositions about many areas in the Christian life and the Word of God.[23]

It is difficult to respond here without sarcasm. If we agreed with his views, we wouldn't have been researching, writing, and meeting with him to bring about correction. If he had just then "realized" that we had major disagreements with him, why had he requested arbitration, which presupposes conflicting viewpoints? It has never been a secret that we hold not only "different" views but in some cases directly opposite views. We wonder why it took four years and all the associated meetings, telephone calls, correspondence, and articles to finally get this point across? In truth, we believe that the only thing Gothard just recently "realized" is that we could not be bullied into silence, and that we fully intended to go forward with the meeting.

The second statement again shows a decided change in

course on Bill Gothard's part. After agreeing on the topics and meeting format, with the only things to finalize being the outside observer, date, and location, he wrote:

> I would like to suggest that we have a "trial run" on one topic which is basic to [Don Veinot's] concerns and which, in my opinion, has ample biblical support. Could you send the enclosed response to him for his comments?[24]

His "trial run" shot over the bow turned out to be twelve pages of what appears to be a piece prepared for public distribution titled *A Response to Midwest Christian Journal*. We now had another decision to make. Should we continue to go forward with our planned arbitration meeting, appearing as it now did that Gothard had no real intention of following through on any of his agreements — given his propensity to stall, obfuscate, and continually change the ground rules? Again, we discussed this with some of the members of our Advisory Board. It was agreed that even though the issues raised were many of the same ones we were to discuss in arbitration, and even though Bill was again backing out of his agreements, we should acquiesce and respond to his latest challenge. Dr. Geisler was quite adamant that with this response, the next step on the agenda would be the finalization of the observer and the actual meeting. No other discussion or topics would be raised until the meeting took place.

We therefore responded with a six-page refutation of his paper on March 13, 2001. Dr. Geisler forwarded this to Bill, and requested possible meeting dates and locations. He also indicated that it was his understanding that *World* magazine would be the outside observer. On March 31, 2001 Bill faxed Dr. Geisler saying that they needed to discuss this and stated that he would call. Dr. Geisler faxed him back the same day pointing out that he was awaiting an indication of Bill's willingness to proceed as agreed. He flatly stated there was no need for further discussion and no new issues to be raised until we resolved what has already been agreed to.

To everyone's surprise, Bill Gothard faxed Dr. Geisler on

April 10, 2001 saying that he had contacted *World* magazine, worked out which reporter would be involved, and said that the meeting would be held at IBLP headquarters in Oak Brook, Illinois. This raised very serious concerns. The contact with the observer was to have been made not by either of the parties of disputation, but by the mediator, Dr. Geisler, in order to maintain as much neutrality as possible. The reporter's neutrality could be unintentionally compromised, depending upon how the issue was presented to him. Frankly, we did not trust Mr. Gothard to to be honest in his presentation of information. Dr. Geisler responded on April 16, 2001 with a reminder that it was his responsibility to make the arrangements on date, location, and observer. He reiterated the points that had been agreed upon and added a point — that neither Bill Gothard nor we must contact the observer until after the report had been published.

Bill Gothard responded with a letter backing out of the meeting and calling for a "Matthew 18" meeting with Don Veinot and the elders of the church where Don holds membership, and possibly with the board of directors of Midwest Christian Outreach. He claimed that he was justified in this action because of an article which had been printed about him in the *Midwest Christian Outreach Journal* prior to his initiation of this meeting which had just come across his desk.

Dr. Geisler answered Bill with a five-point letter on April 25, 2001. He first pointed out that by refusing to sign on the points that he had already committed to, he was backing out of his original agreement. Secondly, he told Bill that if he contacted the neutral observer, he would essentially be engaging in "jury tampering." Third, he asserted that Bill's refusal to proceed with a neutral observer gave the impression that he had something to hide. Fourth, he pointed out that there was an apparent contradiction between Bill's supposed concern for resolution and his unwillingness to meet to bring this about. Lastly, Dr. Geisler explained to Gothard that this was not a Matthew 18 situation but rather a doctrinal disagreement, making a Matthew 18-type approach inappropriate.

Then, Bill Gothard had John Stephens call Don Veinot on April 25 to raise additional issues. This was yet another violation of the established ground rules — no direct contact between the two parties and no additional issues raised until the meeting took place. *All* contact was to be through Dr. Geisler. Don reminded John of these agreements, and John expressed dismay that these agreements should apply to Mr. Gothard. Later that day, Stephens sent faxes to Dr. Geisler agreeing with all points of his April 16, 2001 fax except for the prohibition of contact with the neutral observer.

Next, Ron Henzel received a call from John Stephens, on behalf of Bill Gothard, on May 1, 2001. John said that Bill had just finished writing a new book and wanted to hire Ron for seven days at $500 per day to review the book prior to publication. Ron pointed out that this call constituted *another* violation of the agreement prohibiting contact before the meeting. He also made it clear that it would be an obvious conflict of interest to undertake this project and that the extravagant amount of money offered for this work could be construed as an attempt to bribe him. Only time will tell if Bill Gothard will repent and keep his agreements to mediation or will he abandon them completely?

Bill Gothard's Double Standards

The Scriptures are unambiguous on the qualifications and general demeanor of leaders within the church. It is necessary for a leader to be teachable, to keep his word, to exhibit his integrity by his behavior and to not engage in hypocrisy (such as having two sets of standards, one for others and one for oneself). Followers will emulate far more of what they see than what they are told. The cliché that "What you are doing speaks so loudly I can't hear what you are saying" seems to fit.

Jesus condemns double standards for conduct in Matthew 7:1-2:

> Judge not, that ye be not judged. For with what judgement
> ye judge, ye shall be judged: and with what measure ye

mete, it shall be measured to you again.

Jesus is obviously not telling us that it is wrong to judge others, for beginning in verse 15 of the same chapter he warns us to "Beware of false prophets" and sets forth the criteria for making such judgements. His point is that we are not to judge hypocritically, condemning others for behavior that we engage in, holding them to a standard we refuse to hold ourselves to. Bill Gothard holds a much higher standard for others than he is willing to apply to himself. Even where we disagree with his teachings, we feel that he should live them out – keep his own rules. But he does not follow his own teachings and, as far as we can determine, for all his promotion of authority, he is accountable to no one.

There are certainly good things about IBLP and many wonderful Christians associated with this organization. Unfortunately, there are many legalistic and harmful teachings as well, and many wonderful Christians are being hurt, some badly, by Bill Gothard's ideas.

Chapter 3

The Emerald City

I n the film *The Wizard of Oz*, Dorothy is caught in the chaos of a tornado and ultimately finds herself in a strange place, the Land of Oz. She is not sure how she got there and does not like being there — all she wants is to return home. She meets a scarecrow, who also wants something — a brain. Scarecrow tells Dorothy of someone who could fix both of their problems, the Wizard of Oz, and together they set off for the Emerald City. On the way they pick up other companions in need: the Tin Man, who wants a heart, and the Cowardly Lion, who desires courage. As they travel they encounter various trials, which they solve as a group, but are so focused on the perceived lack in their lives, they never realize they already possess the things they desire to receive from the Wizard! They are convinced that their problems can only be solved by "an expert," so upon arrival in Oz they immediately sign up for a "seminar" with the Wizard.

The Wizard turns out to be an imposing figure and quite awesome — the self-described "Great and Powerful Oz," blowing smoke and flame and giving the appearance of omniscience that one dare not question. In fact, our gang get themselves in big hot water with the Wiz by merely *questioning* an order he gave them to come back at another time. "Do you presume to criticize the Great Oz?," the Wiz thunders. Then, as luck would have it,

Dorothy's dog Toto pulls open a curtain, exposing an elderly bachelor pulling levers and pushing switches. Dorothy and the other "seminar" attendees find themselves in a confusing situation, pitting what they think they "know" against what they now clearly see. They observe the grand deception, yet they hear the great and authoritative Oz bellow, "Pay no attention to the man behind the curtain!" Who are they to believe — the wizard or their own eyes?

The Man Behind the Curtain

By 1973, Bill Gothard and the *IBLP* had become enormously popular. It appears that few Christian Leaders had seriously questioned his teachings up until that time. After all, Gothard was thought to be an evangelical. Like Dorothy, Christians found themselves in a strange and scary world, and no one seemed to be sure of how they got there. Bill Gothard seemed to be the wizard who had all the answers and could bring them back home — back to the way it was before the chaotic years they had just witnessed. Bill was a certain man in an age of uncertainty, and he presented his solutions dogmatically. The way home was the path of "Submission to authority."

Some people, however, including Bible scholars, began paying attention to the man behind the curtain and his strange teachings. One of them was Ronald B. Allen, Th.D., and Professor of Hebrew Scripture at *Western Baptist Seminary* in Portland, Oregon. (Where he taught for 25 years. He currently teaches at Dallas Theological Seminary in Dallas, Texas.) In 1973, his wife prompted him to attend the Institute in Basic Youth Conflicts with her. He was horrified at what he saw and attempted to set up a meeting with Bill Gothard to discuss his concerns. In fact, he attempted without success to meet with Bill for the next 11 years. He eventually committed his thoughts to writing in a 1984 paper entitled *Issues of Concern — Bill Gothard and the Bible*, which begins as follows:

The week that I spent at the Basic Youth Conflicts in

1973 (Portland) was one of the most difficult of my life. In this seminar I was regularly assaulted by a misuse of the Bible, particularly the Old Testament, on a level that I have never experienced in a public ministry before that time (or since). All speakers, myself included, fail to inter- pret (and apply) the Bible from time to time. But in the Gothard lectures, Old Testament passages were used time after time to argue points that they did not prove. I was as troubled by the errors made from the lectern, as by the seeming acceptance of these errors as true and factual by the many thousands of people in attendance.

Gothard's followers may be tempted to view Allen's critical description as an overstatement based on misunderstanding; but if that were the case, Gothard had every opportunity to correct the misunderstanding. When Dr. Allen attempted to arrange a meeting with Gothard through his seminary president, Dr. Earl Radmacher (who was also very concerned about Gothard's seri- ous misuse and abuse of Scripture), in order to discuss these problems, Gothard told Radmacher that "he had no interest in meeting with me [Allen] to discuss these matters."[1] In fact, Dr. Allen contends that Gothard went on to tell Dr. Radmacher, "God is my teacher, I don't need your seminary professors." Dr. Allen extended the offer for well over 20 years, including the invi- tation to meet for lunch or dinner at his expense, if need be.

This unwillingness to be confronted biblically – apparent resistance to being under authority and lack of a consistent bib- lical hermeneutic – has given birth to some very strange and, in some cases, harmful teachings.[2]

Aside from Dr. Allen, Dr. Radmacher and a few other Christian leaders had attempted to and in some cases did meet with Bill in an attempt to correct him privately. However, for the first 20 years or so of Bill Gothard's seminar ministry, his teach- ings received little public scrutiny. A notable exception was Wilfred Bockelman's book, *Gothard – The Man and His Ministry: An Evaluation*. As far as we know this has been the only book- length treatment of Gothard's ministry ever to be marketed to

the general Christian public. (There have been some other substantial published works, but they have had a limited circulation).
While Bockelman worked hard to be evenhanded and found positive things to say, he also had some serious theological disagreements with Gothard, especially on the subject of God's grace.

Nonetheless, Bockelman's book does not appear to have had
much impact on the evangelical community. One reason for this
might have been that his publisher was small, and the book probably suffered from poor distribution. Another factor might have
been the immense popularity Gothard was enjoying in the mid-
'70s (especially among parents and grandparents). Anyone criticizing him naturally would have been viewed with suspicion.

Another thing to consider was Gothard's unique strategy for
marketing his own books and material: you could *only* get them
by attending his seminars. Gothard sold nothing over the count-
er at Christian bookstores or anywhere else. His was the original
"This Offer Not Available in Stores" approach, except operators
were *not* standing by. You had to get in your car and *go* to one of
his public seminars. As Bockelman wrote:

> And if you think you'd like to slip away an extra copy to
> a friend, who could really use one, forget it. The book
> [the seminar notebook] is intended only for the use of
> those who go through the whole program.
>
> During the week there will be twelve times when por-
> tions of the book are distributed. In the front of the book
> is a little card that lists all twelve times and the name of
> the material to be distributed then. When you receive
> yours, that card gets checked off, so you can't go back and
> get a second copy.[3]

One effect of this was that no one who had not actually
attended a seminar had access to what Gothard was teaching.
Thus, very few had the opportunity to privately and objectively
scrutinize his materials outside the arena of his seminars. Not
only that, but at his seminars Gothard publicly discouraged attendees from even discussing the materials outside of the seminars.

As Bockelman, who actually did attend, wrote:

> Bill Gothard is perfectly justified in saying, "If people
> want to know what the Institute in Basic Youth Conflicts
> is all about, let them come to the seminar." He even has
> the right to say, "You can't form an opinion unless you've
> attended the whole Institute." He has reason to be dis-
> satisfied with those who have never attended one of his
> Institutes, but who nevertheless pontificate on them.
>
> Still, I don't think Gothard is being particularly rea-
> sonable when he suggests that people attending the sem-
> inar not even discuss the handbook outside the meet-
> ings.[4]

To many Christians in the 1970s, Bockelman's book probably seemed overly alarmist. But now, reading his comments from
post-Jonestown, post-Waco perspective can be rather troubling.
True, Gothard did not set up a hermetically sealed, cultic community along those lines, but there is one feature he appears to
have in common with them: the avoidance of accountability
through the control of information — specifically, the control of
information about himself and his teachings.

The absence of Gothard materials outside of his seminars
(and the ironic suppression of their content by Gothard himself)
meant that objectionable portions of his teachings were kept out
of the Christian public's view. Since attendees (whom Gothard
dubbed "alumni" after they attended) were discouraged from discussing them, outsiders knew of no reason for alarm.

Since you could not just go out and buy a Gothard book at a
Christian bookstore, Christian book reviewers could not read
them and point out any problems found in them. Therefore,
almost no one was able to read any critical analysis of problems.
It also meant his books were generally unavailable to Bible professors, theologians, and those engaged in apologetics and discernment ministries. Thus, as thousands of Christian college
kids filed into Gothard's seminars, their instructors were unable
to comment on this alternative source of teaching unless they,

themselves, took time out of their busy schedules to attend. And since Gothard was so widely praised, there seemed to be no reason to check up on him.

Gothard materials are understandably difficult to track down these days, unless you actually know some "alumni" who will let you borrow their copies.[5] But some copies of seminar materials from the '60s and '70s have found their way onto the library shelves and into used bookstores, and "alumni" have given us their materials, which we have used these as a basis for evaluating the content of his seminars.

How Gothard Says He Interprets the Bible

An examination of Gothard's materials, from their earliest days, shows there *was* a great deal about which to be concerned. Gothard knew how to disarm his audience, assure them of his competence, and allay potential misgivings. Thus, in his large, red *Basic Seminar Textbook* from 1979, he appears to lay out a sound foundation for what follows in his book:

> WORKING THROUGH THE TEXT: Before any application of Scripture can be made, there must be a thorough understanding of what the text is actually saying.
>
> Why was it written?
>
> To whom was it written?
>
> What were the conditions at the time?
>
> What was the precise meaning in the original language?
>
> What related Scriptures explain it further?[6]

These are, of course, standard procedures for biblical interpretation — indeed for *any* kind of interpretation. It is what would be called the historical-grammatical method.

But it's one thing to know the rules of interpretation (hermeneutics) and to be able to quote them; it's another thing to actually practice them. Not very far into the *Basic Seminar*

Textbook we begin to encounter uses of Scripture that fly in the face of the very sound procedures Gothard himself outlined. For example:

> Undue concern for clothes may be an attempt to cover up or compensate for unchangeable physical features which are rejected. Jesus linked these two thoughts in Matthew 6:27, 28 "Which of you by taking thought can add one cubit unto his stature? And why take ye thought for raiment?"[7]

Gothard makes it sound like Jesus was addressing the problem of shame over blemishes, a big nose, etc. A look at the context, however, reveals that He had nothing of the sort in mind, but instead was addressing the sin of habitual worry:

> Therefore I say unto you, take no thought for your life, what ye shall eat, or what ye shall drink; nor yet for your body, what ye shall put on. Is not the life more than meat, and the body than raiment (Matthew 6:25)?

By teaching that Jesus was linking the two thoughts of clothing and a poor self-image, Gothard also commits the error of anachronistic (chronologically misplaced) reasoning by projecting, if you will, 20th-century psychological assumptions into the teachings of Jesus.[8]

How Gothard Actually Interprets the Bible

Examples like this are not very disturbing at first and seem to be offset by other examples of correct scriptural application. But over the course of nearly 200 pages the errors begin to multiply, especially in areas where Gothard's views tend to be unique — for instance, on page 20, when Gothard begins discussing his favorite subject of "authority."

The essence of Gothard's teaching of submission is not "getting under the domination of authority but rather getting under the protection of authority." According to Bill Gothard, authority is like an "umbrella of protection," and when we get out from under it, we expose ourselves to unnecessary temptations, which are too strong for us to overcome. This is why Scripture, in his view, compares rebellion to witchcraft – "Rebellion is like the sin of witchcraft." (1 Samual 15:23). Both terms have the same basic definition – subjecting ourselves to the realm and power of Satan.[9]

Here a pattern emerges not only of citing Scripture that does *not* prove his point but also of not giving *any* scriptural support for something Gothard considers essential. His citation of 1 Samuel 15:23 is not contextually related to his definition of "submission" as "getting under the protection of authority." And instead of providing us with a Scripture verse that *does* prove that point, Gothard diverts our attention to another issue entirely. He smoothly glides into a comparison of rebellion to witchcraft that is designed to establish the following thesis: Rebellion (getting out from under the "umbrella of protection") is evil; therefore, submission is righteous.

This idea sounds biblical enough so that to most seminar attendees – who are usually balancing a three-ring binder on their knees, feverishly taking down notes, while trying to catch everything on Gothard's overhead presentation – it is not obvious that Gothard has just misused the Bible. But then who *doesn't* occasionally quote a Scripture verse in support of a point it does not prove? We all make this mistake from time to time. That doesn't mean that Gothard's or our teaching is dangerous, does it?

While this reasoning may pacify the conscience of a seminar attendee, it will also set that person up for difficulty because:

1. Gothard's view of submission to authority is the foundation upon which he builds *many* of his other teachings

2. By the time Gothard deals with the subject of authority, quoting verses that do not prove his point has already become something of a habit for him. So for a person to have read all the way through to page 20 in the *Basic Seminar Textbook* without being alarmed by this trend either: *a)* shows that person is not very familiar with the

Bible; and/or *b)* that person is kept too busy by the pace of the seminar to notice. Only the more informed and alert seminar attendees would be likely to pick up on these problems.

Even if it is true that all rebellion is evil and thus, all submission is good, it is still not the same as saying submission means "getting under the protection of authority." When is Gothard going to supply us with a scriptural basis for this idea? He isn't. He basically expects us to accept his assertion and follow quickly to his next point before we have the opportunity to notice he is not teaching Scripture but rather his own ideas. His citation from 1 Samuel, therefore, reads more like sleight-of-hand than a reference for a biblical principle.

But there is more to consider in Gothard's teaching on authority, because an intrinsic part of it can be found in his statement, "Authority is like an 'umbrella of protection,' and when we get out from under it, we expose ourselves to unnecessary temptations which are too strong for us to overcome." With this, Gothard has shifted away from the "authority paradigm" that has been historically presented to young people.

Most young people in the '60s and '70s had been taught that authority was to protect people from social chaos. We need to have government, a police force, a military, and all structures and powers of authority (so the standard explanation went) in order to keep evil from running rampant in the world. It is no secret that many in their teens and twenties, especially in the '60s, rejected this line of reasoning.

Nevertheless, this view *is* the central rationale provided by the Apostle Paul in Romans 13:3-4 (also see Gen. 9), and we have to wonder why Gothard felt the need to supplement Paul's teaching with the notion that not submitting to authority somehow exposed us to "unnecessary temptations which are too strong for us to overcome." Is it not enough that we should fear the inevitable social ills that result from disregarding authority? Must we also fear some mystical, spiritual ill as well? And mystical it will remain, in more ways than one, because Gothard never shows us from Scriptures how this is so.

On the several occasions when we met with Bill Gothard to discuss these issues, he mentioned that he "memorizes large portions of Scriptures and prays for the proper understanding." Now we agree that Scripture memorization is a very valuable spiritual exercise. "Hiding the word in our heart," as King David wrote, is very beneficial to help us in guarding our hearts against sin. It also equips us to share the faith with others in a more confident manner. However, the Holy Spirit does not give mystical interpretations which conflict with His already revealed will nor which would be inconsistent with the written text. Bill calls this "a personal *rhema* from God's Word."[10] This type of mystical impression or "private interpretation" appears to be prevalent in Mr. Gothard's life. For example, Dr. Jay Adams writes:

> In a conversation with me, Bill Gothard asked whether I ever received a prompting to stop my car while driving along, to get out and to go up to a home and ring the doorbell, and witness to the person who answered. I said, "Never." He said, "It happens to me all the time." We discussed this at length, and he said that the spiritual impressions he received were neither sensory nor cognitive in nature. But if that is so, you couldn't really know when a prompting occurred or what, specifically, you were being prompted to do. If you didn't "know" it cognitively, if you didn't "feel" it by means of your senses then, so far as you are concerned it didn't happen. I asked him how he could know he had been prompted. His response was, "When you got it, you know it."[11]

While it is true that we may receive varying *applications* of passages or something may stand out which we had not seen at a prior time, the correct *interpretation* is still the same. By abandoning the standard hermeneutical principles in favor of mystical understandings Gothard has essentially used the same "When you got it, you know it" methodology. Dr. Harry Adams,[12] an occasional writer and contributor to the Midwest Christian

Outreach, Inc. Journal, has observed in a note to us:

> Rhema is the term for a spoken message. It often has the sense of "witness," "testimony," or "statement." It is <u>never</u> used in the sense of the illumination of verses by the Holy Spirit. Gothard's quotation in *The Seven Fold Power* of W.E.Vine is beside the point, for Vine errs in so interpreting Ephesians 6:17, "*the sword of the Spirit, which is the <u>rhema</u> of God.*" Rather, Paul's point in Ephesians 6:17 is similar to John's in Revelation 12:11: "And they overcame him [Satan]... by the word of their testimony." (NKJV) A clear testimony of faith in Christ is the weapon by which we strike a blow for the Gospel. Thus, to suggest we get <u>rhemas</u> from God out of the Bible is close to bibliomancy.[13] The Spirit does illumine the text, but always in a manner consistent with the normal meaning of the text.

This is a fairly serious accusation, so we checked with a second witness, Dr. Thomas Howe.[14] His response was:

> Concerning the word "*rhema,*" I think both you and the Pastor have presented a solid case. Additionally, the term "*rhema*" is close to the term "dabar" in the Old Testament. It can be used to mean a "thing," "matter," "event," or "happening." The question I have is why does not Gothard take the word to mean, "the sword of the Spirit, which is God's thing." This would be a legitimate translation. *Rhema* is not only the word for a spoken message, it is also the word for happening or event. Why doesn't Gothard translate the passage, "the sword of the Spirit, which is God's event," or "which is God's happening"? In other word's, this may be indicating that the sword of the Spirit is what God does to the enemy in our behalf.

Again, we are firm believers in meditation on God's Word, but not as a hermeneutical principle — that is, not as a means of arriving at the meaning of a text. It is true that the Holy Spirit can enlighten our minds to better appreciate the meaning of a text. We sometimes refer to this "understanding" in a sense that is different from cognitive apprehension, which is the normal sense in which we speak of understanding a text.

Sometimes, the Holy Spirit may even help our minds to uncover the actual literal meaning of the text when we are having problems interpreting it. But that meaning will never be any different than that which could be discerned from a literal, historical-grammatical hermeneutical approach. Yet, we feel that Gothard has used his "meditation" or "rhema word" principle to do exactly that: to bypass standard Protestant hermeneutics, with the result that he gets meanings out of the Bible that God never put "in" it!

Of course, we are all guilty of misapplying Scripture from time to time. We are taking that into account. The concern we and others have is that, with Gothard, abuse of Scripture happens so frequently and seems to have gotten much worse in recent years. The elevation of his personal opinions to the status of scriptural authority extends into medical advice (Cabbage Patch dolls interfering with the birth of children), adoption (tracing family lineage to bind ancestral demons), and other mystical elements (hedge of thorns, umbrella of authority/protection, sins of the fathers).[15]

The Links in Gothard's Chain of Authority

Gothard teaches that God had three primary purposes for instituting human authority:

> 1.To [help us] grow in wisdom and character;" 2) "To gain protection from destructive temptations" (as outlined above); and 3) "To receive clear direction for life decisions."[16]

To prove his point, Gothard writes:

> The only recorded incident in the life of Christ between the ages of two and thirty was a discussion

with his parents, which involved authority. This occurred when He was twelve. Should he follow His spiritual calling and be about His Father's business (Luke 2:49), or should he become subject to His parents and leave His ministry at the temple? He did the latter, and the following verse reports, "And He increased with wisdom and stature, and found favor with God and man" (Luke 2:52).[17]

Here Gothard took a story from Luke, designed to illustrate the identity of Christ as the Son of God and Messiah. But in his hands it becomes a story about internal conflict within the Lord Jesus over whether to obey the parental authority of Joseph and Mary, so he can fit it into his system. However, there is nothing in Luke 2:41-52 that even remotely implies that Jesus was struggling with the issues Gothard mentions here. He reads these ideas into the passage, giving unwary readers the impression that they are in the text itself. As illusionists quickly distract their audiences from what they are actually doing, Gothard quickly moves on without providing readers with a verse to back up his assertion.

He apparently doesn't realize the theological problems that result from this sleight-of-hand. If Gothard's interpretation is correct, Jesus deliberately remained behind in the Temple against what He obviously knew (since He was God) to be his parents' wishes as His authority. This would mean that even before the boy Jesus had resolved His supposed "inner-conflict," He had already sinned! This, of course, directly contradicts biblical teaching on the sinless nature of Christ.

The notion that this is a story about Jesus resolving His own internal conflict is also at odds with its climactic scene (which Gothard oddly omits). Luke records this in verses 48-49:

And when they saw him, they were amazed: and his mother said unto him, "Son, why hast thou thus dealt with us? Behold, thy father and I have sought thee sorrowing."

And he said unto them, "How is it that ye sought me?

Wist ye not that I must be about my Father's business?"

This sure doesn't *sound* as though Jesus decided against being about His Father's business! He clearly stated He *must* be about it! Why does Gothard contradict Jesus' words by stating He chose *against* being about His Father's business by being subject to His parents? And where does the text teach that being about His Father's business and being subject to His parents are incompatible, so that He cannot do both at the same time?

Luke's climax also does not uncover any sort of "inner conflict" Jesus may have experienced. On the other hand, he portrays Joseph's and Mary's inner conflict quite vividly. We can read and re-read this passage countless times, but we'll never find Gothard's teachings — however, we may find Luke's.

Luke is telling a story in narrative form. Narratives are often about conflict and resolution. In this case Gothard reads into the text the wrong conflict and is teaching a false resolution. When you read this kind of story (or hear it, or see it in a movie), you can tell what it's about by following the key players in the conflict. A good storyteller knows how to focus your attention on the conflict to build suspense so that the conflict's resolution makes a memorable impact on the readers.

Everyone who has children or young siblings can relate to the terror of losing track of one's young charge, even for a brief period of time. Joseph and Mary were a full day's journey away before they realized Jesus was missing (v. 44), and it took them three days to find Him after they made it back to Jerusalem (v. 46)!

Luke supplies these details because *this* is what the story is about. He wants his readers to ask the same question Joseph and Mary were asking: "Where could Jesus be?" He wants them to feel the same range of emotions any parent would feel, because the lesson for the reader is the same as it was for Joseph and Mary.

How would you know *where* Jesus is? Answer: by remembering *Who* He is!

This is also the only record we have in Scripture of Jesus ever being scolded by His human parents. But, if we believe in the doctrine of the sinlessness of Christ at age 12, then it was a scold-ing He did not deserve. But Gothard's view assumes He *did* deserve it, since he had already gotten out from under their "umbrella of authority."

Fortunately Luke is telling this story instead of Gothard. And as Luke tells it, the *sinless* Christ, at age 12, answered His parents' question with His own questions: *Don't you know Who I am?* And don't you know that *Who I Am* dictates *where I am?* So the basic issue was: Why didn't they think of coming to the tem-ple *first?* It would have saved them a lot of unnecessary worrying!

So this story has nothing to do with any conflict within Jesus over whether to stay in the temple or go home with His parents. Jesus was not contemplating entering the ministry at age 12! Additionally, since Gothard's view is that not being in submis-sion is rebellion and therefore sin (it is "as the sin of witchcraft"), we do not see any way for him to avoid the conclusion that Jesus was a sinner, based on his explanation of the passage. According to Gothard's explanation Jesus had to make the difficult decision of submitting, which means He was not submitted under His par-ents' umbrella of protection at that time. They came looking for Him to bring Him back into submission and Jesus, by choosing to submit, must have ceased from His rebellion and sin. Certainly Bill Gothard would never overtly say such a thing, but his mystical understanding of this passage doesn't leave any apparent escape from this dilemma. When we asked him this question in one of our meetings he was quite befuddled and offered no solution to this conundrum.

Since this is not a story about Jesus making the tough choice to "leave His ministry at the temple" to submit to His parents, neither is it about how His choice to submit was why He "increased in wisdom and stature and in favor with God and man." It wasn't the point of Luke's story. Luke was simply describ-ing the progress of young Jesus' life. He didn't write, *"Therefore* Jesus increased in wisdom and stature..." Luke did not even imply the cause-and-effect relationship between submission to human authority and character development that Gothard forces upon the text. There are many people who have submitted in this way but have *not* "increased in wisdom and stature" nor "in favor with God and man" (e.g., the followers of Peoples Temple leader Jim Jones and Branch Davidian leader David Koresh).

It is always possible that biblical stories can be making other points besides their primary ones. But in such cases, it is obvious from the text. In this case, Gothard invents a meaning that *opposes* the passage's point — specifically, that Jesus is the Son of God. And we know from other Scriptures that the Son of God does not sin!

When in Rome ...

In order to justify his statement that submission to authority is necessary to "receive clear direction for life decisions," Gothard writes:

> Correct decisions are based on faith; that is, visualizing what God intends to do. "Whatsoever is not of faith is sin." (Romans 14:23) One of the most basic aspects of faith is to realize how God gets His directions to us through those He has placed over us.[18]

Here again, we are confronted with two questionable statements and a Bible verse that proves neither of them sandwiched in between. How did Gothard come up with his definition of faith as "visualizing"? He doesn't say. Where does the Bible say following "those He has placed over us" is "one of the most basic aspects of faith"? Gothard doesn't help us out here, either. But he goes on:

> After the centurion asked Jesus to come and heal his servant, it occurred to him that just as his life was structured around a "chain of responsibility," so the kingdom in which God operates must have a similar structure of authority.[19]

The account to which Gothard is referring is found in Matthew 8:5-10:

And when Jesus was entered into Capernaum, there

came unto him a centurion, beseeching him, and saying, Lord, my servant lieth at home sick of the palsy, grievously tormented. And Jesus saith unto him, I will come and heal him. The centurion answered and said, Lord, I am not worthy that thou shouldest come under my roof: but speak the word only, and my servant shall be healed. For I am a man under authority, having soldiers under me: and I say to this man, Go and he goeth; and to another, Come, and he cometh; and to my servant, Do this, and he doeth it. When Jesus heard it, he marveled, and said to them that followed, Verily I say unto you, I have not found so great faith, no, not in Israel.

Is the point of this story that God's kingdom is structured around a "chain of authority" (or "umbrella of protection") similar to that of the Roman Empire? No. The point of this story is the centurion had such great faith in *Who* Jesus was, that he knew Jesus did not *need* to come to his house in order to heal his servant. Jesus was God; He could heal long-distance.

Once again it is possible that this story could be making Gothard's point in addition to its main one, but it would have to be obvious in the text, and it is not. Furthermore, if it does teach that God's kingdom has a similar authority structure to that of pagan Rome, then it contradicts the direct teaching of Christ, Who said,

> ... The kings of the Gentiles exercise lordship over them; and they that exercise authority upon them are called benefactors. But ye shall not be so: but he that is greatest among you, let him be as the younger; and he that is chief, as he that doth serve. (Luke 22:25-26)

The main point this story, as with *every* story in the Gospels, is to highlight for us *Who* Jesus is! By distracting us with his "authority" teaching, Bill Gothard is not only violating the rules of proper interpretation, but he is frustrating the intent of the Gospel authors and diverting our attention from the glory of Christ's person.

Alas, Gothard is relentless. He interprets Matthew 8:5-10 as yet another passage which corroborates his view that submitting to a "structure of authority" will help us "to receive clear direction for life decisions." Once again, we look for a connection between Gothard's thesis ("to receive clear direction") and Gothard's proof-text, but we come up empty. If anything, here we have a story where the *centurion* was telling *Jesus* what to do ("just say the word, and my servant will be healed") instead of *receiving* "clear direction" by submitting to Jesus' authority! It soon becomes apparent that Gothard cites Matthew 8 primarily to support his underlying *premise* (since it does not support his immediate *point*), which is that Christians must get under one of his all-important umbrellas of "protection of authority."

Another group, the Watchtower Bible and Tract Society (more commonly known as Jehovah's Witnesses), writes volumes about this type of authority structure. For example, they state:

> It is a theocratic organization, ruled from the Top down, and not from the rank and file up.[20]

In another publication they state:

> What, can we say, is the basic principle underlying the movement of Jehovah's living organization? It can be expressed in one word: OBEDIENCE.[21]

In the late 1970s and early '80s the Watchtower Society was losing quite a number of members who had actually started studying the Bible on their own. To halt this exodus and remind their followers to get under their authority, the Society published two articles titled "Exposing the Devil's Subtle Designs" and "Armed for the Fight Against Wicked Spirits." In the first article they write:

AVOID INDEPENDENT THINKING
From the very outset of his rebellion Satan called into question God's way of doing things. He promoted independent thinking.... To this day, it has been Satan's subtle design to infect God's people with this type of thinking (2 Timothy 3:1,13).

How is such independent thinking manifested? A common way is by questioning the counsel that is provided by God's visible organization.[22]

In the next article they write:

FIGHT AGAINST INDEPENDENT THINKING

As we study the Bible we learn that Jehovah has always guided his servants in an organized way. And just as in the first century there was only one true Christian organization, so today Jehovah is using only one organization. (Ephesians 4:4,5; Matthew 24:45-47) Yet there are some who point out that the organization has had to make adjustments before, and so they argue: "This shows that we have to make up our own mind on what to believe." This is independent thinking. Why is independent thinking so dangerous?[23]

In these few examples we see how cults teach authoritarianism under the guise of "Thus saith the Lord!" There is little difference between Bill Gothard and the Watchtower Society on this point, and yet we're still left with the question, "Just where *does* the Bible teach this?" Nearly 500 years ago Martin Luther confronted Erasmus of Rotterdam on this very point:

What is this new-fangled religion of yours, this novel sort of humility, that, by your own example, you would take from us power to judge men's decisions and make us defer uncritically to human authority? Where does God's written Word tell us to do that?[24]

If we but turn to the Scriptures and read them in context we find they do not support the premise that Bill Gothard espouses, even indirectly.

The Biblical Hook

In his book, *Scripture Twisting: 20 Ways the Cults Misread the Bible*, Dr. James Sire refers to this method of proof-texting as

"The Biblical Hook."

> When Scripture is quoted, especially at the beginning of
> an argument, which turns out to promote a cult doctrine
> or point of view, it may be that it is being used primarily
> as a hook to grasp the attention of readers or listeners.
> "The Bible Says" gets the attention, but what follows the
> quotation may be far from traditional Christian teaching
> and far from the intention of the Bible itself.[25]

This is not the *only* way in which Gothard misuses Scripture.
The examples we have provided thus far are simply consistent
with Sire's description of "The Biblical Hook."

Gothard's persistent (though incorrect) citation of Bible
verses creates the illusion he is teaching "biblical principles."

Permission to Rebel?

In written correspondence after reviewing our critique in an
issue of *The Journal*[26], Bill Gothard, rather than addressing the
points raised, dodges the issue. He writes:

> The cause-and-effect relationship between obedience of
> children to their parents and the gaining of wisdom and
> favor is clearly established in many other places of
> Scripture. Is it your intention in this article to give chil-
> dren a reason not to obey their parents and not to look
> to Jesus as an example in this area?[27]

While it true that children are taught to obey, honor, etc.,
their parents in other places in Scripture, it is wrong to misuse
Luke 2:41-52 to support Gothard's supposed "cause-and-effect
relationship." It is also wrong (not to say puzzling) for Gothard to
imply that by depriving him of the right to twist Scripture we are
giving children permission to rebel. Gothard's mishandling of
Scripture renders his foundational teachings on obedience, submission and leadership questionable.

This is an issue which Dr. Earl Radmacher from Western
Baptist Seminary spent a great deal of time on with Bill Gothard

in numerous meetings over the years to no avail.

The Biblical Model of Authority

Submitting to authority is taught in Scripture in such passages as Romans 13:1, Titus 3:1, 1 Peter 2:13, and Ephesians 5. Is Gothard's *definition* of submission biblical? In Mark 10:42-44, Jesus gathered the disciples to Himself and said:

> But Jesus called them *to him*, and saith unto them, "Ye know that they which are accounted to rule over the Gentiles exercise lordship over them; and their great ones exercise authority upon them. But so shall it not be among you; but whosoever will be great among you, shall be your minister: and whosoever of you will be chiefest, shall be servant of all."

We can see that Gothard's view is discussed in the Bible, but the idea of getting "under the authority" is what the non-believers, pagans, "rulers of the Gentiles" pushed for as opposed to Jesus' teaching of the leader being the servant of all. In other words, the more of a leader someone becomes, the more accountable they become, not the other way around. Servant leaders live in glass houses ,and everyone around them uses Windex!

In Hebrews 13:17a of Hebrews says:

> Obey them that have rule over you, and submit yourselves.

How are we to understand this? In the Gothard system, like the Watchtower Bible and Tract Society system, it means following orders from the top down. As has been pointed out, Gothard believes that the kingdom of God "operates with a similar structure of authority" to that of pagan Rome. In this system, power brokers assume authority at the top and force those under them to unquestioningly conform. As already pointed out, that meaning would be inconsistent with what Jesus plainly taught. In Gothard's system, leaders themselves are placed above accountability as everyone below them is accountable to them, and the only one above them is God. Leadership as Jesus taught it is exactly the reverse; the more one rises in leadership, the more accountable one becomes to a greater number of people.

Gothard's System in Action

Greg and Karen[28] and Chris and Jack Schultz were members of Crossroads Community Church near Milwaukee, Wisconsin. Greg requested a copy of the church budget. In most church structures this is an item that is made public periodically as a matter of course and accountability. In the four years that Greg and Karen had attended there had never been an annual meeting or any published annual report. Greg reminded the board once a month for six months and finally received a copy of the budget.

The largest single expense, the pastor's salary and benefits, were not shown. Greg later discovered that this was intentional. After more inquiry, he was supplied with the information. None of this was done in a confidential manner, and these things are supposed to be a matter of public record. Several weeks later at a Bible study at the home of Jack and Chris Schultz, the subject of accountability came up with regards to the pastor. Greg shared that he believed the church finance committee needed to be held to greater accountability to the congregation. When asked for some of the specifics of the information, something which should be freely available to all the membership, he shared the details of the financial statement including the pastor's salary and benefits.

On January 26, 1998 the pastor showed up at Greg's house unannounced at 10:00 p.m. He told Greg that he had called ahead but got their answering machine. The problem is that Greg and Karen didn't have an answering machine. This was but one of many false statements the pastor would tell as events unfolded. He went on to say that he was there because "The Scripture says, 'in the day you hear of it,' deal with a problem." He was quoting this seven-word phrase from Bill Gothard's "Deal With Each Problem." He claimed that bringing up church finances at a Bible study is "gossip." Of course, that is possible in Gothard's system where words are redefined to fit his peculiar teachings — especially in the view that leaders are not accountable to those under their authority. The pastor went on to tell Greg that he could *only* discuss church finances with the finance committee and must promise not to discuss it with anyone ever again. This stunned Greg who was given two alternatives. 1) Keep quiet. 2) The pastor would start step two of removing him from the church. Greg could not promise not to discuss the church budget (which again, is to be public information). The pastor asked if he could return with two others to continue with the Matthew 18 discipline. Both proposed "witnesses" were involved in Advanced Training Institute (IBLP's home schooling); and one of them had been involved in IBLP for over 25 years and gave blind obedience to the pastor's authority as taught by IBLP. The following week resulted in numerous phone calls and a meeting with these two men and the pastor which, according to Greg, culminated in the following:

1. Greg was labeled an "independent spirit" and a rebel for not blindly following the pastor.

2. Greg was considered an idol worshipper (by making an "idol" of his own opinion).

3. Greg was pronounced stubborn for not getting back under the authority of his church and keeping silent.

4. Greg was to voice his opinion *only* to church leadership.

5. Greg (and at this point a few others) were told that no one would ever find out the pastor's income, and that if anyone did inquire they would be asked questions which would make them feel so uncomfortable that they would just give up asking.

6. When discussing church leadership Greg was not to use the word "accountable."

7. The pastor commanded Jack Schultz (in whose home the Bible study met) not to assemble if they were going to discuss this issue.

8. And finally, Greg and Karen were told that the people in the congregation should obey their pastor as a child obeys its parents.

Authority Cannot Be Questioned

At about the same time Jack and Chris Schultz were becoming uncomfortable with something else that was going on in the church. They had been attending the church for about five years and were very actively involved. They had opened their home for a Bible study which met every two weeks and had done so for about two years. The study leaders and several others were heavily involved in IBLP and ATI, and when Jack and Chris began questioning what was being taught they discovered that the teachings were from ATI materials. They were also turned in to the pastor for questioning the ATI materials, which were being used at the Bible study. During this period they also realized out that many of the church Bible studies were led by ATI families using ATI material.

Jack had already been told not to allow the Bible study to assemble if the church finances would be discussed and was not under leader scrutiny. Jack and Chris were now listening to the sermons more closely, only to find that they were taken from IBLP and ATI material with a particular emphasis on submission — especially submission and obedience of women to their husbands.

On February 18, 1998 the pastor called Jack at work, requesting that he and his wife, Chris, attend a meeting with the pastor and the newly appointed elder. The pastor refused to explain the purpose of the meeting. The pastor opened the meeting by accusing Jack and Chris of gossiping and being divisive in the church. They were also accused of slander, engaging in corrupt communication, grieving the Holy Spirit, bitterness, wrath, malice, and most significantly being heretics.[29] The meeting was taped with permission of the parties involved, and the Schultzes retained a copy of the tape. The pastor's final taped comment to Jack and Chris was to ask if they could remain in the church and not say anything negative about Bill Gothard, Gothardism within the church, or Gothardism in the pastor's preaching even if someone were to ask their opinion. Jack and Chris said they didn't believe they could do that but wanted time to study the Scriptures that had been used against them and pray about the situation. They said they would give them their answer after church on February 22 and all were in agreement. The next events brought additional stress in an already intense situation. Two days later the pastor called Jack at work, demanding an answer. Jack reiterated that they would answer on Sunday after church as they had agreed. The pastor became enraged that Jack wouldn't "obey" him and stated that Jack didn't have respect for the pastor's position. Jack reminded him that they would give their answer on Sunday after church as previously agreed and hung up.

On February 22 Jack Schultz could not attend church due to military obligations but Chris went and was planning on delivering their answer after church as agreed. This was not to be. When the pastor noticed that Chris was at church he called the only elder (ATI for 25 years) and the head of the Finance Committee (another ATI father) and spoke to them briefly. They in turn asked Chris if they could speak with her in the back of the church. When she arrived in the back of the church she was asked to leave and was told that she was not to be there. She never had the opportunity to deliver their answer. According to Jack and Chris, the elder — who had been a friend of theirs — admitted to them in a discussion at a later time that he didn't know why he was told to escort Chris out but was simply obeying the pastor.

On February 26, Jack and Chris received a certified letter excommunicating them from the church. They were ordered by the "council of Elders" (consisting of the pastor and one elder) not to come to the church or any church-sponsored activity. They were also informed that if they wished to meet with the pastor, they would have to do so through the pastor's attorney.

What Is Christian Submission?

The role of leaders is to teach the Word, correct false teaching, and, if those who are living in immorality or teaching heresy are unrepentant, to bring such ones before the church for a final attempt at correction. These servant-leaders are ones who have grown in grace and knowledge under the watchful eye of the congregation. As they advance in new levels of leadership they grow more accountable to a greater number of people both inside and outside the church. This is more or less opposed by Gothard's view.

Is the kind of submission and control as promoted by Bill Gothard and IBLP what the author of Hebrews had in mind regarding the relationship between leaders and laymen in the church? The answer is, no!

W.E. Vine defines the word "obey" in Hebrews 13:17 in this way:

"to persuade, to win over," in the passive and middle voices, "to be persuaded, to listen to, to obey." ... The "obedience" suggested is not by submission to authority, but resulting from persuasion."[30]

Vines writes of the word "submit":

"to retire, withdraw (hupo, under, eiko, "to yield"), hence, "to yield, submit," is used metaphorically in Hebrews 13:17, of "submitting" to spiritual guides in the churches.[31]

This certainly makes sense, since earlier in the chapter the writer penned these words:

Remember those who led you who spoke the word of God to you; and considering the result of their conduct, imitate their faith (Hebrews 13:7, NASB).

In other words, in the historical, grammatical context, we should "be persuaded" or "won over" and yield as a result of being able to observe the lives of others. Most of us have someone we really respect and really trust. We consider them to have wisdom. We begin imitating some of the things they do in their lives, such as, how they handle people or problems. We go to them for advice — but they are not our "bosses." They become our leaders because they have earned that place by being a servant of all, as Christ said.

The author's kids are grown and married. They still call regularly for advice. They certainly are not obligated, as adults, to follow our counsel, but the fact that they ask for advice honors us — they trust our opinions based upon their long-term observation of our lives.

When they were children, of course, rejecting our instruction was not an option. But the leader/layman relationship is not that of parent/child. The Bible specifically tells us NOT TO BE CHIL-DREN in relation to our leaders, but to test their teachings rigorously so as not to be deceived and blown about from pillar to post.

> That we *henceforth* be no more children, tossed to and fro, and carried about with every wind of doctrine, by the sleight of men, *and* cunning craftiness, whereby they lie in wait to deceive; but speaking the truth in love, may grow up into him in all things, which is the head, *even* Christ: from whom the whole body fitly joined together and compacted by that which every joint supplieth, according to the effectual working in measure of every part, maketh increase of the body unto the edifying of itself in love (Ephesians 4:14-16).

If we are bound to unthinkingly obey and submit to our church "authorities," how can we possibly carry out this command to test what we are being taught? Rejecting false teachings requires *independence of thought*, while rejecting false teachers requires *independence of action*. What a beautiful picture this passage portrays of how relationships in the church are supposed to work, as a body working together in love, as opposed to the heavy-handed authoritarianism of the cults.

Leading by example, from a standing of mutual respect, is far more difficult than IBLP's three-steps-to-this, seven-principles-for-that and twelve-ways-for-something-else. It actually requires relationships with God and other people rather than a relationship with rules. It requires thinking, studying, walking, and praying with others without improper fear. We were never meant to live in a "Christian Ghetto," walled off from all others; we were meant for the much more difficult walk of being in the world while not being *of* it. We realize that this way of life — engagement with the world and the lost people that inhabit it — isn't as nice, clean, and orderly, as the arrangement Mr. Gothard promotes, but it is what Jesus and the apostles taught.

Chapter 4

IBLP:
Institute in Basic Legalistic Practices

Search the Scriptures; for in them ye think ye have eternal life: and they are they which testify of me (John 5:39).

Jesus spoke these 20 words in the middle of a discourse to a group of legalists — the Pharisees — of His day. They had become so focused on the minutiae of the Law that they had completely missed the point of God's revelation to man. The Scriptures, according to Jesus, bear witness of Him and lead to eternal life. The Apostle Paul points out that man can do nothing on his own which will merit salvation (Romans 4:1-2) nor sanctification (Galatians 3:3). We cannot know what motivated the Pharisees. The Pharisees were religionists who created a set of oral traditions which were meant to mechanistically guide and keep them from violating the Mosaic Law. In the process they set their focus on Moses and not on God (John 5:42-47). The result was legalism and self-righteousness at the sacrifice of an actual living relationship with God.

Today, similar "law-focused" groups and individuals are also called "Pharisees" in order to identify them with the first-century Jewish sect of the same name. Another common word used to identify Pharisaical thinking is "legalist," and we used this word to describe Bill Gothard in a series of articles that were published in the *Midwest Christian Outreach Journal*. As mentioned previously, Bill Gothard responded to the first article and to our charge that he is a legalist by saying:

> In your article you present a very interesting overview of recent movements in the evangelical world. Now, at a time when the evangelical church is becoming more and more like the world, we hear an ever-increasing cry of "legalism." Based on many discussions I have had on this topic, the word "legalism" is usually used against someone who would promote a higher standard of Godly living than is generally accepted by Christians in our day. Since this is the label that you have placed upon me and the Seminar ministry, and since you are an educational research ministry, it should be significant to you that "legalism" is not a biblical word. It is fraught with emotional responses and reactions, and is therefore extremely subjective.[1]

He continues:

> Those who condemn fellow Christians for choosing to live by the disciplines of Scripture and reject the Old Testament as being "too harsh," fail to realize that Christ's commandments in the New Testament are far stricter than the Old Testament Mosaic Law. This fact was established in the Sermon on the Mount.[2]

Is this confirmation or refutation of our position? Perhaps we need to revisit the question:

Is Bill Gothard a Legalist?

"Legalism" is a time-honored word Christians use to refer to some kind of misuse of law.[3] Gothard himself, once used it,[4] but now he writes:

> The word legalism is not a biblical term and should not

be used since it has conflicting meanings that are emotionally charged.[5]

It is interesting that Gothard seeks to legislate how Christians
use words and quite ironic that the word which he seeks to legislate is "legalism." It is reminiscent of George Orwell's "thinks-
peak" of 1984. Words are the coins of human ideas, and whoever controls their flow becomes a kind of Federal Reserve Board
Chairman[6] of Christian thought. Should anyone have such
power?

For Gothard to imply that we cannot justly refer to him as a
legalist because "the word legalism is not a biblical term" is simply nonsense. If we limited our vocabulary to words found in
Scripture, then technically we only should speak Greek, Hebrew,
and Aramaic. Even if we extended this rule to include English
translations of biblical words, we still could not use important
theological terms like, "Trinity," "inerrancy," "Calvinism," or
"Arminianism," all of which have conflicting meanings and emotional overtones for various people. Nor could Bill Gothard himself use phrases like "chain of authority" or "umbrella of protection." In addition, the fact that Christians believe the concept of
legalism is found in the Bible is demonstrated by the fact that as
least one important, modern translation – the New International
Version – includes it in their translation:

> If anyone else thinks he has reasons to put confidence in
> the flesh, I more: circumcised on the eight day, of the
> people of Israel, of the tribe of Benjamin, a Hebrew of
> the Hebrews; in regard to the law, a Pharisee; as for zeal,
> persecuting the church; as for **legalistic** righteousness,
> faultless.[7]

Since Gothard has been bombarded with charges of legalism
in recent years, we can understand why he might like to erase the
word from the English language – but this would not be right
and would not resolve the question in any case. Instead, we must
determine the legitimate meanings of "legalism" and consider
whether any of them apply to Gothard and IBLP.

When Christians use the word "legalism," they are usually referring to one or more of the following definitions:

1. Keeping the Mosaic Law as a means of salvation or sanctification[8]

2. Keeping the Law's "letter" without keeping its "spirit"[9]

3. Building a "fence" of unnecessary, extra-biblical laws around biblical laws[10]

4. Imposing obsolete Old Testament (OT) requirements on New Testament (NT) believers[11]

Bill Gothard denies that one must keep the Law in order to be saved,[12] so he does not qualify as the first type of legalist.

Although he would publicly repudiate keeping the "letter" without the "spirit," Gothard's practices would seem to refute that. This would include hypocritical compliance with God's commands. It also includes the way the Pharisees nullified the Law through human traditions (Matthew 15:1-8; Mark 7:6-13).

When we come to the third definition, however, it does not seem that Gothard can be acquitted of legalism. It was precisely the practice of adding extra commandments to the Law that Christ was referring to when He said of the Pharisees, "For they bind heavy burdens and grievous to be borne, and lay *them* on men's shoulders; but they *themselves* will not move them with one of their fingers" (Matthew 23:4).

The Pharisees (and their rabbinic descendents, who wrote the Talmud) were quite unapologetic about this practice. They believed they were protecting the Law by building a "fence" of extra commandments around it[13] and that "tradition" was a "fence" that protected the Law.[14] The idea was this: the more rules you set up for yourself, the easier it is to keep from sinning. Thus, there was a rule against a woman looking into a mirror on the Sabbath. Why? Because, she might see a gray hair, and if she saw it, she might pluck it — and that would be "work" on the Sabbath! Hundreds of other examples could be cited.

It never seemed to occur to the Jewish legalists that the

resulting thousands of pages of rules and regulations would become far more burdensome than the Mosaic Law ever was! It would also suck the very life out of God's people and make hypocritical compliance inevitable under the strain of so many do's and don'ts. Jesus said to those who were being crushed by this system:

> Come unto me, all ye that labor and are heavy-laden, and I will give you rest. Take my yoke upon you, and learn from me; for I am meek and lowly in heart: and ye shall find rest unto your souls. For my yoke *is* easy, and my burden is light (Matthew 11:28-30).[15]

With all the "universal, non-optional principles of life" that Gothard's *Basic Seminar Textbook* contains, it is a kind of "Evangelical Talmud." But this does not apply only to the *Basic Seminar Textbook*. As we work on this book we have literally thousands of pages of IBLP material stacked around us, donated by concerned Christians, all filled with lists of "principles" for living the Christian life. How could anyone who reads them avoid drawing the conclusion that the Christian life is one of extremely complicated rule-keeping?

Gothard even sets up principles for which either a biblical reference is lacking or the one he does supply is questionable. This is a dangerous procedure, as Carl Hoch writes:

> What is legalism to one is not legalism to another. People have their own set of extra-biblical rules that seem appropriate to them. But then each person's set becomes the standard for other Christians. The person who has power and influence will soon gain a large following whose adherents will believe that their "set" is the true set. Those individuals in the group who do not necessarily accept that set as legitimate may still comply out of fear of punishment, ostracism, and "shunning." All of these supererogations[16] become identified with Christianity and build up an unnecessary wall between the church and the world. We should not be surprised when people

reject Christianity for the wrong reason, thinking that they must give up movies or some other item on someone's list in order to become a true believer. What a terrible distortion of Scripture and true Christianity! In essence another gospel has been created that leads to confusion within and without the church.[17]

Bill Gothard believes he has the "true set," and rather than teach the biblical view of grace and the unity of the Spirit, he instead proclaims a uniformity of appearance and actions. He wrote:

> When a soldier voluntarily enlists in an army, he surrenders his individual freedom regarding the clothes he wears, the friends with whom he trains, the activities in which he engages, the music to which he marches, and the social life he wants.
>   When the world sees uniformity and "quality control" of high standards among believers in these areas, they are attracted to the message.[18]

In Bill Gothard's *How to Respond to Legalism* tract, he does not even mention either the third or fourth definitions we have listed, and yet they are among the word's most common meanings. As for the fourth definition – imposing Old Testament requirements on New Testament believers – this takes us into an area of wide disagreement among Christians: the exact role of Old Testament Law in the Christian Life. To evaluate Gothard's tutelage on this point, we must set it in the context of the broad spectrum of evangelicalism.

Gothard Steps in to Fill a Vacuum

Many feel that the Church has not faithfully done its job in preaching the Old Testament. In 1993 theologian Walter C. Kaiser, Jr. wrote:

> The hunger to have someone to give the believing community instruction in the proper use of law is so great

that one popular seminar since 1968, focusing on Proverbs (a veritable republication of the law of God in proverbial form, as can be seen from the marginal references to Exodus, Numbers, and Deuteronomy), has literally had tens of thousands of people in every major city in North America and now all over the world. [A footnote to this sentence reads: "In the Basic Youth Conflicts seminars."] This is an indictment on the church and its reticence to preach the moral law of God and to apply it to all aspects of life as indicated in Scripture.[19]

A widely respected scholar, Kaiser is well known for his independent position on the relationship between the Law and Gospel. He is certainly not a dispensationalist, but he also is not a covenant theologian in the traditional sense; and while his remarks fall short of an endorsement of Gothard and IBLP, they urge Christians to have a greater appreciation for the Mosaic Law.

This quote is a starting point in order to emphasize the diversity of evangelical opinion on how to relate the Law of Moses to the Christian Life. This diversity affects the way one evaluates Gothard's use of the Law. Not all evangelical scholars follow Kaiser's view – in fact, he is in a minority camp. (We agree that Christians have sadly lost an appreciation for the Mosaic Law as an important part of Scripture, although we do not accept his view of how Christians relate to the Law. But our task here is to evaluate Gothard's view.)

Gothard vs. Matthew 5:17

Among evangelicals there are three primary positions on the Mosaic Law. They can be distinguished from each other by one simple test: how they interpret Christ's words. "Think not that I am come to destroy the law, or the prophets: I am not come to destroy, but to fulfill." (Matt. 5:17) More specifically, each view can be identified by how it interprets the phrase "to fulfill" (Greek *plerosai*). At risk of oversimplifying (for variations exist within each viewpoint), the three positions and their adherents are a follows:

1. Christ Revises the Law (Reformed)

2. Christ Replaces the Law (Lutherans and Dispensationalists)

3. Christ Reaffirms the Law (Theonomists and others)

Roman Catholics and Eastern Orthodox hold to a variation of position two in which the "one true Church," through its clergy, mediates Christ's authority in the world. So, in practical terms, they believe the church replaces the Law. Since Gothard claims to be an evangelical, we will focus on comparing his position with the standard evangelical positions.

1. Christ Revises the Law

This broad heading does not do justice to the spectrum of Reformed interpretation of Matthew 5:17, but it accurately conveys its results. In Reformed theology, Christ "fulfilled" the Law in the sense of revealing its true meaning and intent – and, to some extent, transcending it. Reformed tradition divides the Law into three categories: moral, civil, and ceremonial. The moral laws are seen as still in force for the Church, but Christ's ministry helps us better understand them. The civil and ceremonial laws are considered types and shadows of Christ that no longer function as pointing forward to Him, so they have been set aside. Gothard's position clearly is not Reformed, since he promotes ceremonial law in areas of abstinence from sexual relations on specific occasions (Lev. 12 and 15)[20] and circumcision.[21] Gothard's entire rationale for circumcising infants uses the Old Testament in a way that Reformed Christians reject. He stresses the need for an actual circumcision ceremony[22] on the eighth day after the birth of a male child.[23] To document the event, he even provides a "Certificate of Circumcision" with places for signatures from an officiating minister, "medical attendant" (doctor?), family members, and other witnesses.

Regardless of his attempt to justify his use of ceremonial laws by bringing forth alleged medical "evidence" (mostly made up of out-of-context quotes) that "proves" that keeping these ceremonial laws is beneficial to our health, Gothard ultimately does not promote their use for medical reasons. He picks and chooses what he will accept from medical authorities, accepting their legitimacy as an authority in certain areas of agreement, but repudiating them when their opinions and his part company, as evidenced by the following. In his bulletin on circumcision he states:

> In recent years, the time-honored practice of circumcision has been challenged by many groups, including pediatricians.
>
> The attack against circumcision in the United States coincided with the revolt against morality and authority in the 1960s. One of the chief reasons given for not having circumcision was that it decreased a man's sensual pleasure.
>
> Indeed, uncircumcised men have, as a group, been more promiscuous than circumcised men.
>
> Because this is one subject which is so strongly commended and reinforced in Scripture, there is no question what the decision of Christian parents should be on the matter.[24]

While one might wonder what Gothard's sources are about the sexual habits of uncircumcised men, it is clear that he does not present circumcision as an option for Christians. The only conclusion one could reach based on the above quote is that circumcision is a moral requirement. This alone places Gothard outside the Reformed tradition, which interprets circumcision as a moral requirement under Law but not under the Gospel.

2. Christ Replaces the Law
(Lutherans and Dispensationalists)

Despite his popularity among Dispensationalists, it would be a mistake to think Gothard is one of them.[25] The dispensational position on the Law can be summarized as follows: "Christians are not under the Law of Moses as a rule of life." This position reads Matthew 5:17 and 18 together, and the emphasis is on the phrase "until everything is accomplished" at the end of verse 18. Since Jesus has "accomplished" (or fulfilled) the entire Law, all of it has "passed away" (see v. 18) for Christians. The Law remains a vehicle of revelation but not regulation.

Lutherans agree that the Mosaic Law is not binding on Christians, but they differ from Dispensationalists in that they allow for "three uses" of the Law. The first use is to restrain evil in the world; the second use it to bring people to acknowledgement of their sins, so they can understand their need for Christ; the third use is to restrain the remnants of sin that remain in true, regenerated believers.[26]

So, what do Dispensationalists say is the "rule of life" for Christians today? When one considers the fact that a wide range of teachers — from John MacArthur, to Charles C. Ryrie, to Zane Hodges — call themselves "Dispensationalists," the answer obviously varies. But the most common response is that the New Testament itself provides all the moral guidance that believers need.

Gothard's view of the Law is not even close to the Lutheran position. It is more or less opposite to that of the Dispensationalists. While he does not attack the dispensational view overtly, much of what he writes seems intended to refute that position.[27] He does not admit that the Law has passed away in any sense other than, perhaps, that the sacrificial system has ceased.

3. Christ Reaffirms the Law

Theonomists are a small, fringe group of evangelicals whose origins trace back to Reformed scholar Rousas J. Rushdoony, who insisted in his 1973 book *The Institutes of Biblical Law* that the Church should work to bring back Mosaic civil laws and penalties (e.g., the death penalty for adulterers, idolaters, and sorcerers, etc.)

into the law books of modern "Christian Societies." Sometimes called Christian Reconstructionists, they have seen their views spread beyond their Reformed birthplace into Pentecostal circles.

Theonomists depart from the traditional Reformed view in that only the moral aspects of the Law apply today, and they believe that only the ceremonial aspects of the Law passed away with Christ. Thus, Gothard is not a Theonomist. However, we can say that of all the interpretations of Matthew 5:17, this one comes closest to his position. Like the Theonomians, Gothard believes Christ's basic meaning was to reaffirm the validity of the Law for all time.[28]

Nonetheless, Gothard's view goes *beyond* that of the Theonomists. He, too, believes that modern civil laws should be based on Scripture,[29] but he also strongly promotes the ceremonial requirements of the Law for Christians today. In this, his belief comes closer to that of another group outside of evangelicalism: Seventh-day Adventists (SDA).

One of the things Gothard has in common with the Adventists is his admiration for a popular book from the 1960s: *None of These Diseases* by S.I. McMillen, M.D.[30] McMillen primarily interpreted Mosaic ceremonial laws in medical terms. He was an early popularizer of the notion that circumcision reduces risks of cervical cancer in women[31] – a view which has since been repudiated by the America Cancer Society.

Following McMillen's lead, many Bible teachers jumped on the bandwagon, finding medical reasons for the distinction between "clean" and "unclean" foods, the treatment of lepers, the handling of corpses, and numerous other ceremonial requirements which might otherwise seem inexplicable to modern man. For Christians interested in apologetics,[32] this approach also seemed to provide evidence for the hand of an omniscient God at work in Scripture.

But were health and hygiene the primary reasons that the ceremonial laws were given?

While this view of the ceremonial laws enjoyed its heyday

among some commentators,[33] it has been thoroughly discussed by conservative Christian scholars and no longer carries much weight. As Gordon J. Wenham observes, the reasons this view does not work can be found in the Scriptures:

> First, hygiene can only account for some of the prohibitions. Some of the clean animals are more questionable on hygienic grounds than some of the unclean animals. If ancient Israel had discovered the dangers of eating pork, they might also have discovered that thoroughly cooking averts it [sic]. In any event, trichinosis is rare in free-range pigs....
>
> Second, the OT gives no hint that it regarded these foods as a danger to health...
>
> Third, why, if hygiene is the motive, are not poisonous plants, classed as unclean?
>
> Finally, if health were the only or even primary reason for declaring certain foods unclean in the first place, why did our Lord pronounce them clean in his day [Mark 7:19, Acts 10:10-15]? Evidence is lacking that the Middle Eastern understanding of hygiene had advanced so far by the first century AD that the Levitical laws were unnecessary. Indeed, if the primary purpose of the food laws was hygienic, it is surprising that Jesus abolished them.[34]

If ceremonial laws were given for health reasons, then because our bodies are temples of the Holy Spirit (1 Corinthians 16:19), some moral imperative *must* be attached to those laws. The inspired apostles should have recognized this and taught believers to keep ceremonial laws as proper stewards of their bodies — but they didn't. Even when they had a Greek Christian in their midst (Titus), the Christian church in Jerusalem did not require him to get circumcised (Galatians 2:3). Ultimately, however, Gothard does not seek to justify "Christian Circumcision" on medical grounds but as a matter of biblical "morality." He writes:

> Because this is one subject which is so strongly commanded and reinforced in Scripture, there is no question what

the decision of Christian parents should be on the matter.[35]

It is important to note that circumcision was established *before* the Law was given. Circumcision goes back to the faith of Abraham. Thus, those who would seek to dismiss circumcision with the Law, have no Scriptural basis to do so.[36]

To focus on matters of health and hygiene or to interpret Mosaic ceremonies as moral requirements, is to lose the prophetic function of those laws as pointing to Christ and to risk removing Christ from the core of the Bible. Paul's teaching, "Which are a shadow of things to come; but the body *is* of Christ." (Colossians 2:17; cf. Hebrews 10:1), recedes into the background. Keeping ceremonial requirements becomes the main thing, and one ends up trading the substance for the shadow. To all Christians, especially those who follow Bill Gothard, his teaching on the Law should be quite alarming.

The Historic Christian Position

The historic Christian position on Matthew 5:17 which all three views hold in common has not been that Christ came to reaffirm the Mosaic Law, but that, in its original form, the Law was provisional and incomplete at some level. The fact that it was necessary for Christ to come to "fulfill" it is proof enough of that. It is not that there is anything wrong with the Law, but we are incapable of keeping it (Romans 3:19-20, 7:13-14; Galatians 3:21). Its design and function were to show we are sinful, incapable of approaching a holy God on our own merits (Romans 4:1-4) and to bring us to Christ. Once that has happened its task is completed (Galatians 3:24-25).

Romans 10:4 reads: "For Christ *is* the end of the law for righteousness to everyone that believeth." N.T. Wright observes:

> The notorious crux of [Romans] 10.4 can, I think, be reduced to these terms: that the Torah is neither abolished as though it were bad or demonic, nor affirmed in

the sense in which the Jews took it. It was a good thing, given deliberately by God for a specific task and a particular period of time. When the task is done and the time is up, the Torah reaches its goal, which is also the conclusion of its intended reign, not because it was a bad thing to be abolished but because it was a good thing whose job is done. In terms of the Luther-Calvin debate, which has dominated discussion of this issue, we can put it like this. The Lutheran wants to maintain the sharp antithesis between law and gospel; so does Paul, but within the context of a single plan of God, and with no suggestion that the Torah itself is a bad thing. The Calvinist wants to ensure that God did not change his plan, or his mind, in the middle of history; so does Paul (that, indeed, is what Romans 9-11 is all about), but he insists that "the single plan always involved a dramatic break", a cross and a resurrection written into the very fabric of history. The Messiah is the fulfillment of the long purposes of Israel's God. It was for this that Torah was given in the first place as a deliberately temporary mode of administration. In the Messiah are fulfilled the creator's paradoxical purposes for Israel and hence for the world. He is the climax of the covenant.[37]

This is the basic area of agreement between Reformed, Lutherans, and Dispensationalists.

Another area of agreement among evangelicals has been that neither the ceremonial nor the civil aspects of the Law are required of Christians today. Many evangelicals may take different theological routes, but they arrive at the same conclusion: it is not only unnecessary but wrong for Christians to require others to be circumcised, to keep the Levitical purification rites, or (with the exception of Theonomists) to impose Mosaic civil sanctions.

Bill Gothard has not merely adopted a "fringe" position on the Law; he clearly falls *outside* most of historic evangelicalism, having gone much further than Theonomianists.

Ron Henzel explained Gothard's view to Dr. Walter Elwell, professor at Wheaton College, during a personal conversation. Dr. Elwell identified Gothard's position (as it was explained to him) as a "moderate Judaizing" position because Gothard clearly does not require circumcision for salvation, yet he makes it a requirement of Christians.

Full-blown Judaizers, about whom we read in Acts 15, required circumcision for salvation. Then there were Jewish Christians who practiced the Law but did not require Gentile Christians to do so. Moderate Judaizers fall in between Judaizers and Law-observing Jewish believers.

Gothard has embraced the Galatian error on sanctification with his view. The Apostle Paul directed the book of Galatians to a group who had been saved by faith apart from the Law but who were subsequently deluded into believing that sanctification came as a result of keeping the Law.

Gothard's Key Text

Oddly enough, Gothard defends his position on the Law by quoting Galatians 3:24 from the KJV: "Wherefore the law was our schoolmaster to bring us unto Christ..." Should not Christians follow the Law if it brings people to Christ? Several things need to be noted here.

First, Gothard often misquotes Paul's verb tense by saying that the Law *is* a schoolmaster. Paul used a past tense ("was" KJV, NIV[38]) to indicate that the Law no longer functions in this way.

Second, the phrase "to bring us" is not in the original Greek (it's italicized in the KJV). The NIV and NASB add similar phrases, but the NIV provides the alternate translation, *"the law was put in charge until Christ"* in its margin. Many scholars agree that the Greek preposition *eis* has this temporal meaning of "until" which fits the context (especially v. 25).[39] Paul is not so much describing what the Law did (i.e., bring us to Christ) as he is emphasizing its *temporary* role.

Third, Gothard omits Galatians 3:25, *"But after that faith has come, we are no longer under a schoolmaster,"* where Paul makes it clear that the relationship described in v. 24 no longer exists for Christians. By quoting Galatians 3:24 out of context (seemingly his preferred method of misusing the Bible), Gothard attempts to get Paul to say what he wants him to say.

In Intertestamental Judaism, one strain of teaching held that during the Messianic Age the Law would still be strictly applied, but God's rationale for deleting some of the more inscrutable commands would be explained. Of course, we know that Paul does not argue that Christians should practice Mosaic circumcision with the proper understanding as Bill Gothard attempts to imply; Paul says that Christians should not practice it at all (Galatians 5:2-12)! Gothard's view sounds more like one of the Intertestamental Jewish views than it does the Apostle Paul's. It also more closely resembles Seventh-day Adventism with Gothard's habitual resorting to Levitical ceremonial cleanliness laws regarding abstinence from sexual relations for a certain number of days after the birth of a child[40] and even the dietary requirement of keeping dairy products and meat separate (based on an Intertestamental misinterpretation of "Thou shalt not seethe [boil] a kid [young goat] in his mother's milk"[41] (Exodus 23:19)!

But Is It Legalism?

Based on the evidence, we have to conclude that Bill Gothard is a legalist according to the third and fourth definitions previously listed. Several Bible teachers have observed that legalism inevitably leads to license, because it frustrates the work of the grace of God. Instead of being cleansed and made Holy by God's Spirit, legalism depends on one's own efforts; since man is not up to the task, sin invariably boils over in the human soul.

Not only have we written about these issues, but also we met with Bill Gothard and three members of his staff (John Stephens, George Mattix, and Nathan O'Brien) on October 4, 1997 to discuss these questions. This ended up being an approximately six-hour meeting, from about 7:30 p.m. to 1:30 a.m. A large portion of the meeting was spent on legalism.

Gothard's teaching on circumcision is but one among many

examples of his legalistic bent, but it is notable in that his view on this topic is *specifically condemned* in Scripture. We pointed out to Gothard that the Apostle Paul had devoted an entire book of the Bible to this topic. Granted, it is small and might be easily missed, but the book of Galatians is very clear on this issue. As we discussed Bill's teaching on circumcision, he continued to misuse Scripture in an effort to support his view. For example, he partially quoted the Apostle Paul in Romans 2:25, "For circumcision verily profiteth..." We countered by placing the partial verse in its context — Paul's point was that Jews who were relying on Jewish rituals for justification were doomed to failure. The balance of the verse that Gothard omits refutes the very point Gothard was attempting to make. "For circumcision verily profiteth, IF THOU KEEP THE LAW, but if thou be a breaker of the law, thy circumcision is made uncircumcision." Since *everyone* is a transgressor of the law, circumcision is of *no value*. The Apostle was not commenting on the possible health benefits of the practice, nor was he suggesting that circumcision was an antidote to rebellion — Paul was thoroughly repudiating the idea that anything done either *to* the flesh or *in* the flesh has any value in achieving righteousness.

Should Christians Criticize Christians?

One of the complaints of Bill Gothard and some of his followers is that Christians shouldn't criticize the teachings of other Christians. We have found, through our live radio broadcast experience, television interviews, the publishing of our *Journal*, and our teaching ministry, that the information which seems to generate the most angry responses are when we are dealing with false teachers/teachings within the church. Most people in the Christian community agree that it is right and necessary to expose the false teachers/teachings of pagans, Jehovah's Witnesses, liberals, Mormons, etc. But sadly, too large a number feel that we should not critically evaluate the doctrines and practices of teachers *within the church*. However, this view is not supported by Scripture. Indeed, the doctrines taught by

Christian teachers *must* be evaluated, or we are no different than the cults and false religions which claim that their leaders are above correction. Such examples would be: Benny Hinn or other Word Faith teachers; charismatic excess, such as the Holy Laughter Movement; evangelicals who make common cause for political and/or financial reasons with Rev. Sun Myung Moon or Minister Louis Farrakhan; "deliverance" ministries; shepherding movements; and other problems. Christian desire for "unity" offers no excuse for silence on these matters. Sometimes doctrine was vigorously and passionately debated even in the early church guided by the original Apostles (Acts 15). The Apostle Paul criticized Peter and Barnabas for hypocrisy (Galatians 2:11-14). Much of the New Testament was written to correct false teachings and expose false teachers (2 Timothy 2, 3; Titus 3; 2 Peter 2; 1 John 4:1-2; 3 John; Jude). And, we might add, that if Christians criticize us for criticizing Christians, they only make our case for us.

In our scrutiny of Bill Gothard's ministry and in the practice of evaluating and critiquing some of his teachings, we do not presume to judge his motives or his heart. In fact, he may sincerely believe that his prescriptions for Christian living actually conform to biblical truth.

Our concern is that Bill Gothard, though sincere, interprets some biblical texts in illegitimate ways, resulting in a sometimes-damaging misunderstanding of those Scriptures among his followers. We are well aware that false teachings can result in unfruitful or negative effects in the lives of those who accept them, which compels us to pursue this issue. It is our conviction that while God can bless His children even when they do cling to false interpretations of Scripture, such error can frustrate God's work in the believer.

We are certain that we and everyone in the church at large are imperfect in one way or another and have imperfect understanding of the Scriptures. An infallible understanding of the infallible Scriptures is a claim that we disavow for ourselves as well as for others. Having said that, however, we believe that through humility, biblical analysis, and the community of other Christ followers, a consensus can be reached about what God does teach us through the Scriptures and how these teachings apply to our lives today.

We believe that all who want to follow Christ and the Scriptures will welcome dialogue and evaluation of *any* individual's biblical interpretation, since the Scripture tells those who wish to glorify Christ and obey Him to "Prove [examine or test] all things; hold fast that which is good" (1 Thessalonians 5:21).

Finally, the Bereans were considered as having "noble character" (Acts 17:10-15) because they searched the Scriptures to see if what the *Apostle Paul* told them was true. Nobility is commendable; gullibility is not.

Chapter 5

Character First!

O ne of the lessons for today is obedience, and the first graders at the school inside the First Christian Church building in Fort Lauderdale sing about it quite obediently. While the students at the Charter School of Excellence are divided fairly evenly between blacks and whites, they dress alike, with the boys in dark blue pants and green buttoned-up golf shirts and the girls wearing white blouses under plaid jumpers. All eyes are focused on their young and attractive teacher, Mrs. Blocker, who leads them in song:

> Obedience is listening attentively,
> Obedience will take instructions joyfully,
> Obedience heeds wishes of authorities,
> Obedience will follow orders instantly.
> For when I am busy at my work or play,
> And someone calls my name, I'll answer right away!
> I'll be ready with a smile to go the extra mile
> As soon as I can say "Yes, sir!" "Yes ma'am!"
> Hup, two, three!

The ditty is capped off with a collective clap from all the happy children in the classroom. While singing songs about obedience and orderliness, they march in place, stand up straight, and occasionally salute in unison, giving the class a slightly militaristic feel. The little boys and girls, however unwittingly, are indeed in a war of sorts: They stand on the front lines of an ideological battle — popularly known as the culture war — for the souls of America's children.

The lesson the children are learning this morning in South Florida has nothing to do with math or science or history; it's about values, about morality, about set ways of how to conduct oneself in life....

In addition to instantly obeying their authority figures, they are to be grateful for the chance to follow orders....[1]

Certainly, teaching morals is a good thing. Morals are about "oughts." The way we "ought" to live or the way we "ought" to treat others. Bill Gothard represents himself as having the answers to life's very difficult dilemmas, answers which he claims can be handled by using the "Basic Life Principles" that he teaches. Columnist Bob Norman stated:

Gothard doesn't focus on the Ten Commandments — he teaches his seven "universal, nonoptional Principles of Life," and he extends those principles to what food to eat and what clothes to wear. Breaking any of Gothard's principles leads to the highway to Hell, quite literally.[2]

As we noted in the last chapter Bill Gothard is a legalist whose teachings derive from a misuse of Scripture with the result that he is essentially a moralist. The biblical teachings of grace and freedom in Christ are notable for their absence from the endless stream of literature, videos and audio tapes that issue from IBLP headquarters.

The Problem with Moralism

There is an inherent weakness in being a moralist. A moralist is someone who is primarily concerned with regulating the morals of others, based on the belief that if everyone would simply "do the right thing," the world would be a much better place. And there is no doubt that it would, which is why moralism can be so alluring.

The problem is that moralism is utterly incapable of dealing with the very thing that *prevents* people from doing the right thing: sin. The Apostle Paul addresses and condemns moralists in Romans 2:1-16. Moralism offers neither a pardon for the guilt of sin, nor a remedy for the power of sin, nor a hope for ultimate freedom from sin. It is most especially in the area of how to live the Christian life that moralism can be most deceptive.

While morals and laws communicate how we ought to behave, they have no power to cause or even assist us in fulfilling them. For example, the speed limit on the street where the Veinots live is 35 miles per hour. It is a perfectly good speed limit, clearly posted along the street in several places on perfectly good signs. They are easily understood but can only tell the driver what is expected; they cannot prevent the drivers from violating them. Occasionally the area police discreetly park a squad car with a radar gun along the street and within a few minutes officers are obliged to turn on their lights and pull over an offending driver. Was there something wrong with the law? No; it performed its designated role by informing the driver of what he or she ought to do. The weakness is in the driver. The law has dominion over the driver, and the driver who violates it and is caught will be punished as a law-breaker. That is how law works. The law cannot make anyone law-abiding or moral, it can only expose and punish those who are not and keep everyone else at least outwardly "in line" through the fear of punishment (which is a far cry from biblical righteousness, since that is motivated by love for God). To make matters worse in a spiritual sense, everyone is a speeder, and all are caught! That is the Apostle Paul's thrust in Romans 2:1-3:20.

Grace operates differently. Using the same example, the driver is under the law of the speed limit, but you, as his passenger, are not. The law is still there and in force, but only for the driver not the passenger. In a similar way the Law is in force and condemns those who are not in Christ. The Law has no power or authority over those in Christ because He is now the driver, so to speak. He has fulfilled the Law, and we are justified by faith (Romans 3:21-30). In Romans 3:31 Paul is very clear that the Law isn't nullified, but in fact performed its work in making us conscious of sin (cf. v. 20). So the Law has power over non-believers but not over believers who are in Christ and delivered from the Law.

The reason this kind of freedom from the Law is necessary is due to the nature of the Law *as law*. Law, by its very nature, has limitations that grace does not. Earlier we noted that the Law is incapable of helping anyone to obey, or forgiving anyone who fails to obey. While it's true that the Law of Moses included a sacrificial system to cover people's sins, that very system demonstrated the inadequacy of the Law to actually deal with sin. As the author of the epistle to the Hebrews noted, "For *it is* not possible that the blood of bulls and of goats should take away sins" (Hebrews 10:4). Thus the Law, in itself, offered no hope of eternal forgiveness. It could only offer a temporary "covering" for sins that needed to be renewed every year, constantly reminding sinners of their guilt (Hebrews 10:2-3). Grace, on the other hand, removes the bondage of a guilty conscience. Even God forgets about our sins, saying, "And their sins and iniquities will I remember no more" (Hebrews 10:17). This kind of grace, the grace of God in Christ Jesus, is largely foreign to the writings and speeches of Bill Gothard.

It may seem on the surface that Gothard covers his bases by including Gospel presentations at various points in his seminars. But even when one subscribes to a theological system that acknowledges the need for grace (as Gothard's does), when one's *approach* is simply moralistic (as Gothard's is) it becomes legalistic. This virtually nullifies the power of grace. Moralism reduces any Gospel presentation to the level of a polite nod in the general direction of Christ's cross. In a practical sense, moralism cannot define "grace" the same way the Bible does, and eventually one who is truly a bona fide moralist will abandon any pretense of relying on pure, biblical grace. Sadly, as we shall see, this is what Gothard has now publicly done.

A Re-Defining Moment

The fictitious comic Jack Handley is quoted as saying, "A man doesn't automatically get my respect. He has to get down in the dirt and beg for it." Perhaps you've known someone who so completely misunderstood the meaning of a particular word (e.g., "respect") that his own private definition of it was actually the complete opposite of its true meaning.

For a long time we suspected this to be the case with Bill Gothard's private definition of "grace." We wondered how anyone who could outline the Bible's plan of salvation with seeming accuracy could be so far off the mark when it came to instructing others in how to live the Christian life. Did he really understand the Gospel of grace? We wanted to believe that he did, despite the fact that he kept arriving at the wrong conclusions.

And then one day we received a disturbing paper by Bill Gothard titled *Definition of Grace*, and our questions began to be answered. Here Gothard attacks the biblical definition of grace as "unmerited favor," calling it a "faulty definition."[3] And he goes even further:

> In the Old Testament, those who found grace possessed qualities that *merited* God's favor [emphasis ours].[4]

In the context of conservative evangelical theology, the very idea of "meriting God's favor" is shocking. It contradicts the heart and soul of the biblical teaching about grace and stands in defiant opposition to a continuous line of teaching that extends back through the Reformation, the early church, and the New Testament itself.

One might ask, "How does he come to this conclusion?" We certainly did. As we and others reviewed the paper our consensus was the same. Mr. Gothard arrived at a new definition through a misuse and out-of-context quotation of both the Scriptures and other cited sources. For example, his first step in justifying his definition of "grace" is:

> The New Testament word of *grace* is *charis*. It comes from the root word *chairo*, which means to be "cheerful, happy, or well off, to be joyful, or to rejoice." *Charis* is defined in *Strong's Exhaustive Concordance of the Bible* as "the divine influence upon the heart, and its reflection in the life; including gratitude, joy and liberality."[5]

In the next section of this chapter we will demonstrate how Gothard here abuses *Strong's* concordance. But first we should note that by defining "grace" in this way he actually limits the scope of the word's meaning to the realm of sanctification (the process whereby God makes Christians holy), thus excluding justification (the act of God declaring sinners righteous in Christ). This subtly contradicts the New Testament's emphasis on grace as the basis for justification (Romans 3:24; 5:1-2, 16-21; Galatians 2:16-21; 5:4; Titus 3:7).

The theological implications of Gothard's definition are vast and profound. He seems unaware of the fact that it sets him in opposition to the Protestant Reformation and leads directly to a Roman Catholic understanding of the sinner's standing before God. This would perhaps not be so troublesome if not for the fact that Gothard claims to be an evangelical Christian. But before we can address those issues it's important that we draw attention to the dubious method whereby he came upon his definition of grace.

Playing with Words while Grasping at Straws

Gothard avoided a host of acknowledged and respected authorities on biblical words who could have spared him and his followers this regrettable error, but for some reason he resisted any urge he may have had to consult genuine linguistic reference works, opting for the meager resources of an English concordance. Readers should also be aware of the fact that *Strong's* as useful as it is as a concordance, is not a definitive authority on the biblical languages. It provides convenient dictionaries (or lexicons) of Hebrew, Aramaic, and Greek words as appendices, but they are far too abbreviated, and sometimes even outdated, for the serious study of biblical words. For that it is necessary to consult standard lexicons and theological dictionaries.[6] But since *Strong's* definitions *are* so brief, we should at least be able to expect Gothard to provide a full and accurate quotation and interpretation of them. However when we look up the definition for *charis* that Gothard quotes from *Strong's* (word number 5485, on page 77 of Strong's "Greek Dictionary") we read:

> ... *graciousness* (as *gratifying*), of manner or act (abstr. or concr.; lit., or spiritual; espec. the divine influence upon the heart, and its reflection in the life; including *grati-tude*): — acceptable, benefit, favour, gift, grace (-ious), joy, liberality, pleasure, thank (-s, worthy).

It is immediately apparent that Gothard did not quote Strong either fully or accurately. He selected one aspect of the good doctor's definition and tried to apply it to every usage of the word in Scripture.

The last portion of *Strong's* definition, beginning with the word "acceptable" ("acceptable, benefit, favour," etc.), helps us to see the range of meaning (or semantic range) that *Strong's* identifies in the New Testament word for "grace," to which Gothard made no reference whatsoever. Here it is especially noteworthy that Gothard flagrantly skips right over *Strong's* definition of *charis* as "gift" — something that can never be earned or merited (otherwise it ceases to be a gift, and becomes a payment or reward). As Paul wrote, "And if by grace, *it is* no more of works, otherwise grace is no more grace" (Romans 11:6).

True, *Strong's* shows that *charis* ("grace") could *also* refer to "graciousness," either of manner (i.e., a character quality) or of action (i.e., a deed that reflects grace, such as the "grace" of giving, as Paul refers to it in 2 Corinthians 8:7). But the concept of a "divine influence upon the heart" is but one usage of the word *charis* out of several, and is not a complete definition of *charis*, but an example of one kind of *unmerited favor* that comes from God.

The word *charis* occurs 155 times in the New Testament, and is never translated as "divine influence." That meaning, if it exists, must be derived from the context.[7] Even in cases where this sense might be possible, there is nothing in the word *charis* that would signify it as earned or merited.

The idea of "gift," which Gothard omits, is perhaps the most prominent aspect of the word *charis* in the New Testament. It comes out especially in the related word *charisma,* which we find in Romans 6:23: "For the wages of sin *is* death: but the gift [*charisma*] of God *is* eternal life through Jesus Christ our Lord." Whereas *charis* emphasizes the generosity (or "liberality" as in the KJV and *Strong's*) of the giver, *charisma* emphasizes the gift that is generously and freely given. The verb form, *charizomai,* simply means "I freely give" or "I forgive."

For reasons separate from the legitimate concerns of biblical Greek, Bill Gothard engages in a verbal "shell game" with the words *charis* and *charisma.* He takes the emphasis on the gift that we find in the word *charisma* and transfers it to the word *charis,* and then he further narrows the meaning by defining *charis* with only one particular kind of gift given by God. He writes:

> The grace that comes by Jesus Christ is an active, dynam-
> ic energy from God to carry out His will.[8]

The strange idea that God's grace can be limited to some kind of "active, dynamic energy" is foreign to the New Testament, although it is reminiscent of the ancient Gnostic heretics who reduced grace to a "power."[9] What Gothard does here is like someone trying to force the word "gift" to only signi-fy "Christmas presents that are earned by good behavior." Not only does it limit the particular *kind* of gift (thus excluding birth-day presents, anniversary presents, etc.), but also it requires it to be *earned,* thus emptying it of its true biblical meaning.

Does God, in His grace, give Christians the power to carry out His will? Certainly! But that is only one aspect of God's grace, not the sum total. When God gives us the power to obey Him, is it because we've earned it? *Never* (Ephesians 2:8-9)!

There is nothing in the *Strong's* definition that even alludes to Gothard's meaning; not only does it not support Bill Gothard's definition of grace, it is in fact, in opposition to Gothard's view. In addition, Gothard's definition of grace is not supported by *A Greek-English Lexicon of the New Testament and Other Early Christian Literature* by Bauer, Arndt, Gingrich, and Danker, or any other standard lexicon or dictionary now in use. However, to anyone familiar with the theological controversies of church history, Gothard's definition should sound strangely familiar.

The Road to Rome

In the movie, *Who Framed Roger Rabbit?* detective Eddie Valiant goes into the all-cartoon world of Toon Town and soon finds himself being chased by a malicious "toon." Since he's in a cartoon world, he is able to pick up the stripe in the middle of the road, bend it in a 90-degree angle, and lay it at the foot of a brick wall. The toon follows the stripe, crashes into the wall, and is knocked unconscious. "Gets those toons every time!" Eddie mutters to himself with grim satisfaction.

This is an apt analogy for Bill Gothard's definition of "grace." He picks up the stripe in the middle of the road, as it were, but bends it in a 180-degree angle, so that his definition ends up leading people straight back to the Law. This becomes painfully obvious at the conclusion of his *Definition of Grace*, where he writes:

> A child who does not want to be protected from evil will look at parental instruction as unwanted control. However, a wise parent will not only give detailed instruction on how to avoid problems, but will give further encouragement and assistance to carry them out. This illustrates the true nature of grace, which is "the divine influence upon the heart, and its reflection in life."[10]

For Gothard, the primary purpose of grace is to assist Christians in keeping the Law. And a primary purpose for keeping the Law is to "earn" more grace! He offers no way to break out of this vicious, self-defeating cycle.

It is all the more sobering to consider the ramifications of where Gothard's twisted road leads. It is the theological implications of his definition of grace that make it so startling. The ways in which he attempts to work out those implications represent a 180-degree turn *away* from the doctrine of justification and sanctification by faith alone that was recovered by the Protestant Reformation, and *toward* the Roman Catholic doctrine of salvation based on works.

To summarize these ramifications, when we look back in church history to see the concept of grace limited to some kind of "energy" or "power" or "substance" that God transmits to people to make them more righteous, we also find specific theological errors following closely behind. These errors have driven countless souls to spiritual despair:

1. An emphasis on "infused righteousness" to the exclusion of the imputed righteousness of Jesus Christ to the believer

2. The teaching that grace is merited – or earned, or deserved – rather than unmerited

3. A re-definition of "justification" itself in terms of both personal merit and "infused righteousness" – or as God "*making* sinners righteous" rather than declaring, counting, or reckoning sinners righteous

The first thing that confronts the reader of Bill Gothard's *Definition of Grace* is its total emphasis on infused righteousness as opposed to imputed righteousness. Nowhere does Gothard even mention imputed righteousness. While normally this might simply be dismissed as an argument from silence, it becomes quite troubling to note that when he does cite Scriptures that have been traditionally used in support of imputed righteousness, he uses them to serve his notion of infused righteousness.[11]

The second thing that confronts us is Gothard's open denial that "grace" is properly defined as "unmerited favor." He refers to this as a "Faulty Definition."[12] He even goes so far as to claim that "In the Old Testament, those who found grace possessed qualities that merited God's favor,"[13] and that "Two witnesses in the New Testament also affirm that additional grace is merited by a person's humility."[14]

This should come as quite a shock to the vast majority of evangelical believers who have been taught by parents, Sunday school teachers, pastors, and many other Christians that, as J.I. Packer wrote,

> The grace of God is love freely shown toward guilty sinners, contrary to their merit and indeed in defiance of their demerit.[15]

Gothard stands against multitudes of Bible-believing Christians who have always understood grace as God's unmerited favor.[16] He conveys the idea that when the Bible speaks of those who "found grace" it's saying that they merited God's grace. Quite the opposite is the case, as Packer has also written:

> The word translated "grace" in the New Testament (*charis*) is used in the Greek Old Testament to render the Hebrew *chen*, also translated "grace" in the AV, which signifies the "favour" that a suppliant "finds" in the eyes of a superior person from whom he cannot claim favourable treatment as a right.[17]

It is difficult to understand how Gothard can affirm belief that salvation is a free gift when the grace on which it is based must be earned. But in an apparent effort to preserve his affiliation with evangelical Christians, Gothard writes:

> It is certain, based on biblical truth, that we can do nothing to merit the grace of God for salvation. Grace for salvation is a free gift and not the reward for any works that we do to merit it. This distinction was the great battlefield of the Reformation because of the false doctrine that a person could earn salvation by good works.[18]

But even here he can't resist criticizing Martin Luther for

going to "opposite extremes which also breed error" in a manner that demonstrates his failure to grasp the issues.[19] Salvation and sanctification are both the work of God by grace. How seriously can we take this disclaimer of Gothard's when he has already defined grace as "an active, dynamic energy from God to carry out His will" (i.e., as infused righteousness)? In light of his new definition of grace, what could he possibly mean by "grace for salvation?" If grace is simply an energy enabling obedience, then salvation and sanctification must automatically be re-defined in terms of obedience (the carrying out of God's will) rather than faith alone. This conclusion is reinforced when Gothard both denies that grace is unmerited and declares that it was merited in both the Old and New Testaments.

As Gothard continues to expound his anti-evangelical concept of grace, the long shadow of St. Peter's Basilica falls across his pages, which begin to echo with the familiar phrases and doctrines of Rome's hostile response to the Protestant Reformation, "The Canons and Decrees of the Council of Trent" (1546). In a very carefully worded statement, that council declared:

> For, whereas Jesus Christ himself continually infuses his virtue into the said justified, – as the head into the members and the vine into the branches, – and this virtue always precedes and accompanies and follows their good works, which without it could not in any wise be pleasing and meritorious before God, – we must believe that nothing further is wanting to the justified, to prevent their being accounted to have, by those very works which have been done in God, fully satisfied the divine law according to the state of this life, and to have truly merited eternal life....[20]

Even though this Tridentine confession (as it is called) held that all the righteousness that "the justified" (i.e., those who are saved) possess comes from Jesus Christ, nevertheless in the final analysis those saved "have truly merited eternal life." This is because in Catholic theology, the purpose of grace is to enable people to "merit," or earn, salvation. In an attempt to safeguard some semblance of the "free gift" concept inherent in both the Greek (*charis*) and Latin (*gratia*) words for grace, Catholicism teaches that "*initial* grace" (*prima gratia*) is totally unmerited. But all grace *after* that serves to allow people to accumulate "merits" that will eventually "justify" them before God, gaining for them eternal life.[21]

How does Gothard avoid coming to the same conclusion? It's not clear that he does. In fact, the more he writes, the deeper he sinks into the same works-righteousness pit that trapped many of the medieval scholastics, and on which the Tridentine bishops based their confession. On page 3 of his *Definition of Grace* he writes: "... initial grace is a free gift of God and growth in grace is a process after salvation." Since Gothard's "initial grace" is also found in medieval theology (both the phrase *and* the concept!), and his concept of "growth in grace" involves earning grace, this is a statement that would have made the Tridentine bishops applaud!

He attempts to avoid the logical conclusion that in the final analysis salvation itself is earned by simply declaring that "grace for salvation" is not merited. But since by "grace for salvation" he apparently means the same thing as "initial grace," this again is consistent with the Council of Trent, which logically concluded that salvation *is* ultimately merited. What both Gothard and Trent share in common here is the belief that, while God freely gives the first step ("initial grace"), the rest (i.e., all subsequent grace) must be earned.

And since Gothard considers "unmerited favor" to be a faulty definition of "grace," how can "the grace of salvation" (as he calls it) be anything *but* merited? On what basis does he single out his "grace for salvation" as the sole exception to his definition of "grace?" And yet if Gothard himself can demonstrate from Scripture that the "grace for salvation" is unmerited, then on what basis does he make all other grace merited? His bifurcation of the meaning of "grace" — assigning it two radically opposite definitions — is totally arbitrary.

So the only difference between Bill Gothard and the Tridentine bishops was that the bishops were more consistent in their logic and more persistent in driving toward its obvious conclusion. If Gothard shared these virtues he would be forced to apply his definition of "grace" across the board. Only a desire to be considered a member of the evangelical Protestant camp restrains him.

There is but one logical step left for Gothard to explicitly take: to re-define "justification" in a manner consistent with his Romish doctrine of grace. This would involve Gothard admitting that if grace is basically *earning* the infusion of more and more righteousness, then justification (being righteous before God) must be the process of being *made* righteous, rather than being *declared* righteous. Or, as the Council of Trent put it, justification "is not remission of sins merely, but also the sanctification and renewal of the inward man, through the voluntary reception of the grace, and of the gifts, whereby man of unjust becomes just [i.e., whereby an unjust man becomes just; *unde homo ex injusto fit justus*]...."[22] If he ever openly he takes this next logical step – thus completely blurring the distinction between justification and sanctification – then he will have officially adopted a justification that is, practically speaking, based on works, and therefore a salvation that is not strictly by grace through faith.

The multitudes of conservative evangelical Christians who have attended Gothard's seminars during the final three decades of the 20th century must be scratching their heads right now. How could so many people have missed this in his teachings? But maybe a better question would be: How was he able to disguise his true view for so long?

Perhaps the fact that Gothard up until now refrained from actually attacking the true meaning of grace is why the thousands of pastors who have attended his seminars have allowed him to get away with his misleadingly narrow definition, which has actually been his "operational definition" all along. Various versions of it can be found in his materials as far back as the 1970s. He has always excluded any mention of "unmerited favor" from his definition. The only differences between then and now are that up until now (a) he hasn't attempted to defend his narrow definition, and (b) he hasn't openly attacked the historic definition of grace as unmerited or undeserved favor.

Reversing the Reformation

But now Gothard *is* attacking it, and he's trying to use Scripture as one of his weapons against it. In an attempt to support his view that "In the Old Testament, those who found grace possessed qualities that merited God's favor," he cites Noah, Moses, and Gideon as examples. His concept of grace turns out to be astonishingly similar to that of the Jehovah's Witnesses. In explaining why they take their message door-to-door, their official literature states:

> We want to give deserving ones the opportunity to learn of Jehovah's undeserved kindness and the Kingdom hope.[23]

The self-contradicting nature of this statement is apparent to all but those who are too spiritually blind to see it. If Jehovah's Witnesses are going door-to-door out of concern for "deserving ones," then Jehovah's kindness must be deserved rather than undeserved. Gothard's teaching is doomed by precisely the same kind of self-contradiction.

Aside from the fact that "merited grace" is an oxymoron, Scripture does not teach what Gothard says it teaches. There is no verse that says, "Because so-and-so possessed such and such, he *merited* grace." The lack of any direct biblical statement, however, doesn't prevent Gothard from trying to cherry-pick verses which he thinks *sound* like they support his case.

Gothard cites Exodus 33:12, where Moses acknowledges to God that he "found" grace. Gothard then assumes that when the author of Hebrews writes that Moses chose "to suffer affliction with the people of God" (Hebrews 11:25) that this choice on Moses' part was the reason why he received the grace mentioned in Exodus 33:12. Unfortunately for Gothard, there is *no* connection between these verses. In fact, the specific kind of "grace" referred to in Exodus 33 was God's gracious choice in selecting Moses as the leader of the children of Israel and the promise of God's presence as they journeyed to the promise land. These were things God had decided to do *before* Moses finally agreed with God to go back to Egypt (after spending much of Exodus 3-4 arguing with Him about it). So, contrary to Gothard's logic, in the case of Moses the grace of God's choice of Moses *preceded* Moses' choice to obey.

Likewise, Gothard quotes Genesis 6:9 – "Noah was a just man *and* perfect in his generations, *and* Noah walked with God" – as the reason why Noah merited the grace mentioned in the previous verse (Genesis 6:8) "But Noah found favor [i.e., grace] in the eyes of the LORD." But *when* did Noah receive this grace – before or after he walked with God? Gothard would have us believe he found it afterward, but the text does not say that. There is no cause-and-effect relationship between Genesis 6:8 and 6:9, so that Noah's obedience (mentioned in verse 9) was the cause of Noah receiving God's grace (mentioned in verse 8). If there were, we would be left to wonder why Genesis *reverses* the cause-and-effect order that Gothard proposes! It's also important to notice that there is actually a literary "break" between verses 8 and 9: verse 8 climaxes the section found in Genesis 6:1-8, and verse 9 begins a new section. Therefore, verse 8 relates to what precedes, not to what follows, and Genesis 6:9 relates to what follows. Therefore, Genesis 6:9 (Noah's righteous life) does not "explain" Genesis 6:8 (the fact that Noah received grace). Genesis 6:8 does not tell us *when* Noah received grace, nor does Genesis 6:9 provide us with the *reason* why Noah received grace. Further, we do know that it was Noah's *faith* which pleased God (Hebrews 11:7)!

By trying to force Genesis 6:9 to provide the cause for Genesis 6:8, Gothard has not only reversed the flow of the passage, but he's also reversed the relationship between grace and righteousness that is found in Scripture and has been taught in historic evangelical theology. H. C Leupold explains that when the text refers to Noah as "righteous" (Hebrew *tsaddîq*) it is referring to the righteousness that God gives us by His grace and through our faith.[24] In other words, Genesis 6:9 tells us about Noah's righteousness *not* to inform us about the reason why God was gracious toward Noah, but simply to verify that he had true faith.

Bill Gothard argues that the "word *unmerited* is not found anywhere in Scripture."[25] As shown in the previous chapter, this is just a word shell game. There are many words that are not in the Bible but are nevertheless biblical teachings (e.g., "Trinity"). Gothard himself uses phrases like "umbrella of protection" and "chain of responsibility" even though they're not found in Scripture. But before we have a chance to reflect on this, he attempts to move his shells quicker than our eyes can follow, writing that "grace is merited by a person's humility."[26] But where does the Bible actually *say* that grace is "merited?" It doesn't; and thus Gothard violates his own criteria.

Gothard makes several arbitrary statements, such as "It [the definition of grace as unmerited favor] is not a true definition in all cases."[27] But he offers no evidence of an instance in which grace does *not* refer to unmerited favor. While the word "grace" in Scripture often has a specific focus — e.g., on specific *gifts* (or "graces") from God — where can it be shown that these are earned or merited? Besides, Gothard's argument here can just as easily be used against his own definition of grace as a "dynamic energy from God," since *that* definition is not true in all cases. As *Strong's* indicated above, "grace" has a range of meaning. The question is: is "merit" ever included in that range? The answer, by the way, is "No."

Grace for Sale

Proclaiming the totally free nature of God's grace, the prophet Isaiah wrote:

> Ho! Every one that thirsteth, come ye to the waters;
>> And he that hath no money come; come ye, buy and eat:

Yea, come, buy wine and milk
Without money and without price.
Wherefore do ye spend money for *that which* is not
bread?
And your labor for *that which* satisfieth not?
Hearken diligently unto me, and eat ye *that which is*
good,
And let your soul delight itself in fatness.
Incline your ear, and come unto me:
Hear, and your soul shall live;
And I will make an everlasting covenant with you,
Even the sure mercies of David" (Isaiah 55:1-3).

On a purely worldly level, most people understand fairly well
that you can't pay for something if it's free. You can't pay for it
with money. You can't barter for it with goods or services. You
can't earn it with your good looks or your sparkling personality.
Otherwise it wouldn't be free.

But for some reason, people also seem to have tremendous
difficulty in translating this simple, common-sense understanding into the spiritual realm. The root of the problem is pride. We
want to be able to say that we deserve the good things we have.
We worked for them; they're ours. Borrowing from the old
Smith-Barney commercial, "We get our blessings the old fash-
ioned way: we *earn* them!" But if every spiritual blessing in our
lives is purely undeserved, our pride suffers a mortal wound.

Seeing this dilemma, but still trying to find a way to earn the
gift of God's grace, Gothard writes: "The favor of God is unlimited; therefore, according to the definition 'unmerited,' there is
nothing we can do to gain it or increase it. How then do we grow
in grace...?"[28] It is spiritually agonizing to read these words from
an evangelical Christian perspective.

Here we see the tragedy of Gothard's dilemma most clearly:
if grace is not earned, he asks, then how do we get it? When he
tries to fit the biblical definition of grace as "unmerited favor"
into his view that our relationship with God consists of meriting
blessings from Him, it doesn't fit. But instead of re-examining his

view, he throws out the biblical definition! He can't seem to conceive of a relationship with God that is based *purely* on what God *gives,* rather than what Christians "earn." Without understanding the nature of biblical grace, Gothard finds himself at a theological dead-end and can't see any way out other than working his way into God's favor. Gothard's tragic answer to his own question is, "We grow in *grace* through meritorious *works!*" — that are totally incompatible in biblical theology. "And if by grace, then *is it* no more of works; otherwise grace is no more grace. But if *it be* of works; then it is no more grace: otherwise work is no more work" (Romams 11:6)!

But it is also appalling to realize that, if unmerited grace is objectionable because "there is nothing we can do to gain it," then this same objection that Gothard lodges against unmerited grace *after* salvation must logically apply as an argument against unmerited grace *for* salvation. What is more important than gaining salvation? And so, if unmerited grace is also grace that we can do nothing to gain, then how do we gain salvation? To be consistent, Gothard should also insist that saving grace is earned. Otherwise he should acknowledge that his objection is invalid.

The mentality that pursues God's free grace as if it were something to be earned is the same mentality that produced papal indulgences in the Middle Ages. It was a very logical development: if grace can be obtained in exchange for doing certain things, why can't one of those things be paying money to the Church? The issue finally came to a head when Rome began selling "plenary indulgences," which guaranteed purchasers instant entrance into heaven, and Martin Luther had to speak out.

Now, almost 500 years later, Bill Gothard is re-laying the foundation for the very system the Reformation destroyed with the word of God. After growing up in an evangelical home, graduating (twice) from an evangelical college, and speaking to literally millions of evangelical Christians, how did he fail to learn how to receive grace for the Christian life without meriting it?

So how do Christians grow in grace? We grow in grace by growing *in* grace — not by growing in law, not by growing *into* grace (by works). Not by continuously becoming more adept at complying with a never-ending list of rules, regulations, or "non-optional principles" designed to earn us blessings.

How can *you* grow in grace? Here's an idea: just ask! Jesus said,

> Ask, and it will be given you; seek, and you will find; knock, and it shall be opened unto you.   For everyone that asketh receiveth; and he that seeketh findeth; and to him that knocketh, it shall be opened (Matthew 7:8-9).

That's grace! The word grace, both in Greek and in English, is directly related to the words for "gift." You don't earn a gift (Romans 4:4-5). In fact, you don't even usually have to ask for a gift. It is simply *given* to you. But God is such a cheerful giver Himself that if you ask He won't turn you away.

Do you struggle with sin? Do you have a problem controlling your temper? Do you need to overcome some addiction? Then stop depending on your lists of rules, principles, and laws, which cruelly remind you that you have a problem that you lack the power to overcome. (Besides, many of them may reflect someone else's ridiculous scruples rather than God's will.) Halt your endless search for "root causes." Sometimes such insights are helpful, but they won't change you. If you rest your hope on these things, they will cause you to neglect the two primary means for growing in grace: the promises of God's Word and prayer to God as your loving, merciful, and exceedingly generous Heavenly Father.

We grow up into a mature relationship with God that *begins* with grace, *continues* with grace, and *ends* with grace. It leaves no room for any sort of works-righteousness trade-off in which God periodically dispenses more "grace" to us as He notices that we've gone down Bill Gothard's list of things-to-do to "merit grace." God's grace is not some "allowance" He gives us for completing our chores. We grow in knowledge and maturity *because* of God's grace, with the result that we understand God's grace more *fully*, and so continue to grow in our experience of *grace*. This is the glory of our position in Christ!

The Bible's concept of grace is God-centered from beginning to end. We don't earn *any* of it at *any* point. Even the works we do are the product of His unmerited favor. We don't work *for* grace; we work *from* grace (Ephesians 2:10)! Gothard, on the other hand, has an anthropocentric (human-centered) view, based on the ability of sinful human beings to perfect themselves — with some help from God, of course. But while his approach may appeal to human pride, for Christians it comes at a terrible cost.

Christians Can't Handle Freedom

The day that Ron and Wendy Henzel welcomed their son, Benjamin, from South Korea was one of the happiest days of their lives. Since then, Ron has been struck by Apostle Paul's use of adoption as an illustration of what it means when Christians become members of God's family.

In the ancient Roman world, if a man was not the *pater familias* (the male head of the household), there were only two other ways he could be considered "part of the family" (the immediate family, that is). He could either be a son or a slave. Sons had freedom; slaves did not.

The Apostle Paul wanted the Christians in Galatia to understand that when it comes to relating to God, there are only two ways. You can try to relate to Him on the basis of law or on the basis of grace. If you try law, you will always fail. You will be a slave and you will never be free. But if you try grace, you will not only succeed in having a relationship with God, but you will be one of His adopted sons! This was amazing stuff back in the first century because Paul made it very clear in Galatians that even women, who were by no means treated as equals in Roman society, would share the same status before God as men did.

Very frequently, one's starting-point determines one's ending-point, and when it comes to having a close and fruitful relationship with God, *everything* hinges on one's understanding of His grace. Starting with a definition of grace that's based on what is earned,

will lead to a never-ending bondage to performance. In his essay
How His Teachings Will Put You Into The Bondage of Legalism John
A. Miller observes:

> Mr. Gothard teaches a definition of the Grace of God
> that is in complete opposition to what is taught in scrip-
> ture. His definition of grace is "An active force within us
> giving us a the desire and the power to do things God's
> way." This definition has nothing to do with the com-
> plete and unmerited favor of God that I've come to know
> and understand. Consider the following verse: *For it is by
> grace you have been saved through faith – and this not from
> yourselves, it is the gift of God* – Ephesians 2:8
>
> You can't read these verses and come away believing
> anything like what Gothard teaches as a definition of
> Grace. And if there is heresy at the cornerstone of his
> belief system, how can you accept anything Mr. Gothard
> teaches?[29]

Miller raises a valid point. Bill Gothard is in the business
(and a very lucrative business it has been) of telling Christians
how they should live. But if his teachings on the very basics of
the Christian life are faulty, how much more faulty must they be
when he addresses the deeper issues of living out the faith in the
real world?

So how does Bill Gothard expect believers to relate to their
Heavenly Father? Don Veinot interviewed the father of a family
who had been involved with IBLP for nearly 30 years. The family left in large part due to seeing how the Institute actually operated "up close and personal." The family's daughter had gone to
work at the orphanage which IBLP operates in Russia. The father
and mother began receiving long distance calls from their daughter who was very distressed by what she was seeing there. They
flew to Russia and spent time at the orphanage. What did they
experience?

...we sat in on a meeting with seven orphanage couples

and Bill. We were discussing rules, law, grace, etc. and Bill made the statement, "Christians can't handle freedom." The way he said it appeared to us that he was there to set the boundaries for us.

Bill Gothard's starting-point (grace is merited) has determined his ending-point (Christians can't handle freedom). He does not share the Apostle Paul's understanding of the proper way to relate to God. Fortunately, others have. For example, John Calvin (1509-1564) wrote:

> See how all our works are under the curse of the law if they are measured by the standard of the law! But how, then, would unhappy souls gird themselves eagerly for a work for which they might expect to receive only a curse? But if, freed from this severe requirement of the law, or rather from the entire rigor of the law, they hear themselves called with fatherly gentleness by God, they will cheerfully and with great eagerness answer, and follow his leading. To sum up: Those bound by the yoke of the law are like servants assigned certain tasks for each day by their masters. These servants think they have accomplished nothing, and dare not appear before their masters unless they have fulfilled the exact measure of their tasks. But sons, who are more generously and candidly treated by their fathers, do not hesitate to offer them incomplete and half-done and even defective works, trusting that their obedience and readiness of mind will be accepted by their fathers, even though they have not quite achieved what their fathers intended. Such children ought we to be, firmly trusting that our services will be approved by our most merciful Father, however small, rude, and imperfect these may be.[30]

Offer the Father *defective* works — *without* hesitation? Yes! That's what it's like to relate to a loving father, as opposed to a harsh judge.

At the ripe old age of three and a half, Ron and Wendy

Henzel's son, Benjamin, tried his hand at representational art. With pen in hand he proceeded to deface several otherwise perfectly good sheets of computer paper. The results looked more like Picasso than DaVinci (no offense intended to fans of Picasso), but can you guess where they ended up? If you guessed "on the refrigerator," you're right! (If you guessed in the garbage, shame on you!) Like the proud papa that he is, Ron immediately put them on display to show Ben how much he approved of both him and his work. Because of Ron's fatherly love for Benjamin, it is *impossible* for him to disapprove of his son's work, "however small, rude, and imperfect" it may be. Benjamin is not Ron's slave; he's Ron's son. He'll never have to earn Ron's favor or merit Ron's blessing.

Do you have this kind of relationship with God? Are you confident that, no matter how many times you fail Him, He still loves you and still approves of you as a loving Father does a son? You can be. But first you must break free from trying to relate to God as if your obedience were more important than His love and grace. You must stop seeing your Father as someone who lays an endless list of moral demands on your shoulders. As Charles Hodge wrote:

> Redemption from bondage to the law includes not only deliverance from its penalty, but also from the obligation to satisfy its demands. ... The Apostle says, in Galatians iv. 5, that we are thus redeemed from the law, in order "that we might receive the adoption of sons"; that is, be introduced into the state and relation of sons to God. Subjection to the law, in our case, was a state of bondage. Those under the law are, therefore, called slaves, *douloi*. From this state of bondage they are redeemed, and introduced into the liberty of the sons of God. This redemption includes freedom from a slavish spirit, which is supplanted by a spirit of adoption, filling the heart with reverence, love, and confidence in God as our reconciled Father.[31]

You can relate to God either as a loving Father or as a legal Judge. You can come to Him either as a forgiven son or as a condemned sinner. There are no other options. Despite what Bill Gothard teaches, if you begin the Christian life by pure grace but try to complete it by merit, you will fail (Galatians 3:3). So which way do you choose?

Chapter 6

A Black and White Gospel
for a Color World

A s we learned in the previous chapter, the Gospel is about grace, and grace leads to freedom and godliness (Titus 2:11-14). Freedom, in turn, is about choice. Specifically: it is about multiple choices, based on multiple options. It is about enjoying the kind of latitude in decision-making in which more than one choice may often be right, and sometimes even encountering situations in which there are no wrong choices and one may literally do as one pleases. However, true grace produces a truly godly life.

This is not to say that moral absolutes cease to exist or that it is no longer important to distinguish between right and wrong when one becomes a Christian. But the Christian life is not meant to be one of constant dread, lived out warily by rule-burdened souls who view God as One who looks for flaws in every decision they make. That kind of God would understandably make people want to run away and hide from Him. But God is a Father who wants His children to have the nerve to come into His presence at any time, not only when they've been on their best behavior. And the Christian life is meant to be lived out with the kind of boldness that comes from knowing a Father who sees even our bad decisions as opportunities to show us more grace and love (Ephesians 3:12; Hebrews 4:16) — *not* simply as opportunities to allow troubles into our lives.

God is the Father who treats His children like the spiritual *adults* that we are in Christ. This is Paul's basic point in Galatians 3:23-4:7, where he likens the Law of Moses to what we would call a legal guardian in our day. The guardian establishes and enforces rules for a child, but only until the child becomes an adult. At that point, the adult children of the Father are capable of governing their own behavior. They are mature. They understand their Heavenly Father on an adult level, desire to please Him, and no longer need a guardian to tell them how to do that.

In stark contrast to the Bible's view of God and the Christian life, we have that of Bill Gothard, whose concept of "merited grace" leads directly to his system of "non-optional principles of life." Upon these principles he piles rules, regulations, laws, steps, and so on. Enticing Christians with the promise of "success" (which he later qualifies as "God's definition of success"), he lures them into seminar after seminar. While they sit there with manuals on their laps, Gothard builds his never-ending fence of prohibitions around them. Many of these are simply cultural taboos dictated by his own white, American, middle-class, mid-20th century background (e.g., men shouldn't wear beards; women shouldn't work outside the home). Others are the result of his bizarre approach to Scripture (e.g., married couples should abstain from sex on certain days). Either way, Gothard gradually cuts off his audiences from more and more of their Christian liberty until they have little or no spiritual freedom left.

In the end, Gothard puts the adult children of God back under a legal guardian. There is virtually no area of life in which almost every possible decision is not divided between "right" and "wrong" choices, without any middle ground. You may make a "wrong" choice and not even realize it, but rest assured that Gothard's God will let you know in some indirect and unpleasant way. For instance, He may bring a financial setback into your life to let you know that you shouldn't have painted your living room green. You may come down with the flu the week before you were going to leave for college and that could be God's way of telling you that you shouldn't go, but should attend Gothard's Advanced Training Institute instead. Gothard's God has quite an imagination when it comes to getting your attention, keeping you in line, keeping you terrified of making the wrong decision, and keeping you away from grace and freedom.

The Not-So-Well-Hidden Agenda

One of the things we learn from Paul's epistle to the Galatians is that when you surrender your Christian freedom, you surrender it to someone else. You're not surrendering it to God. He doesn't want to take it back from you; He's the one who gave it to you in the first place! Instead, as Paul wrote, "And that because of false brethren unawares brought in, who came in privily to spy out our liberty which we have in Christ Jesus, that they might bring us into bondage. To whom we gave place by subjection, no, not for an hour; that the truth of the gospel might continue with you" (Galatians 2:4-5). When you give up your Christian liberty, you invariably surrender it to someone else's false teaching about God and the Gospel.

The false teacher is not motivated by love for you. He is motivated by the desire to control you and lord it over you, with his goal being that you will give him the glory that rightly belongs to God. The Christian who enjoys the liberty that belongs to God's sons and daughters will end up praising God. The Christian who turns over control of his or her life to some guru's list of rules and regulations will end up praising the guru. We have seen this time and time again with various cults, and we see it with the devoted followers of Bill Gothard. It's as if they can't stop talking about him. And for many people, that kind of personal glory is all the incentive they need.

Whatever their motivations, these kinds of people present a spiritual danger both to individual Christians as well as the church at large because, among other things, they distract believers from the proper devotion to Christ. We couldn't help but wonder if Jerry Bridges was thinking specifically of Bill Gothard when he wrote:

> We've talked about some of the areas in which we practice legalism with each other and with ourselves: fences, differing opinions, spiritual disciplines, and fear of what others think. ...
>
> Aggravating all of these areas is a class of people who have come to be known as "controllers." These are people who are not willing to let you live your life before God as you believe He is leading you. They have all the issues buttoned down and have cast-iron opinions about all of them. These people only know black and white. There are no gray areas to them.
>
> They insist you live your Christian life according to their rules and their opinions. If you insist on being free to live as God wants you to live, they will try to intimidate you and manipulate you one way or another. Their primary weapons are "guilt trips," rejection, or gossip.
>
> These people must be resisted. We must not allow them to subvert the freedom we have in Christ....[1]

In what some might consider a remarkable coincidence (but which we consider a remarkable providence), Bill Gothard responded to an article published in the *Midwest Christian Outreach Journal* with a paper that he first threatened to upload to the IBLP web site but which he later distributed in printed form. He gave it the accusatory (and we consider libelous) title of *A Response to Antinomian Rationalism*. In it, he wrote:

> One day the author of the article explained his chief disagreement. "What bothers me most about Bill Gothard and his teaching is that to him everything is either good or evil, either right or wrong." In other words, there is no room for the gray areas of life.[2]

As we read these words we could hear Bridges' description of the "controller" echoing in our minds: "These people only know black and white. There are no gray areas to them."[3]

The author to whom Gothard refers here is Ron Henzel, and the conversation from which he quotes was one that Henzel had by telephone with IBLP director John Stephens, which Stephens then related to Gothard. In that conversation, however, the main issue was not whether Henzel was "bothered" by Gothard's totally polarized view of life's choices. (In fact, he's never lost a minute of sleep over anything Gothard has taught.) His point was that Gothard's "no-room-for-gray-areas" philosophy is one of the most fundamental errors in Gothard's system, since it plays a foundational role in Gothard's approach to the Christian life. In other words, Henzel was advising Stephens that Gothard's insistence that *each and every* personal choice that anyone makes can and should be classified as either "good" or "evil" is a false assumption that leads to a host of other errors. The issue is not one of personal dislike for Gothard's black-and-white philosophy, but of whether it is *biblical.* Henzel told Stephens that, from a biblical perspective, while there are many things that are always right and many other things that are always wrong, some choices are morally debatable, while others are purely neutral; to say otherwise may lead to legalistic bondage.

Gothard clearly disagrees with Henzel on this score. In his opinion, precisely the opposite is the case. Nothing is ever debatable or neutral. He writes:

> However, when it comes to basic morality, there are no "gray areas" that are "off-limits" for biblical examination and judgment. God has established only two classifications: good or evil.
>
> He does not allow for gray areas or amoral activities that are determined by culture, tradition or personal tastes.... One day every deed will be judged as either good or evil....
>
> Gray areas are a mixture of light and darkness. Such a mixture contradicts the character of God, Who is "light, and in him is no darkness at all" (1 John 1:5)....[4]

Reasonable people would try to give Bill Gothard the benefit of the doubt at this point. If, by his reference to "basic morality," he is simply affirming the existence of moral absolutes, then he is surely correct. And if, by declaring that no area is "off-limits" to biblical scrutiny he is simply saying that Christians should be morally discerning and ready to avoid even the appearance of evil, then we certainly have no argument with him.

But this is not all that Gothard is saying. He takes the matter one step further. He insists that Christians who appreciate moral absolutes and examine all their options in order to avoid evil will *never* find a choice in any area of life that is morally neutral or strictly a matter of personal preference. He declares that God "does not allow for gray areas or amoral activities that are determined by culture, tradition or personal tastes."[5] In even the most mundane of choices Christians run the risk of displeasing God and inadvertently bringing negative consequences into their lives. In other words: you have to walk on eggshells around Gothard's God. You never know when you might violate one of his "principles." And to leave no room for misunderstanding him, Gothard writes:

> Those who believe in gray areas and amoral activities conclude that if something is not directly forbidden in the Bible, believers are free to decide for themselves whether it is right or wrong. Such a freedom was not even shared by the Lord Jesus Christ....[6]

In the summer of 1999 Bill Gothard invited Ron Henzel to meet with him personally and specifically requested that Don Veinot not attend. In that meeting, Gothard presented Henzel with an earlier (and much shorter) draft of his *A Response to Antinomian Rationalism* article — a version which mentioned Henzel and Veinot by name (the published version does not). Gothard had John Stephens read the document to Henzel and threatened to upload it to the IBLP web site if he did not remove texts critical of Gothard from his web site. Henzel was unmoved by this tactic. He advised Gothard that he misunderstood the meanings of the words "antinomian" and "rationalism" and was utterly mistaken in applying them to Henzel and Veinot. He also told Gothard that if he insisted on accusing him of being either of these things, he would respond in an appropriate manner.

Henzel also directly challenged the reasoning of Gothard's article. He had been in Gothard's office for two previous meetings with him, and each time he couldn't help but notice its dark red carpeting.

"How did you choose the color of this carpet?" Henzel asked Gothard.

"What do you mean?" replied Gothard, looking a bit puzzled.

"If you had chosen green, or blue, or some other color, would those choices have been morally wrong?" asked Henzel. "Was this the *only* 'righteous' color available?"

"Are you saying that the Holy Spirit can't lead us in the choice of carpeting?" retorted Gothard.

"No, I'm not suggesting that," said Henzel. "But are you saying that there was no other choice that the Holy Spirit could have blessed? Are you saying that the choice of *this* dark red color was inspired by God?"

Gothard did not directly answer this question, and Henzel did not persuade him in that meeting. It is also obvious that Gothard has not changed his mind since then, for now he writes:

> In an effort to push the discussion to what might be considered ridiculous, our critic looked at our carpet and asked, "Is this carpet good or evil?," ignoring the fact that at the final judgment God is not going to judge carpets, but people. The following three tests can be applied to any decision, including decisions involving a carpet.[7]

Why Gothard asserts that we think this is about "judging carpets" rather than judging people is puzzling, but is consistent with his tendency to misrepresent our views. In any case, at this point what he gives with his right hand he simultaneously takes away with his left. First he says, "God is not going to judge carpets, but people," and then he provides his readers with three "tests" so they can know that God will judge their choice of carpets favorably.[8] But before he does, Gothard accuses Henzel of trying to make his reasoning appear ridiculous. This is obviously not true; Henzel didn't have to try.

Playing the Fear Card

Bill Gothard has been exploiting the issues of juvenile delinquency and youth crime as a marketing tool since he founded his Institute. He knows very well how effectively it attracts the attention of concerned parents and has consistently portrayed governments and law-enforcement authorities as impotent in this area while he himself has all the answers.[9] As experienced marketers know, inflicting fear on prospective customers can be a very effective way to sell a product. Gothard is a master at it.

The fear of youth rebellion and violence was the springboard from which he launched his Institute in Basic Youth Conflicts (now the IBLP) in the 1960s. So it's not surprising to see him feign expertise on this subject by returning to it in his debate with Henzel. Seeing Henzel's statement to Stephens as an exploitable weakness, Gothard proceeds to rise to the defense of his "no-gray-areas" approach by writing:

> Such a disagreement is no small matter. The exploding youth crime of our day is a result of teenagers who do not distinguish between right and wrong.[10]

It's worth pausing at this point to consider Gothard's reference to "the exploding youth crime of our day." This is yet another echo of what Gothard has been saying since the '60s. Those listening to him since that time should be forgiven for believing that youth crime was *always* "exploding" in the second half of the twentieth century and that it continues to do so at the dawn of the twenty-first century. But this makes us wonder: if youth crime has been constantly "exploding" for the past 35 years (i.e., getting worse and worse), why don't we (i.e., the authors of this chapter) personally witness such crimes being committed on our own streets, or somewhere nearby, at least *once* every few years? We live in fairly average suburban neighborhoods in the Chicago area and occasionally read the "police blotter" sections of our local newspapers. Where is all this ever-increasing youth crime? Things don't get worse and worse to such an extreme degree as to be considered *continuously* "exploding" for three decades or so without being regularly observed by average people.

The reason Gothard can seemingly get away with exaggerations like this is because, in addition to exploiting natural parental fears, he also exploits the common cultural ignorance that results from most people relying upon the media for information (which is ironic, considering Gothard's opinion of the media). In the late 1990s, media coverage of several tragic shootings in public schools across the United States not only tapped into every parent's nightmares, but fed public perceptions that youth in general were becoming exponentially more violent. For the past few years American airwaves and newspapers have almost regularly featured images of teenagers in different parts of the country using everything from handguns to military-style assault weapons to kill their teachers and fellow students.[11] When the media haven't been racing to the scene of the latest schoolyard tragedy, they have been analyzing the causes and consequences of the previous ones in grim detail.

But media images do not tell the whole story, and several exceptional cases of shocking violence — as deeply disturbing as they are — do not constitute "exploding youth crime." If one truly wants to know whether youth crime in America is indeed "exploding" these days, one would do better to consult information supplied by the U.S. Department of Justice's Bureau of Justice Statistics[12] than Bill Gothard. There we learn that from 1996 through 1999, incidents of violent crime[13] in general actually declined by slightly more than 20 percent, while incidents of violent crime among juveniles (all youths under age 18) declined by nearly 31.25 percent.[14] In fact, incidents of juvenile violent crime actually began declining a year earlier than violent crime in general, dropping nearly 32.25 percent in 1999 from the rate in 1995.[15] And when we examine the *rate* of violent offenses per 100,000 people, the rate for youth crime actually dropped 39.4 percent over the same period – nearly doubling the 22 percent rate decline for the general population. At the end of the 1990s, incidents of violent crime committed by minors had reached their lowest levels since the late '80s, while the rates came close to figures seen in the mid-'70s.

At the time that Gothard referred to "exploding youth crime," youth crime was actually going through its steepest decline in 30 years. This being the case, preying on people's fears served his purposes better than did pursuing facts.

Distinguishing Between Sense and Nonsense

In his *A Response to Antinomian Rationalism* article Gothard pursues the defense of his thesis that every choice we make, no matter how mundane, is either "good" or "evil," and in the process he equates a belief in "gray areas" with a failure to distinguish between right and wrong. But this is absurd.

The fact that people are able to detect shades of gray does not mean that they are unable to detect black and white. The ability to distinguish between shades of gray is actually *based* on the ability to distinguish between black and white. Otherwise we wouldn't be able tell if one shade of gray were darker or lighter than another.

Likewise, just because people acknowledge the existence of a morally neutral category doesn't meant that they don't know good or evil when they see it. Just because we believe that the color of carpet we choose is a morally neutral decision doesn't mean that we don't know that it's wrong to steal carpet. The ability to discern that a particular choice may be right, wrong, or morally neutral, depending upon the circumstances (thus causing it to fall into a "gray area"), is *based* on the ability to distinguish between right and wrong.

But Gothard's preposterous logic here is not as troubling as his problematic theology. When he writes, "The exploding youth crime of our day is a result of teenagers who do not distinguish between right and wrong,"[16] he implicitly contradicts the biblical doctrine of human sinfulness. People – even young people – do not commit crimes because they fail to distinguish between right and wrong. They commit crimes because, in spite of the fact that they *know* the difference between right and wrong, they deliberately choose what is wrong (Romans 1:28-32, 3:23; Genesis 6:5; 8:21; Psalms 25:7).

This is no light matter, but potentially a grave theological error. In our previous chapter we questioned whether Gothard actually holds to the biblical doctrine of justification and or sanctification by grace through faith. Now we must ask whether he holds to the biblical doctrine of the inherited sinfulness of human nature on which Scripture bases the need for God's grace.

"Antinomian Rationalism" and the Art of Name-Calling

In the 1930s, Roman Catholic priest and radio commentator Fr. Charles Coughlin discovered a very effective way of discrediting people he considered political threats. He would appeal to the anti-Semitism and isolationism shared by much of his audience by denouncing various individuals as "atheistic Jews" or "imported radicals." It mattered little to Coughlin that the sources of his "information" were often untrustworthy. He knew that once he used the power of the broadcast medium to slap labels on people, those people would find it very difficult to remove them from their reputations.

In the 1950s, Wisconsin senator Joseph P. McCarthy used the new medium of television to boost his political career by taking advantage of Americans' fear of Communism. No evidence was too slight, no testimony too tainted, no logic too specious for him to use in labeling various individuals as "Communists" or "subversives." Reputations were destroyed. Careers were ruined. For decades after McCarthy himself was discredited and died his victims struggled to rebuild their shattered lives. McCarthyism has come to be synonymous with intimidation through labeling and blacklisting, and has often been mistakenly portrayed as a "right-wing" tactic. The fact is, however, that McCarthyism is equally useful to demagogues of all political persuasions. In truth, it has become a favorite tool of the left for stifling opposition to their agenda today.

Conservatives are often labeled "Uncle Toms," if they are black, or "racists" if they are white, for daring to voice opposition to any aspect of the left's "civil rights" agenda. People who oppose gay "marriage" are labeled "homophobic." Men and women who oppose abortion on moral grounds are dangerous "extremists," and so it goes. Thus, opposers are allegedly motivated by "hate" or "fear" rather than rational disagreement. Name-calling, becomes a very effective substitute for rationally defending one's case—legitimate viewpoints are summarily de-legitimized, and thinking is short-circuited by knee-jerk reactions to an emotional appeal. Whenever you hear someone slap a label on someone else without providing careful definitions and clear evidence you are more than justified in suspecting that you may be listening to a propagandist, rather than someone who truly desires to inform the public.

This is why we took such great pains in the *Midwest Christian Outreach Journal* to establish the definition of the word "legalism" and carefully document our sources in Bill Gothard's writings before concluding that he is a legalist.[17] We do not want to be mere propagandists.

We wish we could say the same about Bill Gothard. But like Coughlin, McCarthy, and many others before him, what Gothard's name-calling lacks in definition and evidence, it more than makes up for in vagueness and inaccuracy.

A "rationalist" is someone who relies on reason as the primary source of knowledge[18] or the basis for establishment of religious truth.[19] Francis Schaeffer states:

> Rationalism means that man begins from himself and tries to build all the answers on this base, receiving nothing from any other source and specifically refusing any

revelation from God.[20]

Despite the fact that he includes a section titled "Defining Antinomian Rationalism" in his *A Response to Antinomian Rationalism*, not only does Gothard fail to define "rationalism" for his readers, he provides no evidence that we are rationalists. An antinomian is one who is without law and is opposed to any restraints. It appears to us that for some reason he wasn't satisfied with simply calling us "antinomians" and felt the need to add the epithet "rationalists" for good measure — as if to say, "And not only that, but you're ugly and your mother dresses you funny!" He never even tries to make a case for calling us "rationalists." But just for the record: we rely on the Bible, not reason, as the primary source of knowledge about God, the Christian life, and the basis for establishment of religious truth.

Moving on, the only "evidence" Gothard uses to prove that we are "antinomians" is the fact that we believe that (a) in addition to "black" and "white" choices, there are also choices that fall into "gray areas," and (b) the Bible should not be used as a medical textbook. We'll deal with point (b) later. Meanwhile, if point (a) makes us "antinomians," then it does the same for such well-respected Christian authors as Jerry Bridges and Erwin Lutzer (and a host of others). After noting that the Bible lists things that are always right and other things that are always wrong, Lutzer observes:

> But the fact is that there are many questionable activities which are difficult to classify categorically as "sinful" or "not sinful." What about movies, Sunday sports, television, or a myriad of other choices? Is it possible to do these things without being worldly? Or should such a list be used to define precisely what worldliness is?
>
> One Christian, who had become weary of the disagreements that exist regarding the specifics of Christian conduct, made this suggestion: a group of church leaders ought to form a list of sinful activities so that the average Christian could know at a glance what is sin and what is

not. Then we could just follow instructions rather than constantly face such decisions on our own.

On the surface, this suggestion might seem feasible or at least worth a try. But a closer analysis will show that such an assignment can never be done. It sounds simple, but in practice, it is impossible.[21]

But ever since the 1960s Bill Gothard has pursued what Lutzer called the impossible (to which we would add unbiblical) enterprise of eliminating all "gray areas" from the Christian life. And now he concludes that anyone who can still find "gray areas" *must* be an antinomian!

So much for Gothard's "evidence" that we're "antinomians." It consists only of a circular argument based on his own idiosyncratic definition. So now we must examine that definition, which he proceeds to give as follows:

> In the sixteenth century, a small group of people formulated a new philosophy: The Old Testament had no value in the life of New Testament believers. They claimed that Christ had done away with the Law and believers were not to follow it. These people were known as the *Antinomian Sect*. (The term *antinomian* is derived from the Greek words *anti* meaning "against" and *nomia* meaning "Law.") They are described in the dictionary as "one of a sect who maintain, that, under the gospel dispensation, the law is of no use or obligation, or who hold doctrines which supersede the necessity of good works and a virtuous life." This sect originated in Germany around 1538 through the teachings of John Agricola [sic].

Here Gothard demonstrates his lack of familiarity with church history in general and the history of the Reformation in particular. The dictionary definition of antinomianism that he cites was hardly a "new philosophy" in the sixteenth century. It was, in fact, one of the errors refuted by the Apostle John in his first epistle. Nor can it be properly said that an *"Antinomian Sect"* existed in the 1500s — at least not as Gothard describes it.

It's true that there was an antinomian *controversy* and that this controversy centered around the teachings of Johann Agricola (1494-1566) a one-time pupil of Martin Luther (1483-1546), but that controversy lasted only about three years (1537-40). It's possible that Agricola influenced some people who for a while may have become his followers, but they were never an organized sect. Eventually, after he narrowly escaped a heresy trial by fleeing to Berlin, Agricola published three different recantations of his former views, the first of which came on December 6, 1540.

Gothard distorts what Agricola taught. Agricola did not deny the value of good works or a virtuous life. He simply denied any role to the Law of Moses in assisting Christians to lead such a life. As nineteenth century church historian Philip Schaff explained,

> Agricola taught with some truth that genuine repentance and remission of sin could only be secured under the gospel by the contemplation of Christ's love. In this Luther (and afterwards Calvin) agreed with him. But he went much further. The law in his opinion was super-seded by the gospel, and has nothing to do with repen-tance and conversion. It works only wrath and death; it leads to unbelief and despair, not to the gospel. He thought the gospel was all-sufficient both for the office of terror and the office of comfort. Luther, on the contrary, maintained, in his disputations, that true repentance con-sists of two things — knowledge and sorrow of sin, and resolution to lead a better life. The first is produced by the law, the second by the gospel.[22]

No matter how one might disagree with him, Agricola was obviously concerned for the proper means of bringing about repentance and forgiveness. It is a serious mistake for Gothard to equate him with those "who hold doctrines which supersede the necessity of good works and a virtuous life." In addition to this

historical misrepresentation is the fact that Martin Luther himself coined the word "antinomianism" to describe Agricola's
teachings (which makes Gothard's criticism of Luther all the
more ironic and unjust). Only since the 16th century has common usage expanded the word's meaning to include a reference
to the previously existing heresy that Christians need not be concerned at all about good works or virtuous lives.

So the sixteenth century witnessed an antinomian *controversy,* not an "Antinomian Sect," and there's no evidence that
Agricola's teachings led to the development of *any* sect. Agricola
did not teach that it was unnecessary for Christians to live virtuous lives, but that the Law of Moses shouldn't be preached as
part of the Christian message — a position he later recanted on
more than one occasion.

But in the midst of all this fuss about Reformation church
history, it's easy to lose sight of one crucial question: what does
any of this have to do with whether or not one believes in the
existence of "gray areas?" Does Gothard cite *anything* that
Agricola supposedly taught on that subject? No. Then why even
bring him up? Even the most licentious forms of antinomianism
have little or nothing to do with "gray areas!" Those "who hold
doctrines which supersede the necessity of good works and a virtuous life" don't bother with pesky "gray areas." To them black
is white, and so is everything else! They believe that people can
sin as much as they please! So then just what *is* the connection
between antinomianism and gray areas?

That's just it: there isn't any. That's why name-calling is so
easy, and at the same time so effective. Most people don't have
time to research all these things anyway, so many of Gothard's
loyal followers will simply accept what they hear as true. And on
that single fact the propagandist's livelihood depends.

The Joy of Being Misunderstood

As we have already noted there *is* a brand of antinomianism that
tries to give people permission to sin. It is this licentious type of
antinomianism with which Gothard is actually attempting to

identify us. He simply picked the wrong brand of antinomianism by citing Agricola as his main example.

So on the one hand, we respond to this charge by categorically denying that there is anything in our theological position that would encourage people to live a life of sin. On the other hand, we also are grateful for the fact that Gothard's labeling of us as "antinomian" puts us in extremely good company. The Apostle Paul was slanderously accused of teaching "Let us do evil that good may come" (Romans 3:8). In other words, his enemies called him the functional equivalent of an antinomian. Martin Luther's enemies did the same to him. D. Martyn Lloyd-Jones went so far as to insist that if our Gospel preaching is not confused with antinomianism we're probably not preaching the true Gospel when he wrote:

> There is a sense in which the doctrine of justification by faith only is a very dangerous doctrine; dangerous, I mean, in the sense that it can be misunderstood. It exposes a man to this particular charge. People listening to it may say, "Ah, there is a man who does not encourage us to live a good life, he seems to say that there is no value in our works.... Therefore what he is saying is that it does not matter what you do, sin as much as you like".... There is thus clearly a sense in which the message of "justification by faith only" can be dangerous, and likewise with the message that salvation is entirely of grace.... I say therefore that if our preaching does not expose us to that charge and to that misunderstanding, it is because we are not really preaching the gospel....
>
> That is my comment; and it is a very important comment for preachers. I would say to all preachers: If your preaching of salvation has not been misunderstood in that way, then you had better examine your sermons again, you had better make sure that you really are preaching the salvation that is offered in the New Testament....[23]

Steve Brown puts it even more bluntly:

> Now hear something very important: while the apostle Paul was not antinomian, *he was very close to it.* Just so, while the Reformation leaders were not antinomian, *they were very close to it.* Also, while the Christian faith is by no means antinomian, *it is very close to it.*
>
> What's the point? Paul would never have had to write a defense of his teaching on freedom if he had not been very close to heresy. Martin Luther would never have had to come back from Wartburg (where he was in hiding) to straighten out the libertarians in Wittenberg if his teaching had not at least implied something close to what they were doing. The Christian faith would not have had to deal with the heresy of antinomianism unless there was something in it which seemed to imply that particular heresy.
>
> That brings me to a syllogism with two premises and a conclusion. Premise: The real Christian faith is close to antinomianism. Premise: A lot of modern day Christianity is not at all close to antinomianism. Conclusion: A lot of modern day Christianity is not real Christianity.[24]

So it seems that we should not be discouraged when Bill Gothard falsely accuses us of antinomianism, because true Gospel preachers are commonly accused of this. On the other hand, this does not seem to bode well for the authenticity of Gothard's version of the Christian faith, since as far as we know, no one has ever mistaken his "non-optional principles of life" for antinomianism.

Moses M.D.?

Henny Youngman once wisecracked, "When Moses sat on top of Mt. Sinai, you know what he really said? 'This would be a good place for a hospital.'"[25] Youngman was kidding about the number of hospitals named "Mt. Sinai." But Gothard isn't kidding when he insists that the Bible, and particularly the Law of Moses, can be used as a medical textbook. He writes:

> Some might deny being an Antinomian Rationalist, yet still vigorously oppose any attempt to apply Old Testament truth to health or medical decisions. They insist that the Old Testament's primary — and possibly only — function was to foretell the life and work of Christ. They reason that it was only a shadow of things to come, a schoolmaster to bring the human race to Christ; but now that Christ has come, there is no further need for a schoolmaster. The problem with this thinking is that Christ died years before Paul became a believer, yet Paul found the law essential to his understanding of sin. This would also be true of every other person in the world.[26]

If Gothard's logic is difficult to follow in this paragraph, it is with good reason: there is no logical connection between the issue of whether the Old Testament contains medical information and Paul's description of the Law as a "schoolmaster" or "tutor" in Galatians 3:23-25.

But it's clear that he's also changing the subject. Without establishing any logical connection he has now moved from the question of whether gray areas exist to whether he is justified in using the Bible as a medical textbook, as he does in his "Medical Training Institute of America" booklets and elsewhere. This was one of the things we took him to task for in the *Midwest Christian Outreach Journal.*[27] He seems pretty upset about it, for he writes: "To vehemently state that the Old Testament is not a medical book is to do injustice to the deep wisdom of God in His unfathomable and unsearchable Word."[28] So now he makes it clear that you not only have to agree with his "no gray areas" approach, but you also have to accept his opinion that the Bible is a "medical book" to avoid his label of "antinomian rationalist."

Over and over in his *A Response to Antinomian Rationalism,* Gothard misrepresents our view,[29] such as when he attempts to identify us with "Those who find no significant value in the Old Testament"[30] and "those who have set aside the Old Testament."[31] And as he does so his reasoning becomes more and more bizarre. Under the heading, "The Origin and History of Independent Thinking," Gothard writes:

> There is nothing new about a philosophy that provides for gray areas and amoral activities so that people are able to decide for themselves what is right and what is wrong. This was the substance of Satan's first temptation to Adam and Eve. If they took the forbidden fruit, they would be able to decide for themselves what was right and what was wrong. "Ye shall be as gods, knowing good and evil...." (Genesis 3:5).[32]

This is, indeed, a curious interpretation of the phrase "knowing good and evil" (Genesis 3:5), because it makes "the knowledge of good and evil" an inherently evil thing even though God *Himself* possesses it (Genesis 3:22). But "the tree of the knowledge of good and evil" was good, because God declared it to be so along with the rest of His creation (Genesis 2:9; cf. 1:31), and "knowing good and evil" is not a bad thing. If it were then God would be bad. Thus Gothard is clearly confused about the meaning of the phrase "knowing good and evil."

"Knowing good and evil" is not an ability to *decide*, as Gothard teaches, but an ability to *discern*. (But if Gothard's view is correct, then how could Adam and Eve have decided to eat the fruit before the fruit gave them the ability to decide?) God provided two ways of gaining the ability to discern between good and evil, one of which He prohibited. If they had persevered in obedience, they eventually would have gained the kind of discernment that God possesses. Instead, they succumbed to "the substance of Satan's first temptation" – which, contrary to Gothard's view, was not an offer of "independent thinking" (which isn't even mentioned anywhere in the Bible), but the offer to "become like God" (Genesis 3:5).

Satan told Adam and Eve a half-truth. It was true, as the Lord

Himself later acknowledged (Genesis 3:22), that partaking of the fruit did make them to some extent like God, in the sense that they had attained a knowledge of good and evil. But Satan did not tell the whole story and left Eve to draw her own false conclusion: that the fruit would make her "wise" (Genesis 3:6). It actually made her and her husband quite the opposite.

Additionally, the knowledge of good and evil cannot in itself be a bad thing, because God also possesses it (Genesis 3:22), and He is perfect Goodness. Rather, it was the way in which that knowledge was obtained that made eating the forbidden fruit sinful. Had Adam and Eve waited for God to instruct them in the knowledge of good and evil, they would have gained it by being obedient. Instead, they acquired it by being disobedient.

But again, as in the case of Gothard's misrepresentation of Johann Agricola, we're forced to ask, "What does Genesis 3 have to do with 'gray areas?'" Partaking of the forbidden fruit wasn't a "gray area," nor did Satan promise our first parents that all their decisions would become choices between different shades of gray. Genesis 3 has nothing to do with this subject, and the only way Gothard can get this meaning *out of* that passage is by first reading it *into* the passage.

Subsisting on a Diet of Worms

Christians are easy to guilt-trip. If you find someone who claims to be a Christian but who denies ever feeling guilty about anything, look out! He'll probably lie about other things, too. As for the rest of us, we find our entire beings trembling "amens" to every line that Isaac Watts wrote when we sing,

> Alas, and did my Savior bleed,
>   And did my Sov'reign die?
> Would He devote that sacred head
>   For such a worm as I?[33]

The problem is that a lot of times we confuse having a biblical understanding of sin with having an extremely low opinion of ourselves, and the two are not the same. But to take advantage of this phenomenon, spiritual abusers have developed something we call "Worm Theology." The basic tenet of Worm Theology is that we must always look at ourselves in the worst possible light, and the favorite verse of Worm Theology is Jeremiah 17:9. Bill Gothard exposes himself as a Worm Theologian when he writes:

> Establishing gray areas simply allows us to do our own will and constitutes iniquity. It is unrealistic to think that we can make right decisions with a heart that is "deceitful above all things and desperately wicked" (Jeremiah 17:9) and with the law if sin in our members which motivates us to do the things that we know are wrong (Romans 7:19). Based on these facts, God warns, "he that trusteth in his own heart is a fool" (Proverbs 28:26).[34]

Notice the logic Gothard starts out with here. It can be summarized with the following equation:

Gray Areas = Doing Our Own Will = Iniquity (Sin)

But is it true that when we *Christians* "do our own will" that it "constitutes iniquity?" Where in Gothard's equation is the New Testament teaching that "if any man be in Christ, he is a new creature: old things are passed away; behold, all things are become new" (2 Corinthians 5:17)?

It's true that Christians continue throughout their lives to carry around within themselves the remnants of in-born sinfulness. To some extent, the truth of Jeremiah 17:9 still applies to us. But it's not the whole story, something new has happened to us, and this new thing has transformed our *wills!*

Even the verse in Romans 7 that Gothard tries to use to discredit our wills actually defends them: "For the good that I would I do not: but the evil which I would not, that I do" (Romans 7:19). Paul *wanted* to do the right thing, but indwelling sin prevented him. So obviously "doing his own will" did not "constitute iniquity."

Furthermore, as we shall now see, if "Establishing gray

areas...constitutes iniquity" we are forced to conclude that God is the author of iniquity, because He Himself established them as part of the Christian life.

The Strong, the Weak, and the Tyrants

So turning for a moment from Bill Gothard's attack on Christian freedom, it is time to inquire into what the Bible says on the subject of gray areas. Of course, this exact phrase is not used in Scripture, but Paul clearly referred to it when he wrote:

> Him that is weak in the faith receive ye, but not to doubtful disputations. For one believeth that he may eat all things: another, who is weak, eateth herbs. Let not him that eateth despise him that eateth not; and let not him which eateth not judge him that eateth: for God hath received him. Who art thou that judgest another man's servant? to his own master he standeth or falleth. Yea, he shall be holden up: for God is able to make him stand. One man esteemeth one day above another: another esteemeth every day alike. Let every man be fully persuaded in his own mind (Romans 14:1-5).

If a "gray area" is something that is simply a matter of personal preference and is neither "right" nor "wrong," then it's obvious that Paul considered an individual's choices about diet and the observance of "holy days" to be gray areas. True, in the example he gave, Paul did refer to the vegetarian as someone with weak faith, and it's likely that he would place the person who esteemed one day above another in the same category. But he doesn't call either of these people "wrong," just as he avoids calling omnivorous Christians and those who regard every day alike "right." He does not identify what is "black" here so we can distinguish it from what is "white." He leaves that to each individual's personal discretion and walk with God.

Furthermore, the "strong" are not to receive the "weak" for the purpose of "setting them straight" — or as Paul put it, for the purpose of engaging in "doubtful disputations."[35] In other words: the person who enjoys his freedom in the Christian life (i.e., the strong) should welcome the one who doesn't allow himself as much freedom (i.e., the weak), but not in order to argue about who's right and who's wrong. Paul doesn't even allow himself to be drawn into that argument, and he carefully resists legislating these areas for all believers.

This is a different issue from what Paul confronts in Galatians, where the Judaizers were not simply "weaker brethren" who imposed unnecessary limits on their own choices, but *false* brethren, spiritual tyrants, who were bent on limiting other people's choices (Galatians 2:4). We won't go so far as to label Bill Gothard a "false brother," but we would be remiss if we didn't point out that his goals go far beyond limiting his own personal choices.

Paul makes it clear in Romans 14 that believers will disagree with each other on the practical details of how to live the Christian life. When you encounter these disagreements in your own fellowship with other believers, as you inevitably will, you should read the sign that Paul has placed between you and them, which reads: "None of Your Business."

In 1 Corinthians 7:1-17, Paul deals with another question: "To marry, or not to marry?" In this passage he presents a series of considerations to guide each person's individual decision, and he makes it abundantly clear that there is no one, single, "right answer" for every situation — or even for one specific situation, such as the one that the Corinthians were facing. In fact, he makes sure that his readers understand that all the advice he gives in this chapter is conditioned by a "present distress" (7:26), probably a persecution crisis that threatened to shorten the lives of Christians in Corinth (7:29). But even for this most important of life's decisions — marriage — contemplated under distressful circumstances, Paul did not indicate what the "right" choice would be. He gave "permission" instead of a "commandment" (7:6), and offered his own personal "judgment" rather than lay down a Divine law (7:25). He gave them latitude ("...let him do what he will, he sinneth not: let them marry," 7:37).

He didn't give the Corinthians ten steps for knowing whether it's God's will for you to marry, or seven reasons why Christians shouldn't marry during times of persecution. He did something far better. He helped them, in a brotherly way, to think through the ramifications of their choices, and then he gave them the freedom to make them!

Dubious Interpretations

So now we must ask, "Doesn't Bill Gothard's Bible have Romans 14 in it?" The answer may not be as simple as you'd think, for in a very misleading section of his *Antinomian Rationalism* article, he writes:

> In Scripture we have examples of questionable matters that produced "doubtful disputations." The chief example was the meats that were sacrificed to idols, and sold in the open marketplace at a significant enough discount that Christians bought the meat (See Romans 14).
>
> Some believers felt that it was not right to buy the meat, since it was offered to an idol. Others reasoned that the meat itself was untainted and therefore it made no difference. Paul himself affirmed that there was nothing intrinsically wrong with the meat. However, because of the damaging effect that the whole matter had on weaker Christians, the Jerusalem council, under the guidance of the Holy Spirit, unanimously agreed that this meat should not be eaten, even by Gentile believers. (See Acts 15.) In Revelation 2, churches are rebuked for having members who encourage the eating of meat offered to idols (See Revelation 2:14, 20).[36]

One thing out of several that make this so misleading is that, from the outset of this section, Gothard tries to portray Romans 14 as a discussion about meat sacrificed to idols, even though the word "idol" doesn't even occur in the passage. Paul takes up that subject in detail in 1 Corinthians 8 and 10:25-33, not in Romans

14. If we read Romans 14 without importing ideas into it from other passages, the issue it deals with isn't eating meat sacrificed to idols, but whether or not to eat meat *at all* or to be a vegetarian (14:2)!

True, Paul's reference to the "weak" brother may imply that the one who only eats vegetables is trying to be careful to avoid the taint of idolatry. It's also true that Paul was discussing the same "weak" Christians in 1 Corinthians 8, where he explicitly refers to the issue of meat offered to idols. Nevertheless, the *subject* of Romans 14 is how to deal with "doubtful disputations" — i.e., honest differences of opinion among Christians on peripheral matters. Otherwise, Paul would not have raised the issue of esteeming one day above another (14:5-6), which had nothing to do with idolatry.

Not only does Gothard distort the purpose of Romans 14, but he also legislates the very thing that Paul refused to legislate, *both* in Romans *and* in 1 Corinthians! Gothard declares that the New Testament forbids Christians to eat meat that had been previously sacrificed to idols. To make this declaration, Gothard had to commit several significant errors of interpretation.

First, Gothard had to completely ignore the fact that Paul refers to the one who abstains from meat as "weak" in faith (Romans 14:2; 1 Corinthians 8:7, 10), implying that the one who eats the meat has "strong" faith.

Second, he had to ignore the clear teaching of 1 Corinthians 8 that the only time Christians should sacrifice their liberty to eat meat sacrificed to idols is when it might cause a "weak" brother to stumble. It is within this context that Revelation 2:14 and 20 are best understood.

Third, he had to contradict direct instructions from the Apostle Paul in 1 Corinthians 10:25-33 to go ahead and purchase meat from the marketplace and freely eat meat on social occasions without even asking whether it had had been sacrificed to an idol. (A kind of "don't ask, don't tell" policy.) This practice obviously placed Christians at risk of eating sacrificial meat, but the only time Paul instructed Christians not to eat it was when it might offend someone else.

Fourth, he had to distort the decision of the Jerusalem Council, which declared, "But that we write unto them, that they abstain from pollutions of idols, and from fornication, and from things strangled, and from blood" (Acts 15:20, KJV). The phrase "pollutions of idols" refers to the same thing as "things offered to idols" in Acts 21:25, where Paul reiterated the council's decision, so it obviously included meat offered to idols. But Gothard misinterprets the *reason* that the Jerusalem Council instructed Gentile believers to abstain: "For Moses of old time hath in every city them that preach him, being read in the synagogues every sabbath day" (Acts 15:21, KJV). In other words, it was to avoid offending those in nearby Jewish communities who might see Christians eating meat sacrificed to pagan idols and use that as an excuse to reject the Gospel. It was not, as Gothard says, "because of the damaging effect that the whole matter had on weaker Christians." It was to minimize the possibility of offense in situations where Jews were present.

The Jerusalem Council did not issue a universal prohibition against Christians eating pagan sacrificial meat. If they had, it would have directly contradicted Paul's instructions in 1 Corinthians, and he would have hardly gone along with it. Instead, both they and Paul granted all believers the very thing Gothard withholds from his followers: freedom governed by love.

What We Have Seen and Heard

Where does all of this lead? What kind of results can we expect from the kind of teaching that robs Christians of their spiritual freedom?

Most of us know that Jesus was comparing false teachers to trees that produce bad fruit when He said, "Ye shall know them by their fruits" (Matthew 7:16). Well, we've been hanging around Gothard's tree for several years now, and the fruit we've seen is not the kind you want to write the folks at home about — except maybe to warn them.

We at Midwest Christian Outreach have received numerous phone calls, letters, and emails from families broken upon the hard rocks of Gothardite legalism. We have seen the members of churches that have been rent asunder by the divisiveness of ATI families. We have met with people who have been excommunicated from their churches for expressing even moderate disagreement with IBLP literature. We know of elderly parents whose children have turned against them in the name of Gothard's "principles" and have alienated their grandchildren from them. We know of many who shun anyone who does not follow Gothard's dress code, medical manuals, or one of dozens of other things.

A man contacted us because the pastor and congregation of his church helped his wife and children move to another state while he was gone. Why did they do that? Because he resisted being indoctrinated into Gothardism.

Someone from a close-knit rural community with a majority population of evangelical Christians emailed us. Because of their remote location, most of the families there had been home-schooling for years, and until recently it was the kind of town where everyone looked out for each other. But when one of the local pastors started pushing the ATI homeschooling curriculum, trouble started. Those who switched to it tried to pressure all the other families into using it, too. Eventually the ATI home-schoolers refused to allow their children to play with non-ATI homeschooled children, and the community was torn in half — by Gothardism.

The Pharisees had many traditions that were structured in such a way that they could turn a cold heart to others and feel quite spiritual about doing it. For example, they had a "principle" called "Corban," which means "given to God" (Mark 7:10-11). The idea was that one could dedicate his money, property, and other possessions to the temple. He had free use of the possessions for himself, but under the Corban principle he could not use them to help family or friends who might be in need. It sounded extremely spiritual. What could be more righteous than giving one's possessions to God? And so the Pharisees' version of "biblical principles" allowed them to say, "Mom, Dad, I would really like to help by paying your rent but I am committed to following God's principles." The result was harming those in need and disobedience to God. If your "non-optional principles of life" are making you less loving than you used to be, they're not truly biblical principles.

We have heard too many accounts of spiritual devastation from victims of Gothardism for us to conclude that these are somehow deviations from the norm. They are the norm. They're the direct result of a legalistic system. But if we take away all the principles, rules, steps and what-not, what will Gothard's followers do?

"They Will Kno-o-w We Are Christians by Our ..."?

Jesus said, "By this shall all men know that ye are my disciples, if ye have love one to another" (John 13:35). The Apostle Paul wrote, "he that loveth another hath fulfilled the law ... love is the fulfilling of the law" (Romans 13:8, 10).

How will your pagan neighbors know that you're a Christian? By your "biblical principles?" By your collection of seminar textbooks, "Wisdom Booklets," "Men's Manuals," "Character Sketches," "Medical Training Institute of America" booklets, videos, and cassettes? By the fact that you homeschool your kids and don't let them watch regular television or listen to contemporary Christian Music?

When someone asked the question, "If you were accused of being a Christian, would there be enough evidence to convict you?" they weren't asking whether you had more scruples than a televangelist or were more judgmental than Church Lady.

Go back and read Christ's story about the Pharisee and the tax collector in the temple (Luke 18:10-14) and ask yourself, "Which one of these two people am I more like and in what way?"

When you think about your Christian friends who aren't followers of Bill Gothard, do you find even a small part of yourself, somewhere deep inside, subtly looking down your nose at them? How about when you think of your non-Christian neighbors and co-workers?

On the other hand, when you mingle with other followers of Gothard, do you find yourself feeling like you'll never "measure up?" Do you leave their presence berating yourself for not being as "spiritual" as they are?

Living the kind of legalistic lifestyle that Bill Gothard prescribes will keep you on a never-ending spiritual treadmill. Sometimes you'll feel as though you're doing pretty well on that treadmill. Other times you'll feel that you're not doing such a good job of keeping up. Either way, your focus will be on the treadmill and your performance rather than on sharing the love of Jesus with those who need it.

When you think you're doing well, you'll become smug and self-righteous. When you think you're falling behind, you'll get frustrated and depressed, and you'll either lash out or withdraw in anger from those you should love. When you tell other Christians that they should get on the treadmill too, and they refuse, you'll imagine that you're being "persecuted" and try to find comfort in that thought. When you notice that your treadmill never takes you close enough to the lost for you to share the Gospel with them or have any impact on their lives, you'll reason that God will bring them to you in His own good time.

None of this sounds very spiritual, does it? Maybe it's time to get off the treadmill. But how?

Some Things Are Easier Caught Than Taught

Legalism is like a paralysis. It deadens spiritual nerve endings. It atrophies spiritual muscles. After you've been a legalist for a while, the needs of others no longer move your heart like they used to. That space inside of you where the love of God was shed abroad seems to have dried up, and you find yourself doing less and less for others and requiring more and more from them.

In the case of physical paralysis, you don't need a clinical description to recognize it. You can usually spot a paralyzed person fairly quickly. But the spiritual paralysis caused by legalism is a bit trickier to identify. A big reason for that is that there are so many legalists among us, and legalists are well practiced at appearing spiritual while not exercising any spiritual muscles.

But there are certain situations that separate the legalists from the non-legalists. In these moments the truly spiritual are easy to distinguish from those suffering legal paralysis, because their actions give them away. You may not be able to give a theological definition of a spiritual Christian, but you know one when you see one. Rebecca Manley Pippert relates the following story about a young college student:

> His name is Bill. He has wild hair, wears a T-shirt with holes in it, jeans and no shoes. This was literally his wardrobe for his entire four years of college. He is brilliant. Kinda esoteric and very, very bright. He became a Christian while attending college.
>
> Across the street from the campus is a well-dressed, very conservative church. They want to develop a ministry to the students, but are not sure how to go about it. One day Bill decides to go there. He walks in with no shoes, jeans, his T-shirt, and wild hair. The service has already started and so Bill starts down the aisle looking for a seat.
>
> The church is completely packed and he can't find a seat. By now people are looking a bit uncomfortable, but no one says anything. Bill gets closer and closer and closer to the pulpit and when he realizes there are no seats, he just squats down right on the carpet. (Although perfectly acceptable behavior at a college fellowship, trust me, this had never happened in this church before!) By now the people are really uptight, and the tension in the air is thick.
>
> About this time, the minister realizes that from way at the back of the church, a deacon is slowly making his way toward Bill. Now the deacon is in his eighties, has silver-gray hair, a three-piece suit, and a pocket watch. A godly man, very elegant, very dignified, very courtly. He

walks with a cane and as he starts walking toward this boy, everyone is saying to themselves, You can't blame him for what he's going to do. How can you expect a man of his age and of his background to understand some college kid on the floor?

It takes a long time for the man to reach the boy. The church is utterly silent except for the clicking of the man's cane. All eyes are focused on him. You can't even hear anyone breathing. The people are thinking, *The minister can't even preach the sermon until the deacon does what he has to do.* And now they see this elderly man drops his cane on the floor.

With great difficulty he lowers himself and sits down next to Bill and worships alongside him so he won't be alone. Everyone chokes up with emotion. There seems to not be a dry eye in the entire congregation.

When the minister finally gains control he says, "What I'm about to preach, you will never remember. What you have just seen, you will never forget."[37]

Chapter 7

The Orwellian World of Bill Gothard

Squealer consoles the animals, saying, "Do not imagine comrades, that leadership is a pleasure. On the contrary, it is a deep and heavy responsibility. No one believes more firmly than Comrade Napoleon that all animals are equal. He would be only too happy to let you make your own decisions for yourselves. But sometimes you might make the wrong decisions, comrades, and then where should we be?" (*Animal Farm*, by George Orwell)

While doing a radio interview on Chicago's WYLL in the early 1990s, the program's host, Sandy Rios, asked during the commercial break if we had any information about Bill Gothard and IBLP. I explained that we had just started looking into the group due to requests for information we had received. We then asked her about her interest. She relayed that at one time she had lived overseas and one of her friends there was very involved with IBLP. When they would discuss various issues of the faith, her friend would run to the "red book" from IBLP for the answer. Sandy was quite concerned that the Institute's teachings seemed to supersede the Bible and that her friend's every decision was made with reference to Bill Gothard's material rather than from the Word of God.

From the former Gothardites we have talked to, this excessive reliance upon IBLP material for decision making seems to be more the rule than the exception. If we were to distill all of IBLP's precepts down to one concept, it would be *obedience to authority*. Leaders must be followed unquestioningly. Individuality and independent thinking are discouraged. People are expected to conform in dress, hairstyle, music, and other aspects of life to prove their spirituality in IBLP's world.

Totalistic, authoritarian groups mistake uniformity for unity. Uniformity, however, is external and overtly apparent, whereas true Christian unity is an internal bond, powerful but invisible. In Jesus' prayer for believers in John 17:21 He asks that "they may all be one," just as He and the Father are one. How *are* we one? Is it just in the sense of unity of purpose, appearance, and allegiance, or are we in some sense truly *one*? First Corinthians 12:13 teaches us that by the indwelling Holy Spirit we, as believers, are actually one entity. Legalism substitutes the invisible spiritual unity of believers with the visible physical appearance of uniformity and conformity to rules and regulations.

In IBLP, the "God approved" fashion is short hair and clean-shaven faces for men and long hair and dresses at all times for women. Those who do not externally conform are classified as "in rebellion." If they should question they are labeled "bitter." There really is no acknowledgement of Christian liberty in these areas.

Former Gothardite Jenice Miller writes:

> Mr. Gothard does not teach these wonderful truths which will set us free from the power of sin (the law) and to allow the Holy Spirit to empower us to be everything we were meant to be. No! He teaches how to be enslaved to the power and the penalty of sin. There is no freedom of the Spirit to lead in one's life. Gothard must think he has the blueprint for one's life. By the time you have "progressed" to the elite "home education" seminar, he will

dictate when to get up in the morning, how to dress, what to eat (dietary law), what music to listen to, how to use the TV (never) and the newspaper (let others screen it for you), not to use contraceptives, when to have sex with your mate (based on Levitical law), what colors and styles to use in your dress, how to clean your house, how to check your mail, choice of toys, whether a man should wear a beard or not, how to use your money, how you should worship, how to be cleansed from sin, how to be right with your brothers, friendships, dating, and the list goes on. Gothard's blueprint is indeed a "how to" religion which gives people no room for a personal Christianity. It is a way of controlling and cloning people. What area of life would the Holy Spirit be able to interact with a person under this system? Does Gothard know the mind of God so well that he can dictate so many details in the lives and hearts of God's people? Wouldn't this also isolate these people from any truth or added information from sources outside of the Gothard camp? Would it enhance an arrogance of superiority in the body of Christ because no one but Gothard knows God's way?[1]

It might be that Bill Gothard, like Comrade Napoleon book *Animal Farm*, would be only too happy to let you make your own decisions for yourselves. But sometimes you might make the wrong decisions, and then where should we be?

Resistance Is Futile — You Will Be Assimilated!

Those of you who are Star Trek fans remember the Borg — it was a civilization made up of conquered peoples who, upon capture, are altered in such a way that they could no longer think or act independently of the collective consciousness. All struggles of an individual to remain free are met with the same chilling admonition Resistance is futile; you *will* be assimilated. And sure enough, they were. And then, as soon as they were assimilated, they dutifully did their part to enslave and assimilate others. So successfully assimilated were they, that individuality became anathema to them.

People who get caught up in extreme authoritarian/high-control groups are not weak-willed individuals who are just begging to be dominated. Many are highly intelligent thinking people. So how are they transformed into people who are convinced that they have no right to decide for themselves how to dress, who to associate with, etc.? How do they end up in the Borg? It's really quite simple to explain, and we see it repeated over and over as we examine such groups. The leader, whether Bill Gothard or Marshall Applewhite, has essentially one task: To convince their followers that they represent God, that whatever they say is tantamount to God speaking. Who wants to fight against God? If God wants you to shave your beard, you are going to do it! If God says Cabbage Patch dolls are evil, let's get them out of the house!

The second issue is peer pressure. You may initially laugh at the idea that a Cabbage Patch doll might prevent delivery of a baby (see chapter ten), but if you see that your "godly" friends are not laughing, you begin to think the "problem" lies in you. Can ten thousand "straight faces" be wrong? Added to this, the leader constantly reinforces this idea — saying right out that if you don't see things their way, the problem lies with you — you're rebellious, worldly — perhaps you are not really a Christian at all! The result of this conditioning is that the next time you hear something that in former days would have struck you as unusual or even silly, you won't laugh or raise any objection. Even asking questions could be dangerous to your spiritual standing. You are now part of the Borg — part of the problem: you have been assimilated.

Many "alumni" who were part of the IBLP system and left refer to IBLP women as "Stepford Women."[2] Melody Pake confesses that she was caught up in this phenomenon but is not quite sure just how it happened to her.[3] She first became involved in ATI (Advanced Training Institute) for the home-schooling aspect, and before she realized it she had become a model IBLP woman. She is still unsure how she, a thinking woman, had succumbed to the peer pressure and lost her personal identity.

As with other totalitarian systems, the punishment for non-conformists and those who "break away" from IBLP and ATI can be very harsh indeed. A woman we met at a counter-cult conference who had been part of ATI for years was fearful of identifying herself because of the shunning she knew would occur if her family and friends discovered that she had spoken out against the system. She shared with us her reason for leaving — as she had studied the *Communist Manifesto* in her home schooling preparation, it became apparent to her that IBLP matched it in all points except one (she didn't specify which one). We find the same type of oppressive uniformity practiced in other totalistic[4] groups such as the Jehovah's Witnesses. But at least the Jehovah's Witnesses operate outside of Christian churches, not within them. IBLP does not stand outside and pick off the unwary; it comes right into the sanctuary to create divisions where there should be unity in the Spirit.

Churches in Turmoil

We are aware of a growing number of churches in grievous turmoil which is directly attributable to IBLP influence. Churches whose leadership is involved with IBLP use the "submission to authority" card to eliminate any questioning by non-IBLP families or individuals. The leadership under IBLP control generally sees itself as above correction, certainly not accountable to the little people who are beneath their "umbrella of protection" (or under their thumb, as it were). Such leaders often charge those who disagree with Gothard's teachings with being divisive and rebellious and demand that they meekly submit to their "God-given" authority.

Churches whose leadership is not supportive of IBLP are finding that Sunday School attendance and youth groups shrink as Gothard adherents get involved and recruit within the church. Of course, they do not "submit" to the authority of these churches, since Bill Gothard has become their authority. They view non-IBLP pastors and elders with suspicion and create factions in their attempt to replace the church's teaching with Bill Gothard's standards. As Pastor Keith Gibson points out:

> Gothard is very dogmatic regarding all of his positions. To disagree with him is, in effect, to disagree with God. For instance, it is his view that Christians who listen to contemporary Christian Music are not exercising personal freedom and conviction... they are carnal. Many of his followers develop a similar level of dogmatism. This can create division in the body. Several times I have had a family come to me with an ultimatum declaring that if our church was not going to follow "God's way" (i.e., IBLP teaching), they would have to leave the church. I have had this same testimony repeated to me from other pastors as well. In Gothardom, every issue is a test of fellowship.[5]

Totalistic Groups and Authoritarian Rule

A belief common to totalistic groups is that God has given to a particular man or group of men the right to rule — and rule they do! This man may be the founder of the particular cult or authoritarian group and upon his death rulership passes to another man or group of men.

The Children of God followed David "Mo" Berg until his death. Until their fiery end at Waco, the Branch Davidians were following the dictates of the self-appointed prophet David Koresh. Members of the Solar Temple burned to death under mysterious circumstances while following cult masterminds Luc Jouret and Joseph di Mambro. Many of us can still remember what happened to those who followed Jim Jones to Guyana. Not all authoritarian groups lead their followers to physical death in such dramatic ways, but they do bring their followers into bondage and dependence on them.

Authoritarian leaders demand uncritical allegiance and unquestioning obedience from their followers. For example, the *Watchtower*[6] tells its readers to "avoid independent thinking,"[7] likening independent thought to Eve's sin in the garden. To question the dictates of "God's organization" is to follow Satan's invitation to "decide for yourself what is good or bad." "To this day," the article warns, "it has been Satan's subtle design to infect God's people with this type of thinking. How is such independent thinking manifested? A common way is by questioning the counsel that is provided by God's visible organization." What a powerful tool for dictatorial rule! To question "the organization" is to follow Satan and sin against God. We looked at this with regard to IBLP in chapter two.

Are we as true Christians to blindly follow our leaders? Ephesians 4:11-16 makes it abundantly clear that we are to test what we are being told, not to be children tossed about by crafty teachers, but mature in Christ and being led by the Holy Spirit. We are to check out what a teacher communicates, and independent thought is essential to this evaluation process. Our devotion is never to be to our church or our leaders, but to God alone, and the Bible must be our standard. Thus, all Christians with all of our differences, various gifts, callings, personalities, and temperaments complete the Body of Christ.

Sally's Solitary Confinement

After an interview about cults on *Cross Talk* on radio station VCY America, Ingrid Schlueter, the host, asked about Bill Gothard and IBLP and then related the story of a family she was trying to help. The parents of a young teenage girl (we'll call her Sally) had come to Ingrid's father, Vic Eliason, looking for information on Bill and IBLP. This was a home-schooling family that had come into contact with Gothard and IBLP through his ATI program. They had sent their daughter to a seminar for young women at IBLP's Indianapolis facility. Sally was a fairly typical and very pretty 13-year-old girl. During that seminar a personal counseling session was scheduled between Sally and Bill. After the session Bill Gothard called the parents and explained that he "sensed" her heart wasn't right with God, that she would be pushing all boundaries and was potentially very rebellious. He recommended that she be left there (the Indianapolis facility) "for a few more weeks."

Anyone who has reared children knows that the teen years can present varying degrees of difficulties, depending on the temperament of the child. Some kids are by nature compliant and are not "risk takers." Others are strong willed and more difficult to handle. In the Gothard system, a truly godly family, properly submitted to authority, will have perfectly behaved children. If a youngster exhibits independent thinking or questioning of authority, that is a sure sign of rebellion and a spiritual problem. As Sally's parents thought about it they agreed that she was sometimes late for her curfew and was beginning to have an interest in boys. (This is considered spiritually unhealthy — interest in the opposite sex is discouraged until the father chooses a potential spouse. More will be said about this later.) The parents believed Bill was the spiritual leader and an expert in these matters; they trusted his wisdom and agreed to leave her. After several weeks Bill again called and said that Sally still wasn't ready to go home. In fact, he suggested that they give Sally to the Institute as Hannah had given Samuel to God. They reluctantly agreed.

Meanwhile, young Sally was in misery. She called regularly, usually in desperation, begging to come home. A staff member monitored every phone call.[8] As if being held against her will were not bad enough, Sally was regularly put into solitary confinement. Solitary confinement is something generally associated with prisons, where it is used to deal with those who have actually broken the law, either for the protection of other inmates (due to violent behavior) or for their own protection from other inmates. Yet solitary confinement, often used as punishment for hardened criminals, is being used by IBLP to "assimilate" powerless children who exercise independent thought. Sally's parents became concerned about their daughter's welfare and went to the Indianapolis facility to meet with their daughter and the director. After a brief meeting the director handed Sally's father a belt and demanded that he give her a good, hard spanking in front of him. The father could not bring himself to do it, and the parents were berated for not loving their daughter.

Sally's parents finally took her back from the Institute after a year and a half. Naturally enough, the experience alienated Sally from her family and the Christian faith. She eventually ran away from home and moved in with her boyfriend. The family is trying to rebuild a relationship with her and is praying regularly for her to come back to God. However, the parents still believe in Gothard — they hold no ill will towards him and think he is a good and humble man. They believe that the problem lies with the employees, who they see as irresponsible and unqualified. When I spoke with them they were confident that "If Bill knew, he would do something about it." This die-hard loyalty is very common among Gothardites and is very hard to shake: no matter what he does, he can do no wrong. Pastor Keith Gibson calls this the "power of persona."[9]

> Hands down, this is the most common defense to which those involved in IBLP appeal. Bill Gothard presents himself extremely well. His followers are convinced he is one of the most godly, sincere, humble, gracious, you-name-it, men who has ever lived. One young lady expressed it this way, "Here is a man who loves people and families so much that he spends every waking moment seeking God's direction about how to help them."[10]

We have no doubt that Mr. Gothard sincerely wants to help people and families live godly lives, as he defines that. But, like the Pharisees of Jesus' day, Gothard has gone way beyond biblical standards and has piled heavy burdens upon his followers' shoulders.

> For they bind heavy burdens and grievous to be borne, and lay *them* on men's shoulders; but they *themselves* will not move them with one of their fingers (Matthew 23:4).

There is no grace in Gothardom and no acknowledgment of the damage he inflicts upon the very families and churches he claims he desires to help. He uses anecdotal cases in an attempt to prove how successful his ministry is but dismisses those stories that powerfully demonstrate the destructive nature of his teachings. Sally and her family are but one case among many examples that have been brought to our attention.

Rachel's Story

In addition to the numerous phone calls, e-mails and letters we receive on this issue we find similar stories on the worldwide web, such as the web site by Rachel Stevens attempting to expose the authoritarian abuses associated with IBLP:

> My story begins in fall of 1979 when my parents attended their first Basic Seminar. They were both new Christians, and immediately soaked up the overwhelming surge of information that was provided at this seminar. Mr. Gothard, who claims to have rediscovered long forgotten and overlooked spiritual truths, seemed to be a fast-ride provider to spiritual maturity. Claiming to have enlightenment from the Lord, which provides him with a much keener insight than your local minister, to some, Gothard becomes very alluring.
>
> My parents attended an Advanced Seminar in the summer of '86, and that fall they joined the IBLP, which is one of the major branches of Gothard's original seminar ministry. At this point, my parents began to seriously concentrate on living a life of complete separation from society. This was a direction that they began in 1979, a direction in which they are still going. This has resulted in the unfortunate story that I am about to relate to you.
>
> I am the oldest of 6 children, and my parents homeschooled all of us, with the intention of doing so through college-level. Our one social contact was our local church. All of my mother's family, including her mother, are still in shock over the negative and drastic change that my mother underwent when she married, and became involved with Bill Gothard.

I grew up with no friends my own age, very limited contacts with older adults, and a handful of pen pals. My parents were very physically abusive with all of us,[11] also, and even looking down at the wrong time became grounds for a severe beating. Naturally, I was almost always in fear, and constantly trying to avoid being beaten, or reprimanded. All of these ideas on handling children were directly taught by, or derived from Bill Gothard's teachings.

As I grew older, I committed my life to Christ, and began to study the Bible in depth whenever I could. The Holy Spirit began to open my eyes, and show me how some things that I had learned from Bill Gothard and from my parents were wrong. Much of this search for truth was spurred on as a result of statements that our pastor made to my father. Statements such as, "I really have cautions about your curriculum," or, "why don't I see any display of God's grace through this teaching," were quite common.

Now for a brief explanation of Gothard's key teachings! Gothard teaches that the Christian life is built on a series of seven principles that, if we attain, will bring us ultimate success.

1. We must accept the way that God has designed us, and make no changes to it, except changes that will attract attention to God. Out of this principle stem two other key teachings (a) we must have bright eyes. This is based on Isaiah 60:1, which is a clear misuse of Scripture. (b) No forms of birth control are acceptable even for use within marriage. God has designed us to reproduce!

2. We have a responsibility to God to be perfect in every action, word, deed, and thought. This puts followers into a continual confessing process where they are scared they have forgotten to confess

some misstep. This step is really tied into the third principle.

3. We must be under authority. This is Gothard's favorite principle, and the one he spends the most time on. When you join Gothard's group, you become part of a "chain of authority," originating directly with God. The "chain of authority" diagrammed as a pyramid, places God at the top, Mr. Gothard directly underneath, then his aides, then the fathers of every family in his program. Of course, the mother and children are placed under the father. Mr. Gothard also has a very comical diagram of the chain of authority: within a family, and connected teachings to this principle which promote the practice of exorcisms, all with twisted Scripture interpretations to back it up.... This principle is tied to the second one in that children and wives are to confess all improper words, actions, thoughts, and deeds to the father, as they would to God.

4. We will suffer for committing to such a high standard of living. The endless lists of rules and regulations which are imposed on all members of this cult by the religious hierarchy are explained away as a special standard of living which God expects of those who are so much closer to the truth and to him than the rest of the world.

5. We are owned by God, and by our fathers. This is how Mr. Gothard promotes his teaching of arranged marriages, and a ritual that engages a daughter to her father until her time of marriage. I admit, it's bizarre!

6. The more that we submit to authority, and continually examine our minds for where Satan might

be inhabiting us, we will find true freedom.

7. All of this brings true success, and success will
    continue as long as we continue studying Bill
    Gothard's teachings. Well, if you aren't complete-
    ly baffled yet, the best is yet to come.

At the age of 15, as I continued to move in the opposite
direction of my parents, they put even more restrictions
on me. We left the church we had attended, and my parents began inflicting even more physical abuse. They also
began asking constantly what I was thinking. I was able
to get help from a family at church, and I ran away from
home. I was placed in a foster home, then my parents satisfied state regulations, and I was going to be forced to
return home. So, at age 16, I ran away again. My simple
motivation was to escape the abuse and false teachings of
my family. After almost 5 months on the run, I was
found, and taken by my parents to Indianapolis, IN,
where Mr. Gothard runs a detention center for juvenile
youth, among other things. For almost 6 months, the
Gothardites held me here as a prisoner, treated me worse
than a criminal, and kept me indoors with never a step
outside for two months. Then one day in mid October of
'98, the Lord miraculously answered my prayers and
opened a way for me to escape Indianapolis. For safety
reasons, I will not state the circumstances of my escape.
When I reached my home state again, one of my uncles
who is a lawyer gave me a place to stay with him and my
aunt. We are now in the process of going through a series
of hearings so that I will have protection from my parents
and the Bill Gothard cult.[12]

Don Veinot spoke at length with Rachel and she is recovering
from this experience. She is a dedicated believer, actively involved
with her church and growing in the grace and knowledge of Jesus
Christ. She is attempting to establish a healthy relationship with

her parents but is being shunned due to her rejection of Bill Gothard and IBLP.

Gaining Christ

Carmen was a healthy 18-year-old high-school graduate who had enrolled in college. Her parents had begun using the ATI materials to home school her two younger brothers. Her parents became persuaded through the ATI seminar that college is a dangerous place. We would agree that for those who are not grounded in the faith and taught how to think, college could be a dangerous place. This is why is it so important for parents and churches to teach their young how to think and give them solid reasons for believing in Christ, rather than just force-feed them with *what* to think and demand they believe it, as IBLP does.

Carmen dropped out of college at her parents' request and, in hopes of joining one of Gothard's apprenticeship programs, began going through the ATI curriculum. While in Indianapolis attending a Girl's Counseling Seminar, she met Bill, who almost immediately (within a week) invited her to move from her home (and from the umbrella of her parent's protection, by the way) to the Institute headquarters in Oak Brook, Illinois, which she did. For the next 10 months she was Bill's personal assistant, attempting to live by what she calls the countless "godly and orderly rules."

Conflict arose between her and her parents over her independent thinking and questioning of her family's church traditions. This independent thinking resulted in her being dubbed a deceiver with a rebellious spirit and ostracized at the Institute and removed against her will. It is difficult indeed to fulfill the "countless godly and orderly rules" (which Gothard imposes on all but himself), but to fall short is dealt with quite harshly, as we have seen. Carmen has had time to recover from this part of her life and writes:

> During the time that has elapsed since then I have gone from emotional and psychological hell through a period

of healing, to forgetting and ignoring that part of my life. However, that 10 month (and then 2 year) experience has affected my life in a way that I know nothing else ever will. I am a changed person, changed for the better thanks to the love and grace of my Lord Jesus Christ. He makes everything work together for his good purpose, and I praise him for what he has done to bring me around after what could have been irrecoverable devastation. I also praise him for removing me from the situation when he did in order to save me from further harm. I jokingly say, "I got out while the getting was good."[13]

Carmen is a lively and vibrant Christian who praises God for growing her in the grace and knowledge of Him in spite of Bill Gothard and IBLP. She is thankful that she has learned that her acceptance by God is based on her relationship with Christ and not on blind obedience to a set of principles.

Prophet Bill Speaks

Pastor Johnny Jones had been part of a prison ministry, and through that organization had attended IBLP's pastors' conferences since 1983. He had been able to watch Bill Gothard, as he says, "from a distance," and was impressed with his teaching and seeming humility. He was introduced to Bill at one of those conferences, and the two men had conversed from time to time when Bill was in California, where Jones lived. Pastor Jones met and married his wife, Shantelle, who had been an IBLP "alumna" since 1982. Pastor Jones attended his first *Basic Seminar* in 1989. In retrospect, Pastor Jones concedes that there were a few red flags raised by a friend who pointed out to him verses that Bill was misusing by ripping them out of their contexts. Nevertheless, Pastor Jones dismissed these cautionary signals because Bill and the Institute looked so good from the outside. Jones regularly attended the ATI Advanced Seminars as well as the Pastors' Seminars. In fact, since approximately 1995, Pastor Jones and his wife have participated in any and all IBLP meetings in their area. They really believed in Bill Gothard's teachings and invited a number of their friends and other pastors to get involved.

Pastor Jones and Shantelle homeschooled their five children,using ATI resources. They are African Americans with a real heart for the Lord and a desire to break through the racial divide. They had some concerns about the fact that "African-American people were not visible in the material." Pastor Jones discussed this with a chaplain friend of his who was participating in the homeschooling program as well. The chaplain called Bill to discuss the issue but, in his opinion, the conversation didn't go well. As a result, the chaplain and the Joneses decided to stop using this material. There was another area of IBLP teaching that troubled them somewhat. It was Bill's stand on music. It appeared to them that the only "Godly" music, in Gothard's view, was of white European origin; any other music was deemed of the devil. Still, they were willing to overlook what seemed to them to be evidence of latent bigotry, because they believed Bill to be an extremely godly and humble man. They remained very active in IBLP and ATI because they didn't want to "throw the baby out with the bath-water."

In 2000 Pastor Jones had just finished a three-year pastorate in an Asian church and was seeking God's direction for the future. He was assisting two other churches on a part-time basis and doing some consulting work while he was waiting upon the Lord. In June of 2000 Pastor Jones and Shantelle began fasting and praying in the mornings, which they continued for six weeks. They came to believe that God was leading them to create a retreat center for pastors and church leaders to get away and be refreshed for the ministry. They found a ten-acre piece of property in the hills of California which they believed would be perfect for this ministry endeavor and began the process of purchasing it.

On the Fourth of July weekend in 2000 Johnny and Shantelle attended the ATI conference in Sacramento, CA. In addition to the general sessions, the conference had breakout sessions for the ATI fathers and another one, at the same time, for mothers. As

Pastor Jones sat in the fathers' meeting he became very concerned about the things he heard during the question-and-answer time. There was a great deal of talk about the rejection by the local churches of the "Godly standards" as taught by Bill Gothard, which the fathers believed the churches should be upholding.

Some of the fathers suggested that they start their own churches. Johnny's pastoral heart was pierced by what he was hearing. He kept asking himself the question, "What's up with this? The local church isn't good enough for us anymore?" The last question put to Bill in that session came from Pastor Johnny Jones. He asked Bill what the ministry was doing to help strengthen the pastors and help the local church. This question was never answered. Instead, Bill looked at him and said, "What are you doing right now?" Pastor Jones told Bill and the audience of about 700 fathers that he was seeking God's will for his next ministry assignment. Bill's response caught him completely off guard — he said that he had been praying for a man for six years and that the Lord just showed him that Johnny was that man. Bill asked Pastor Jones on the spot if he would go to Flint, Michigan to head up a ministry there — IBLP had acquired a hotel in Flint, which they were going to reopen as The Character Inn. Pastor Jones regained his composure and answered that he would certainly pray about it. The room erupted — so thrilled were some of the men that God had chosen Johnny through Bill for this assignment that they ran up to Pastor Jones to give him money and congratulate him. There was a great deal of hand-shaking, hugs, and excitement. The men raised $3,700 that afternoon to pay Johnny's expenses for the trip to Michigan. When Pastor Jones reminded them that he had yet to seek the Lord's will in the matter, they told him that if it turned out that God hadn't called him to Flint after all, he was to keep the money for whatever ministry God gave him. Bill asked Johnny to join him backstage for the general meeting.

Have You Heard?

As the meeting broke up, several of the fathers who were present asked Shantelle if she had spoken to Johnny yet. She responded that she hadn't seen him yet and asked why. She was told, "Just pray before you see him." When she and Johnny caught up with each other, she was surprised to learn of the proposed assign-ment. They agreed to pray more before making a decision, but it seemed to them that this was God's leading. After all, they had just spent the previous six weeks fasting and praying, and in the past God had answered their prayers in miraculous ways.

Pastor Jones met with Bill backstage and was introduced to a Dr. McDonald. As they talked, Dr. McDonald expressed that he had been praying for some time that God would raise up an African-American presence in IBLP. Bill reiterated that God had revealed to him that Pastor Johnny Jones was that person, and that God had called him to be the director of the Character Inn. Dr. McDonald was greatly encouraged. Bill then asked Pastor Jones how soon he could fly to Flint. Pastor Jones cautioned Bill that he and his wife would need to pray about this decision before giving him a final answer.

In the evening meeting, Bill Gothard stood before the group of approximately 3,000 ATI parents and relayed the story of the acquisition of the hotel in Flint which the Lord had allegedly led him to open as the Character Inn. Bill Gothard said he had met with the mayor of Flint, an African American who didn't like white people very much, and claimed that he had asked the mayor's forgiveness for what whites had done to his people. He said that the mayor was touched and responded that no one had ever said that to him before. Bill allegedly promised to have African-American leadership at the Character Inn and asserted that he and the mayor were now very good friends. Bill then called Pastor Jones up on stage and introduced him to the 3,000 ATI parents as the new director for this work, which he again stated that God had revealed to him. He then gave Pastor Jones $500 cash with the promise to send him the rest as soon as it was properly receipted and the checks deposited. It truly seemed to the Joneses that God was behind all of this.

Pastor Jones spoke with Bill Gothard and Jim Voellar by

phone two days later to work out the details. They agreed that God was indeed directing this plan. Pastor Jones wanted to know how soon he needed to arrive in Flint and Bill suggested that yesterday would be perfect. Pastor Jones indicated that he would begin making arrangements right away but voiced his concerns about housing his family in Flint, moving expenses, financial remuneration, etc. Bill responded by telling him that IBLP was purchasing houses for the staff and that furnishings would also be provided by IBLP. He was assured that he didn't need to bring anything with him but himself, his family, and their personal possessions. They also agreed on a stipend.

Pastor Jones and his wife had long had a vision of ministering to pastors, strengthening the local church, and cross-cultural ministry that appeared to line up perfectly with the goals that Bill laid out for their involvement with the Character Inn. Bill had explained to them that they would be working with the mayor of Flint and the city officials to rebuild Flint as a city of character. This was to be a whole new type of ministry for IBLP — a convention center that would be a national and international training center for leaders. Johnny and Shantelle were very excited about this opportunity. They went home and set about packing their personal possessions and giving away their furnishings, two cars, a piano, and a year-old Dachshund. After all, Bill had told them that they wouldn't need any of that stuff and that everything would be replaced when they got to Flint. So convinced were the Joneses that this move was God's will for their lives and that Bill Gothard was a man of his word, that Johnny opted not to travel to Flint in advance of the move to check things out. Their trust in Bill Gothard's integrity turned out to be a major mistake.

The First Woe

After a short period of time when they still hadn't received the remaining $3,200, Pastor Jones called Pastor Glen DeSoto who pastors the IBLP church at the Character Inn. Pastor Jones explained that he hadn't yet received the balance of the money that had been raised for his relocation. Glen called IBLP's head-quarters and was told (and relayed to Jones) that a check would be sent out right away. When, the Joneses received the check, however, it was only for $1,000 – $2,200 short. Pastor Jones and his wife did not understand this discrepancy but did not let this possible oversight cool their ardor for the mission, though they did agree that they would wait on the Lord's provision before beginning the trip. In a short while the Lord provided some additional funds through friends, and they embarked on their journey to Flint and a whole new life. They took only what they could fit in their mini-van along with their five children. The bal-ance of their personal belongings they left in a warehouse owned by some friends of theirs. The cost of moving these possessions to Flint would be approximately $5,000. Pastor Jones talked with peo-ple at IBLP headquarters about having some IBLP trucks, which were still in California, bring their remaining belongings with them to Flint. They were told that the trucks would be returning empty and that they would be glad to make the pickup.

So the Joneses said their good-byes and headed for Flint, Michigan. They spent their first night in Nevada. On the road again the next morning, they were very surprised to receive a call on their cell phone from Bill Gothard. Bill asked them to make a stop in Oklahoma City. Now, Oklahoma City is decidedly not on the way to Flint, Michigan, but Bill was insistent that they go there to participate in a character-training seminar that was to begin two days later. Pastor Jones pointed out that he had already been through the character-training, but Bill explained that he would like him to go through a "refresher." Johnny agreed and headed for Oklahoma under the impression that he and his fam-ily would only be there for a week before going on to Flint. All they had with them was their traveling clothes (for seven people) that could fit in their van, but they didn't believe this to be a problem, since they expected their trucked possessions to be waiting for them in Flint when they arrived the following week.

The Jones family arrived in Oklahoma City and enjoyed the seminar and the fellowship. At the end of the week, as they were making preparations to leave for Michigan, they received another call from Bill. They were told to stay there for two more weeks and work with Oklahoma City director Dr. Tim Levendesky. Pastor Jones asked Bill why the holdup — were they not ready for them in Flint? He was beginning to get the feeling that something was very wrong. What was supposed to have been a one-week sidetrack for a "refresher course" had become a three-week hiatus. Pastor Jones asked Tim if this flip-flop scenario was normal procedure for Bill, and Tim replied that it was. Evidently a three-week delay was not bad, relatively speaking. According to Tim, it was not uncommon for someone to be sent somewhere for a week and end up there for *three months*. Johnny told Tim that he and his family were not prepared to stay long term since they had only their traveling clothes — everything else was en route to Flint. The reader should understand that IBLP has a strict dress code. In order to conform, Pastor Jones and his family went to a local second-hand store and used their little remaining funds to purchase suitable IBLP attire for what they had been told would be an additional two-week stay.

A Shocking Revelation

The two weeks came and went and they still had received no word as to when they would be leaving. Then they were hit by a thunderbolt from the blue. Pastor Jones picked up a copy of IBLP's newsletter from the front desk. To his shock and horror, there was a picture of another African-American, Emmett Mitchell, and his family with the announcement that *he* was the new general director of the Character First Inn in Flint, Michigan. The family was heartbroken and thrown into turmoil over this new turn of events. Pastor Jones called Bill to confront him with what now was obviously an undeniable betrayal of their trust. Bill had presented this opportunity to them as a prophetically ordained mission — had said that God Himself had told him that Johnny Jones was the man for the job. He had made promises to them concerning their housing and other needs in Flint, where he was in a great hurry to send them. He had not

sent them the money that had been raised and designated specifically for them. He had thoughtlessly sidetracked them to
Oklahoma City without their belongings and with very little
money. Now they learned that he had, without warning or discussion, appointed someone else to their promised and "God-
ordained" position. Incredibly, Bill casually responded that
Emmett believed that God had been preparing him for this work
and this position perfectly fulfills his vision. Pastor Jones then
asked, "Where does this leave me? What is my position now?"
Bill told him that he wanted Pastor Jones to go to Flint and work
with Emmett.

How is it possible for us to understand Pastor Jones's acqui-
escence to Bill's wishes at this point? He was understandably hurt
and felt sure that he had not been told everything. But, on the
other hand, he was sure that God had called him to this work in
Flint. As he wrestled with these conflicting feelings, Bill
informed him that the hotel was still under construction and
that he and his family should stay in Oklahoma City until Bill
called him to go to Flint.

While they were cooling their heels in Oklahoma, the
Joneses attempted to track down their personal possessions,
which the Institute staff had picked up in California. They
learned that although they had been told there would be no
problem in bringing their possessions back, it turned out that the
returning trucks were fully loaded — not empty as planned — and
so could only take about 80% of the Joneses boxes. To make matters worse, no one seemed to know where their boxes had been
taken.

Another problem arose over their personal mail. Their mail
was being forwarded to Flint, Michigan, since that is where they
had thought they would be. The staff in Flint crossed off their
name and wrote in Dr. Tim Levendesky's name, and sent it on
to him in Oklahoma City. The whole mess was about to head
from the incredible to the absurd. Tim Levendesky called Pastor
Jones and his wife into his office to talk with them about "objectionable" mail they were receiving. Pastor Jones first asked him,

appropriately, What was he doing with their mail? Dr. Levendesky informed Pastor Jones that Bill was concerned over some unapproved (by IBLP) magazine subscriptions the Joneses were receiving. The magazines were African-American publications: *Ebony*, *Jet*, and *Black Enterprise*. Dr. Levendesky pulled out these publications and pointed out the "worldly people" that graced their covers. He went on to say that the Institute didn't feel this was appropriate for the young people at the hotel and might cause them to stumble. Since there didn't seem to be a problem with *Life*, *People*, and other non-Christian publications Johnny and Shantelle wondered if the *color* of the "worldly people" on the covers was the real stumbling block. Johnny and Shantelle began to realize that they were being negatively singled out for some reason but they didn't know why. They had done nothing wrong – indeed, they had tried hard to make the best of a bad situation.

In order to fill his time and serve God while in Oklahoma, Pastor Jones began working in the kitchen. The food had been marginal, and while not claiming to be a chef, Jones knows his way around the kitchen. He and his family had been in Oklahoma City for six weeks when Bill Gothard the prophet finally called. He said he had received another rhema[14] – now God had revealed to him that Pastor Jones would have a three-fold ministry in Flint. He was to open the restaurants in the hotel, work with Emmett, and assist pastor DeSoto with the church that met there. In a short six weeks, Pastor Jones, receiving the "Word of the Lord" from prophet Bill, had essentially gone from general director to cook. Again, he was torn. On the one hand, he thought about returning home to California, but on the other, he believed without a doubt that God had called him to Flint. He was unsure at that point *why* God had called him there, but he packed up his family and headed for Michigan.

No Reception Party

Pastor Jones, with family in tow, finally arrived at the *Character Inn* in Flint, Michigan. The staff seemed less than happy to see them. There was no furnished house as promised. They were shuffled through several different room assignments, each one more run down than the previous one, and finally were settled into the old manager's apartment. When they asked why they had been placed in the most rundown unit instead of one of the newly remodeled units like other staff, they were simply told, "we can't do any more for you." This seemed to them strangely reminiscent of the days when African-Americans were consigned to the "back of the bus." The attitude that they felt directed towards them at that time was, as Johnny puts it, "Real cold. Disdained. Almost as if we were some kind of a disease."

One morning he came down to the front desk to pick up his mail and discovered that his bank statement, along with other items of his personal mail, had been opened[15]. As a matter of course, if mail is accidentally opened or damaged during delivery, the United States Postal Service marks it as such and seals it in plastic to protect it. This was not the case, which led him to believe that someone at the Character Inn had opened it after delivery. Pastor Jones went to see IBLP staff member Donnie Barr to express his concern over this matter. He pointed out that IBLP had tampered with his mail before and wanted to know why his bank statement had been opened. Donnie assured him that no one at the Character Inn would have opened his mail. Donnie then went to see another staff member, Pat LaMantia, who was in charge of the front desk office, and indicated wrongly that Pastor Jones had accused her of opening his mail. (Johnny had accused no one specifically — he had simply asked why it was opened.) When Pastor Jones and Pat LaMantia ran into each other in the office, Pastor Jones told her that he didn't like the fact that his mail had been opened. Pat denied being the culprit. Pastor Jones said that he did not accuse her of doing so, but pointed out that since she is in charge of this area and all mail comes through her, she should know who did open it. He then told her that if someone had accidentally opened it, it would have been appropriate to write a note to that effect. He reminded her that mail tampering is a federal offense and that she had previously tampered with his mail by addressing it to Dr. Levendesky in Oklahoma. Her response was, "I only did what my authorities instructed me to do." Pastor Jones advised her that her authorities had instructed her to break the law.

Is IBLP Racist?

The "racist" label is not one that should be casually affixed to a man or an organization. Racism has been endemic within our culture and is undeniably still a factor to be considered in matters of personal or organizational mistreatment when other explanations do not readily present themselves. On the other hand, racist motives can easily be falsely ascribed in our now race-obsessed society. Because this is so, it behooves Christians to be very careful in drawing such conclusions. Midwest Christian Outreach has volunteers, advisory board members, and supporters who are African-American. We discuss these issues amongst ourselves in an attempt to keep biblical balance in our views and attitudes. It is our conviction that Pastor Jones has this same heart and spirit in this area. He did not come to Flint with a "victim" chip on his shoulder, or sign on to IBLP to look for signs of covert bigotry. Indeed, he seems to have given Bill and IBLP every benefit of the doubt, refusing to take offense when offense was clearly given. He and Shantelle want to work with Christians of all races and ethnicities. But, once on the inside of IBLP, he could not help but note that there was virtually no African-American staff or leadership. Soon, other troubling race-related issues began to come to Johnny's attention.

Over the next several months it began to become a little clearer to the Joneses why Emmett Mitchell had been brought in as General Director instead of Johnny. Emmett, as it turns out, is five-percent owner in a string of banks in Kansas City. The bank raises grant money for inner-city ministries. Emmett was working with his bank to procure a $1 million grant for the Character Inn. When Emmett brought the hotel staff together to discuss the inner-city ministry vision and how best to implement it, the staff (other than Johnny) were bewildered. This was the first they had heard of it. That's when Johnny began to suspect that Bill was telling two different stories — one to African-Americans inside and outside IBLP, and another story to the rest of the staff.

Another strange thing occurred which made Johnny and Shantelle feel that they were being watched or investigated for some unknown reason. In addition to the opened mail, it became apparent that someone was going into the Joneses storage space and sifting through the family's personal possessions, which had eventually found their way to Flint. Why someone would want to do this, they had no idea; what they did know was that the only persons with keys to their storage area were Johnny, Shantelle, and the front desk. As Johnny pondered these issues, he stayed focused on getting the kitchens open in his position as cook. He maintained a low profile and kept his concerns to himself.

Big Brother Is Watching

Pastor Jones was soon to realize that Emmett Mitchell was not really the man in authority at the Character Inn. Although Mitchell held the title of general director and Donnie Barr was in charge of the construction, Pastor DeSoto was the pastor of the church, and Pastor Jones was in charge of the restaurants, Ms. Pat LaMantia seemed to be the person in charge to whom everyone was expected to submit. After a time of feeling progressively more harassed by Pat, he finally spoke out and told her that Emmett is the authority, not her. Other staff quickly advised him, though, that indeed Pat was the one actually running the *Character Inn*, while the others were mere figureheads. After the incident with Pat, Bill called Pastor Jones and told him that if he had any problems, he was to call him directly. Pastor Jones reminded Bill that Emmett is his authority there and so he should be reporting to him. At that, Bill let him know that Emmett was really there for public relations and reiterated that Johnny should report directly to him. This struck Pastor Jones as somewhat odd. He felt as if he was being recruited to spy on the others for Bill, and the thought made him uneasy. But soon he found out that he was not singled out for this mission. As it turns out, Bill regularly called each member of the staff to give out information about the other members of the staff. This was another serious blow to Johnny's confidence in Bill Gothard and IBLP. The Character Inn was not a spiritual place where Scripture was studied, where the staff prayed together for the needs of the body, and encouraged one another. It wasn't a place where biblical confrontation, reconciliation, and healing occurred. The atmosphere of the Inn was taking on the character of George Orwell's book, *1984.* He discovered that inside IBLP, power struggles and back-stabbing under Bill's orchestration are the norm. Johnny's refusal to join in these unholy practices caused him eventually to be labeled a "bitter man" by Gothard. But there was more disillusionment to come.

The Final Straw

As Pastor Jones was considering these things and praying about the state of affairs at the *Character Inn*, another event caused him to have even graver concerns. A sixteen-year-old girl came into the kitchen one day to cook something for Bill Gothard. Pastor Jones asked her why he had not been asked to do this, since he was in charge of the kitchen. He also asked her when Bill had given her this direction. She responded that Bill had asked her to do this when he called her. This took Johnny a little aback. He pushed a little further, asking her how often Bill called her. She said that Bill was her best friend and that he called her all the time. Johnny became instantly concerned for the young girl's welfare, and was also shocked by this revelation. It appeared to Johnny that Gothard's actions seemed to align perfectly with his peculiar definition of dating.

This was the final straw for Pastor Jones, after all of the personal disappointment and broken commitments and disillusionment with the ungodly way IBLP was administered. He turned in his resignation, and he and his family left the Character Inn on May 2, 2001. He still hadn't received the balance of the offering that had been taken up for him in July of 2000.

While being interviewed by the authors he reflected about whether or not God had actually called him to Flint. He came to the conclusion that God indeed called him there in order to show him that Bill does not live up to the principles which he espouses in his seminars and materials. He has a growing concern for the people who are being devastated by Bill Gothard and IBLP.

Chapter 8

Alpena Mountain Home

F requently, those who have never been involved in cults or cult-like groups assume that a lack of intelligence or an overabundance of gullibility leads people to join totalitarian groups. This is simply false. Very intelligent people become involved in destructive religious groups and/or false teachings. Those who are perhaps most vulnerable are people looking for answers to life's difficult questions who are not finding them in their current church situation — one thing all cult groups offer is "answers." Other potential joiners are those who are in a life-change situation — a death in the family, a job loss, a divorce, a suddenly rebellious teenager — who are seduced by the promise of understanding and help. Many are highly idealistic folks looking for a worthy cause to give their lives meaning.

Bill Gothard promises to supply the answers needed to repair and protect families in a very scary world. He has been very successful at marketing himself as an Evangelical — although his teachings are far from Evangelical — and there has been very little critical evaluation of his teachings and methods to allow people the chance to make an informed decision about trusting him and the religious movement he founded. Worse, he has been praised and recommended by big-name Evangelicals, and thousands of

Evangelical pastors and churches have sent their people to his seminars without reservation. Certainly the average person in the pew would have no reason to suspect any harm would come from attending his seminars or getting involved with his organization.

Steve Hamm and his family are devoted followers of Christ who have been involved with IBLP for nearly three decades. Steve went to his first Basic Seminar in 1971. He and his wife became area coordinators of the Basic and Advanced Seminars in the Phoenix, Arizona area. They, like so many others, were attracted to the homeschooling curriculum. They really wanted their children to have a solid Christian foundation and were concerned that the public school system would undermine their faith, a concern that many parents share today. They enrolled in ATI in 1986. Steve's father had been involved with IBLP for many years as well. In fact, Bill Gothard writes:

> My first recollection of the Hamm name occurred when we began receiving boxes of the most delicious oranges[1] that I have ever tasted. Each fall, we were sent significant quantities for the Headquarters staff and other training centers.
>
> The name Hamm became synonymous with generosity. Therefore, when you offered to provide property for a Log Cabin ministry in Northern Arkansas and also pay for building the cabins, I rejoiced that your father's generous spirit was also in you.[2]

Steve's offer, which Bill Gothard refers to, came about as the result of a challenge that Bill put forth at a men's conference in 1994. Steve Hamm was one of the men in attendance. Bill talked about the problem of juvenile delinquents and the programs that the Institute had in place to assist in solving these social ills. One of the programs mentioned was the log cabin program in Indianapolis, Indiana, where the Institute had one cabin. Bill asked the men to pray that God would provide land and the ability to build multiple cabins. After consideration and prayer, Steve contacted the Institute and offered to allow IYFS (International Youth and Family Services, a part of the IBLP) to build the cabins on a mountainside portion of his property in Alpena, Arkansas. After several months, two IBLP staff, Donnie Barr and Bob Bulmer, made a trip to the site and agreed that the location, surroundings, and general atmosphere were perfect for such a project. In addition, Steve was so committed to the ideals of this venture that he offered to pay for the necessary construction materials and lease the property to the Institute for a only $1 per year. That's ONE dollar. The Institute's obligation was to provide the construction management and the labor for construction, as well as interior finishes and furniture. One of the verbal agreements was that the Institute would not take money from the state for the delinquents in the program — that the ministry would be funded by Christians and so remain independent of government and its dictates.

As they prepared to begin the project, named Eagle Mountain, they held community meetings to explain what they were planning and answering the questions raised by the area residents. The residents were concerned about the type of offenders that would be brought in. The Institute's representatives assured the community (a meeting of 300 as well as smaller gatherings) that dangerous criminals such as sex offenders and murderers would absolutely not be brought into this program. Rather, the cabins would house those who had committed misdemeanors and less-serious crimes such as truancy, running away from home, rebellion against parents, and shoplifting.[3] With those assurances the community supported the project as well.

In July of 1995, Steve and his wife received a letter from IBLP outlining the purpose, use, portion of property to be used, and mutual responsibilities. The project was off and running to implement Gothard's well-intentioned vision — with a willing benefactor and program volunteer in Steve Hamm, the construction expertise of Institute staff, and the support of the community.

In April of 1996, a friend of Steve Hamm came in from out

of state for a visit. The friend happened to be a builder who has built homes on mountainsides. Steve and his family were understandably proud of this ministry and took their friend to look at the cabins that were nearing completion at this time. Their friend pointed out what appeared to be structural cracks in the cabins' foundations. Steve had no construction experience and had been depending on the Institute staff for the construction expertise, so he was completely taken aback by this very unsettling revelation. The friend then asked if the construction team had obtained building permits and had periodic inspections during the course of construction. Steve had purchased a copy of the codebook and lent it to the Institute but had no knowledge of the details of the project. He had been depending on the "professionals" at IBLP. Somewhat alarmed, Steve contacted the Institute staff and was assured that indeed, everything was being built according to code and was structurally sound. Steve requested that the Institute obtain occupancy permits, which would be provided by the building department upon final inspection. Five cabins were completed with the potential of 45 more to be built over the next one and a half to two years.

A Log in Someone's Eye

Time passed, and the occupancy permits were not forthcoming. As it turns out, IBLP had not taken out building permits nor were any inspections performed. Through much of what followed, Bill Gothard insisted that there were no building codes to follow nor permits to be acquired. This is patently untrue. In fact, in an article in the *Arkansas Democrat Gazette* we read,

> State building codes do apply in unincorporated areas of counties. The Arkansas Fire Prevention Code "applies in its entirety to unincorporated areas of a county," according to a 1995 state attorney general opinion.[4]

The problem in the state of Arkansas is that building regulations fall under the jurisdiction of the state Fire Marshall, and there is no real code enforcement on single-family dwellings outside of the major cities due to a lack of personnel. An unscrupulous individual or organization who desires to flaunt the authority is able to due so since the state is currently so understaffed. In addition, due to the type of activity that was intended for the cabins, these buildings would fall under commercial use and therefore building permits absolutely should have been obtained, according to Jim Hughes of Hughes Inspection Services. He writes:

> Since these structures cannot be classified as one or two family dwellings, due to the proposed use, they are required to be constructed under the requirements of the Standard Building Code even though they are classified as a Residential Occupancy.[5]

Steve Hamm hired a private inspection company whose subsequent report enumerated a number of code violations. These violations included: improper stairs, no supporting concrete piers for the wood posts supporting the porch roof, improper fasteners in the pressure-treated lumber, masonry walls which were supported on wood, improper foundation walls, water piping which was not approved, and more. In all, 19 code violations were noted upon a visual inspection of the buildings.

Steve and his wife were bewildered over this, but were confident that Bill Gothard and IBLP would take the necessary steps to comply with the state building codes on the log cabins. After all, Bill teaches the absolute need to submit to authority, the necessity of integrity in all aspects of life, and claims to be an expert in conflict resolution. Perhaps, the Hamms reasoned, these problems were due to the use of ATI program teenagers on the construction crew. After all, they weren't really skilled labor, and it was possible that these code violations occurred during times when the skilled supervisors were elsewhere. With assurances from Bill and the IBLP staff that the project would be in compliance, plans were made for the dedication service. And so, on September 29, 1996, the program was launched with Arkansas governor Mike Huckabee and Little Rock mayor Jim

Daily as keynote speakers.

But despite all assurances, and even though some remedial work was done, the cabin's foundations continued to deteriorate. And even though cosmetically the cabins looked pretty good, there appeared to be even more structural problems than had been initially seen through the visual inspection. Steve Hamm had Jim Hughes and an engineer, LaVerne Nelson, return for a more thorough inspection and, if necessary, to engineer remedies. Steve was out of town, though, when this inspection occurred, and an IBLP staff member, Donnie Barr, met the inspector and engineer, directing them to inspect the porches but not the foundations. Even so, they did express concern that two of the cabins didn't seem to have reinforcement in the footings.[6] Of greater concern were the other three cabins, which didn't appear to have proper footings. Jim Hughes explains:

> The other three cabins have foundations of rubble stone gathered from the area with mortar or concrete (unknown) placed over the top level of stone to provide a level surface for the hollow concrete masonry units, which form the foundation wall.[7]

It would later come to light that these concerns were well founded. The backhoe[8] that had been used had not been maintained properly by IBLP and ATI staff and had broken down. Rather than to repair the backhoe or bring in the proper machinery, the decision was made by the IBLP "construction professionals" to *hand dig* about six inches below the surface of the ground and stack stones and rubble and build from there up. It gets worse from there:

- Hollow concrete block was used for the foundation walls from this point up.

- There were no steel dowels to connect the hollow block to the stones and rubble. (Steel rods or "rebar" are typically installed to prevent the blocks from sliding off the foundation as the seasons change.)

- The blocks were left hollow when they should have been filled with concrete to add structural integrity.

- The wood structure was not secured to the foundation wall but was simply resting on it.

- It would be discovered in 1999 that the chimneys (the cabins are heated with wood-burning stoves) did not have proper foundations and were not correctly built, presenting yet more hazards.

We could continue with a description of these houses "built on sand," but suffice to say that serious remedies were needed prior to any actual use.

Throughout 1996 and 1997 the Institute continued operating the LIT (*Leaders In Training*) program, remodeling the staff house and giving the Hamm family assurances that the structural problems on the log cabins were being taken care of. However, the Institute continued to put up roadblocks to any actual resolution.

Conflict Resolution... Gothard Style

The situation went from bad to worse as the Eagle Mountain staff began taking liberties with the personal property of the Hamm family. Although, as we have said, there were many assurances that the cabins were being brought up to code, more and more the staff and L.I.T. students were being sent to other IBLP projects in other parts of the country. Then, Bill Gothard sent a sex offender to Eagle Mountain despite his assurances to the trusting community that no sex offenders would ever be part of the program. When an astounded Steve Hamm found out about, he contacted the director, Bob Bulmer, who told him that it was "Bill's deal" and that he had nothing to do with it. He assured Steve that he would get hold of Bill and have the sex offender removed right away.

Steve Hamm and his family, area residents (many of whom were "alumni"), Steve's neighbor, Roger Kobie (an IBLP alumnus also), and even Steve's home church had been supportive and excited about IBLP and IFYS working in their area. Early on in the venture, Roger Kobie had traveled with IBLP staff member Bob Bulmer to Little Rock to visit the mayor's office, Department of Human Services, and governor's Office. On the return trip Kobie was asked by Bob to be the director of the Log Cabin ministry. (As Roger prayed about it, however, he did not believe God was leading him in that direction, even though such an opportunity had been a lifelong dream of his.)[9] Roger, who was now getting a good look at the Institute work up close and personal, was shocked to find that they do not themselves employ the "Basic Principles" upon which the Institute is supposedly based.

Fisher's List

Our brief look at the history of IBLP shows that although Bill Gothard *teaches* conflict-resolution "principles" in his seminars, he does not personally use them. Pastor G. Richard Fisher[10] compiled a list which he calls "Bill Gothard's 21 Steps to Conflict Resolution." We would have to agree, along with others who have attempted to bring Gothard into correction over the years, that Fisher's piece portrays an accurate representation of the process employed by Bill Gothard when confronted with a problem. The 21 steps are:

1. Initially shift blame – don't answer charges – maybe it will go away.

2. Offer less-than-acceptable solutions.

3. Slander the opponent – lay charges – suggest ulterior motives.

4. Offer a meeting – muddy the waters before hand with other issues – make more accusations – generate many letters to further obfuscate.

5. Finally, have a long, drawn-out meeting for hours and hours to exhaust everyone and wear them down.

6. Bring up issues of new revelations and discoveries.

7. Further discredit key players.

8. Deny blame — accuse others.

9. Have another meeting but lay down rules to really control and thwart solutions.

10. In the long meeting — he steps back and goes silent — gives the appearance of deep reflection — makes general concessions he will not keep.

11. Send more letters to accuse.

12. Manipulate authorities around and play politics.

13. Generate more paperwork to further obscure, confuse and ignore any former commitments to fix anything or change.

14. Fall back on the notion that he is under God's orders and answers to a higher authority. Now we are dealing with God! God's blessing and increase on his work are the obvious signs and proofs.

15. Make further phone calls to wear them down.

16. Send more letters (you hurt us and God's work) — wear them down, grind them down.

17. Threaten pending disaster.

18. Now, out of "deep concern," warn opponent of dire consequences (David and Saul — Ananias and Sapphira). Use Proverbs 6:19 in a pinch (what God hates — you are at fault — it is all you).

19. Agree to meet with opponent for their welfare only; grind them to powder.

20. Admit to staff along the way a tiny infraction to do damage control and explain away other problems. This is also great for the appearance of deep humility and repentance:

"I practice what I preach AND LIVE BY MY OWN PRINCIPLES."

21. Keep attacking opponents behind the scenes, spread rumors; claim "I tried everything." Pull away – cut losses.

The Hamm family, Roger Kobie, Judge David, and Melody Pake, as well as Pastor Lannie and the Osage Baptist Church, were able to witness this process firsthand.

In late 1998 and early 1999, the Eagle Mountain staff became less communicative with Steve. He was becoming more concerned with the structural problems of the log cabins and the increase in the size and number of cracks in the foundation walls. He made several appointments with Bob Norvell, the assistant director and on-site representative for IFYS, but Mr. Norvell failed to keep the appointments. Steve then contacted Bob Bulmer (moving up the "chain of command") and sent a list of unfinished items and concerns. Bill Gothard also was scheduled to come to Eagle Mountain in August of 1999. Bob Norvell began doing some of the items on the list in preparation for Bill's arrival. Still, despite Steve's best efforts, *no* attention was being paid to the structural problems. Of additional concern to Steve was the fact that the septic tank on the "staff house" was also in need of replacement and was running open sewage on the ground.

Step One

On September 1, 1999, Steve Hamm and Bill Gothard discussed these issues again by phone. Again, assurances were given but no action was forthcoming. Thus, recalling Fisher's list, Step 1 of Gothard's *personal* conflict-resolution style was now in action. Concerned about the liability if something should happen due to the structural defects of buildings on his land, Steve had his attorney send an Indemnification Agreement[11] to the Institute for signature. The following month Steve sent a letter to Bill Gothard, as well as board member James A. Sammons, recounting the history of this project. In it he pointed out:

Bob Bulmer and Donnie [Donnie Barr, another IBLP staff member] were encouraged by the fact that the local pastor and several neighbors were Seminar alumni, supported this ministry and wanted to work together as a team. We feel that if these original intentions had been honored, many of the serious matters that have occurred would not have happened. After four years no one seems to be ultimately responsible to see that the original intent and commitments for Eagle Mountain are kept. There seems to be no accountability and even some of the neighbors and people in the community have made comments to us.[12]

Here is a man who is deeply grieved to see the lack of integrity and commitment in an organization in which he had invested much, emotionally and financially, and which claims to teach exactly those character traits in their seminars. He continues:

It deeply grieves us that there was ever a need for a list or for us to have to contact legal counsel because of decisions to do several things illegally here without our knowledge that have put this ministry and our family in a dangerous liability situation. For this reason we are requesting that you would sign the enclosed release form and return it in the envelope provided to our attorney by October 11.

We cannot understand why the staff members who have come here do not feel the need to live by the law of the land and God's principles learned through the Seminar.[13]

This was a very difficult period for the Hamm family, for they had believed for nearly 30 years that Bill Gothard was a man of integrity who respected and submitted to authority and taught others to do so as well. This was only the beginning of sorrows as they worked their way through "Bill Gothard's personal 21 steps of conflict resolution."

Steve learned from his neighbor, Roger Kobie, a few days

before writing this letter that Bob Norvell, the assistant director, had mentioned to him that they were "pulling out" and wouldn't need to complete the work. This blatant disregard for the law, the laissez-faire attitude toward commitments they had made, and their outright rebellion against authority, etc., was a side of Bill Gothard and IBLP that Steve and his family could never have imagined existed.

James A. Sammons called Steve's attorney on October 11, acknowledged the Hamms' reasoning for wanting an indemnification agreement and "requested to see a list of the problem areas you are concerned with so he can check into the matter more closely."[14] This led to a telephone conversation between Steve and James Sammons. According to Steve, Mr. Sammons stated that he was unsure if he could do anything because "Bill calls the shots," but he said he would attempt to bring the matter before the IBLP board. In a later correspondence he pointed out that Bill Gothard would have to approve any decision made by the Board.

Steve and Karen Hamm responded to James Sammons's phone call with a partial list of problems on October 22, 1999. The list included:

- the cabin chimneys were not built to code, the rock veneer was not complete, and proper flashings had not been installed and in some cases were leaking

- exterior trim boards were missing

- raw sewage was running on the ground (cabin 3)

- foundation problems were worsening and center support beams sagging

About cabins 2–5, they wrote:

All the foundations are not to code. In fact, there are no foundations, it's just piled rocks on the ground. Mr. Barr did this after their backhoe got broken, and they never fixed it.[15]

In addition, Steve paid $5,000 of his own money to repair the septic tank on the staff house in order to eliminate the open-sewage problem.[16] Steve received no further contact from Sammons subsequent to this letter.

Step Two—or, How to Fudge Issues and Not Resolve Anything at All

On October 20, Steve's lawyer received a letter from IBLP's general counsel, Robert Barth. Barth pointed out that an inspector had already looked at the property and that, as far as IBLP was concerned, his "conclusions should erase any questions."[17] The problem, though, with that report, as we mentioned earlier, is that it dealt only with the porches, not the structural integrity of the footings of the log cabins themselves. Barth went on to say:

> While the fact that the cabins are on block foundations rather than concrete may be an issue of preference, it certainly is not an issue of safety.[18]

This is an unacceptable excuse because, although a block foundation vs. a concrete foundation may be a personal preference option, and not a building code violation in certain parts of the country the footings upon which the blocks are supposed to sit were improperly constructed. Rather than digging down below the frost line, the builders simply dug an approximately 6" deep trench, filled it with rubble, and poured some concrete over the material. The block was not filled with concrete or properly attached to the footing. In addition, the log framing was not attached to the foundation wall. The issues of concern had nothing to do with personal preference but structural integrity.

Deborah K. Sexton, attorney for the Hamm family, responded on October 27, 1999 to the October 20, 1999 correspondence from Robert Barth. She acknowledged receipt of his correspondence and a copy of the 1996 letter from Hughes Building Inspections and Nelson Engineering. She then apprised him of the problem with the inspector's report that he was relying upon to draw his conclusions:

The next day my client spoke with the engineer, Mr. Nelson, who did the report. The engineer indicated that he did not inspect the footings, foundations and stemwalls. He only inspected the porches, as requested by Mr. Barr.[19]

She also points out:

My client is still very much concerned regarding a contingent liability due to your client's negligence in building and maintaining the cabins. We would appreciate your review of the Indemnification and Release Agreement, which I have previously submitted. If you and your client really believe the cabins are "quite safe," there should be no concern about signing my form of such agreement or a revised form to which both parties would agree.

We also would welcome a visual inspection by your client. We feel somewhere along the way there has been some miscommunication that a physical inspection might clear up.[20]

With all their stonewalling, Mr. Gothard and IBLP have forced the Hamms and other area residents to expend time (several years now), energy, and funds in an attempt to remedy this situation. Ironically, the Hamms have faithfully followed Gothard's teachings on conflict resolution, while Bill Gothard followed his own personal set of "principles" in order to sweep the entire mess under the rug and avoid accountability. Bill refused to sign the Indemnification and Release Agreement, which caused Steve to write yet *another* letter to Bill Gothard and the board of directors of IBLP, again outlining the history of this situation. Steve Hamm then states, in good IBLP-trained style:

We have honestly tried to work through our authorities in order to make you understand the importance of this situation. We have spent a good deal of time and money on calls, research, inspections, and counsel, to try to factually provide for you any information and details you may need and make available qualified, respectable, and interested people who have been involved in this situation from the beginning. We have spent hours and days of fasting and prayer, seeking God's will and crying out to Him.[21]

He went on to express his liability concerns, and to informed Gothard of the legal advice they had received:

Mr. Kobie [retired police lieutenant], has expressed his concern in the event of a liability suit, no court would have mercy on our family, since we are aware of the possible dangerous situation on our property.

Our lawyer has advised us that since the Institute refuses to release our family from liability, for the situation they have created, has violated the lease, and has not extended to use the courtesy of any communication, that we cannot legally afford to have them on our property.[22]

This was sent with a cover letter from his attorney on November 22, 1999 with the request that IBLP vacate the buildings (please note that Bob Norvell had already stated that they were pulling out and wouldn't be completing the work). On the same day, Bill Gothard mailed a letter to Steve and these two correspondences crossed in the mail. He wrote with regard to the structural problems, "...whatever is not right or safe will be corrected."[23]

Blame Shifting

Incredibly, Bill then went on to attempt to turn the situation around and present the conflict as a spiritual problem on Steve's part. Here we see the balance of the Gothard steps to conflict resolution coming into play. He writes:

It now makes us all wonder if you were exaggerating actual dangers and creating list after list of repairs in order to discourage the program so you could use the property for your own personal needs.[24]

This is an outrageous charge. The repeated lists were necessary because:

- IBLP staff did not perform the items on the initial punch list so the items were brought back to their attention through subsequent "reminder" lists.

- Additional structural problems appeared over time.

Bill, however, attempted to turn this around by saying that the structural problems were not real problems; that Steve, greedy for the praise of men and greedy to have the property enhanced for his own use, never truly intended to allow IBLP to use it. He also asserted that Steve was lying to his attorney, and by implication to everyone else, in saying that there were improper foundations. He then went on to relate gossip that he had heard about Steve, which flies in the face of what he himself teaches about not listening to a talebearer. Finally, he suggested that there is a bad spirit emanating from the *property itself*:

> Yesterday, one of the leaders at Eagle Mountain West[25] was told that he would be going back to one of the log cabins in your property. He actually began to cry and appealed not to have to return there because of the spirit of anger that permeates the premises.[26]

Steve responded with a letter on November 29, 1999:

> We are very disappointed that you would choose to believe so much misinformation, without ever coming down here to talk to us, the neighbors, or anyone else who has been offended by your ministry here. If you really want to know the truth about the cabins, your staff's behavior and management skills, and the accusations that were made by the two young men, we would be very happy to have a meeting to discuss these matter with all parties involved. Pastor Lannie would be happy to make Osage Baptist Church available for the meeting.

The Spiritual Danger in Land Ownership

At the same time a letter was on its way from Bill Gothard to Steve Hamm which clearly shows Gothard's shameless manipulation techniques. In the letter, he offered some possible solutions to the situation. With incredible chutzpa, Gothard suggested that Steve give the property outright to IBLP — "Deed the Property as a Gift to the Lord."[27] He went on to give Steve the "spiritual" reasons why this should be done, including the fact that since the property had been publicly dedicated, it should be viewed as "belonging to the Lord." Incredibly, he brought up the sex scandal (see chapter 5) that had occurred at IBLP in the 1980's, suggesting that it was Steve Gothard's private ownership of the Northwoods property that resulted in his moral and spiritual downfall!

> In reviewing the tensions that have developed in Eagle Mountain, I could not help but recall similar factors years ago before the Northwoods Conference Center was established. My younger brother found the property and bought a portion of it for his personal use. He built a lodge on his property and then wanted to have the Institute use it because he could not afford all the related expenses. He often talked of giving it to the Institute, but I urged him to keep the ownership in his name.
>
> The private ownership created tension with other staff members, and ultimately, Satan was able to bring about disastrous spiritual and moral defeat on that property. It was only after my brother followed through on his original idea of giving it to the Institute that the tensions were resolved and the greater blessing of the Lord was experienced.[28]

This creative rewrite of past events blames *private ownership of property* for sexual immorality. It seems almost unbelievable that a prominent Christian leader would use his own and his brother's failure in an attempt to bully and scare one of the Institute's benefactors out of his own property. The implication was clear — if Steve wanted blessing from God rather than disastrous spiritual and moral failure, he would give up that land!

The question arises — is this someone who is familiar with truth, integrity, trustworthiness, etc? Is this someone who should be creating homeschool curriculum and promoting *Character First!* in the public schools?

Don't Criticize God's Anointed

When that ploy did not work, Gothard wrote Steve Hamm yet another letter, berating him for questioning his God-given authority, and the authority of others whom God had supposedly placed over him:

> By finding fault with him [Bob Norvell] and complaining about the work of Donnie Barr, Bob Bulmer, and me, are you not in a position of murmuring against those whom God has made responsible for this work?[29]

Some readers might see this as silly posturing on Gothard's part, as indeed it is. But, in order to understand how such words would be received by Steve Hamm, you must recall that people who are involved for very long in authoritarian groups see the leader as God's man whose words come from the Lord Himself (but without the stone tablets). To stand opposed to such a man is a very scary thing indeed.

The Pakes Get Involved

In January of 2000, Judge David Pake (on the board of governors for IBLP's Law School) and his wife, Melody, became aware of the situation. They attempted to act as mediators, using IBLP principles. So, another meeting was scheduled for February 23, 2000, with the Hamms, Pakes, building inspector Jim Hughes, neighbor Roger Kobie, and Bill Gothard. In preparation for the meeting, Judge Pake sent confidential correspondence to both Steve and Bill, laying out a number of questions to assist in bringing this to resolution in a biblical way. Bill was asked to meet at

Steve and Karen Hamm's home, together with the other parties, in order to look at the cabins in the daylight. Bill Gothard had committed to the appointed time, but he arrived four hours late. Jim Hughes wanted to get to the hospital where his son was struggling against cancer, but he waited so he could take part in the meeting. When Bill arrived this was relayed to him, but rather than show compassion for this man, he went on to describe that such conditions as cancer were the result of sin in someone's life. All parties were shocked. Due to the lateness of Bill's arrival, they were unable to look at the buildings, survey the shoddy workmanship together, and actually see the foundational cracks for themselves. (A cynic might presume that this was the reason for the delay.)

As the meeting began, Bill attempted to impugn the credibility of Tim Hughes, to no avail. He then tried to get Hughes to say that even though there might be code violations (Bill was unwilling to admit that there were) that the cabins were safe for habitation. Mr. Hughes insisted that they would *not* be safe. Finally, Judge David Pake pointed out that while safety was an important issue, a primary consideration was respecting the authority of the government by complying with the building code. Pake then said, "I have just one question, Bill. Are you going to submit to the authorities, which in this case is the building code, as you teach in your seminars, or are you not?" After a period of silence Bill said that he would make things right.

Steve and Karen followed up soon after the meeting with a letter to Bill. They thanked him for coming, getting the facts, and committing to take action quickly. They reiterated the decisions made as follows:

- Mr. Hughes would prepare a comprehensive list of code violations to be corrected.

- IBLP would be liable for the expense of correcting the code violations.

- The State Fire Marshall would perform an official

inspection and note any additional violations that needed to be corrected.

- Bill Gothard would appoint another director for the Eagle Mountain training facility.

- A new lease would be drafted by Judge Pake with changes requested by Bill Gothard and agreed to by the Hamms.[30]

Here we go again

All were hopeful that Bill Gothard and IBLP would stand by this commitment and were excited to see resolution, so that Eagle Mountain would become what they had all envisioned. Instead, more foot-dragging and obfuscation occurred, and it became obvious that Gothard was again breaking his commitment to them. Sadly, there had been no real repentance on the part of the Institute (although Bill admitted to spreading gossip[31]), and needless to say, the relationship between the Hamms and Bill Gothard continued to deteriorate.

In early April, Steve entertained the idea of selling the property. That brought a quick response from Bill by way of a phone call. Steve again catalogued the history of the project, IBLP's lack of follow-through, and its breaking of commitments. Steve reminded Bill that IBLP staff had previously stated that the Institute was pulling out and would not be making the required repairs and stated that their continued absence had confirmed this to be the case. Bill followed up this discussion with an April 18 letter, that attempted to pressure the Hamms (he tried to make *them* feel guilty!) into either donating the property to IBLP or making a substantial monetary contribution if the land were sold. This attempted spiritual manipulation did not work. The Hamms had their attorney send a letter to Bill Gothard directing him to remove all Institute "property from the premises by May 31, 2000." Bill responded by letter on May 29, 2000 — suggesting darkly that Steve was fighting against God:

In the past you have allowed me to be your instructor and the overseer of your home education program. I have invested my life to do good to you and others. Now, we are receiving reproach, accusations, and significant loss to an important aspect of this ministry. God warns, "Whoso rewardeth evil for good, evil shall not depart from his house" (Proverbs 17:13).[32]

He said further:

You may find fault with the human inadequacies of Institute Leadership, however, the fact remains that this is a work of the Lord and He is supernaturally blessing it. Thus, your actions are primarily against the Lord. I would therefore appeal to you to reconsider what you are asking us to do.[33]

His letter the next day was even stronger, containing dire warnings of impending judgement and doom:

By calling the "Institute leadership" liars, you are putting yourself in the position of judging us, this places you in jeopardy of the warning of Romans 2:1-8.[34]

He concluded his letter with these two paragraphs:

I am sincerely concerned for the judgement of God that will come upon you for the actions you are taking. You are dealing with God's work and God's money, both are things you and others have dedicated to the Lord. If God judged Ananias and Sapphira for giving a false impression of generosity to the early Church by withholding part of the money they received for selling their property, how much more serious is it for you to use the Lord's work to unjustly increase your assets.

I would be pleased to meet with you for the sake of your spiritual welfare if you so desire.[35]

In June, Institute staff came under the cover of darkness to remove Institute property from the premises. Subsequently, they sent a letter to the Hamms' attorney demanding reimbursement for lost income and other expenses related to the property. This is interesting. IBLP was the one who continually violated their agreements over the previous four years. IBLP was the one who refused to submit to the governmental authority (the building codes). IBLP was the one who threatened the Hamms — whose only "sin" was their attempt to hold IBLP accountable to keep the very principles Bill Gothard and IBLP teach and supposedly believe — with impending judgments from God. And IBLP now wanted to be paid for its failures and incompetence. On May 29, 2001 the State Fire Marshall, Lt. Lloyd A. Franklin weighed in on the situation. After reviewing the report done by James. R. Hughes, Lt. Franklin stated that the building codes apply to the entire state unless a city or county adopts a more stringent set of building codes. He also suggested that the Hamms contact the Carroll County, Arkansas prosecuting attorney and county attorney for legal assistance. He also suggested that Steve find out if the Institute were licensed and bonded to do this work in Arkansas. If not, this would be a violation of other state laws. We really need to ask the question again. Should an organization which so flagrantly violates the laws of the state in which it is operating really be trusted with teaching character in the public schools?

A Cracked Foundation

While we were interviewing Steve and his family and were checking out the foundational cracks and other structural defects of the buildings for ourselves, Steve waxed philosophical about the situation. As we stood looking at one of the crumbling foundations with multiple structural cracks and no footings, he said, "This is really a picture of the Institute. Like the cabins, it looks great; but there is no solid foundation, so it will keep breaking apart."

Steve and his family have expended more funds to rectify the structural deficiencies and are moving on with their lives. They still love many of the people that work with the Institute but are being shunned by them for making their own decisions, in opposition to Gothard's will. Perhaps Bill Gothard would be only too happy to have let them make their own decisions for themselves. But sometimes they might make the wrong decisions, comrades, and then where should the Institute be?

Chapter 9

The Courtship Game

C ourtship has become a "catch-all" phrase to describe something better than dating. It's the word used by people for everything they think boy-girl relationships should be, a wish list for how things should ideally unfold – The boy goes to the father, the boy courts the girl in safe family settings, boy and girl fall in love, and the sun shines at their outdoor wedding – and this is all good. We should have high standards; we should be idealistic. But misguided idealism can make for a rather unpleasant collision with reality. Unfortunately, what looks good on paper doesn't always go as smoothly as planned in real life. Relationships are confusing no matter what you call them.

–Joshua Harris[1]

There has been a lot of talk in recent years concerning something-called "courtship." In the American homeschooling culture, courtship has become such a popular theme that in nearly every homeschooling conference, book sale, catalogue, or magazine, you are sure to find a large section devoted to this topic.

The concern is understandable given the importance of the

subject of marriage and the high divorce rate, even among Christian people. Currently the divorce rate inside the church is nearly equal to that outside the church. That Christian marriages are crumbling at a rate comparable to the culture around us is a major problem, but it is not our only moral problem. Living together prior to marriage in order to determine "compatibility" has become common in culture and, sadly, is a growing trend within the church as well. Even popular media have gotten involved in that act. In the 1970s we saw *The Dating Game*, where contestants asked and answered questions to determine compatibility before beginning a "relationship." Although we would not recommend finding a suitable mate in this way, it looks good compared to a new "reality" television show called *Temptation Island*. Four couples unmarried but are in a "committed relationship" are taken to an island where the uncommitted-committed males and females are separated from one another for a period of two weeks. During that time they will be subjected to as much sexual temptation as possible by 26 beautiful singles to see if their professed love for one another is true and solid. This is truly a fool's paradise.

The Courtship of Gothard's Followers

In reaction to the current trend, and in Bill Gothard's zeal to create a cradle-to-grave, step-by-step systematized way to live, he has become a leader in the aforementioned "courtship movement." We would, of course, agree that marriages are troubled, that the divorce rate is very troubling, and that loose living seems to abound both outside and inside the church. It is important to have sound biblical teaching on marriage and, indeed, on relationships in general in our throwaway society. Some of the things which Gothard teaches, as Dr. Ronald B. Allen points out, "...make sense and may be used by couples for good as they seek God's guidance in their lives."[2]

In looking at this we need to begin by asking some questions. What is meant by "courtship," and how did this movement begin? The term "courtship" comes from the days when instead of dating, the custom was for a man to call on a woman at her parent's house to "court." Back then, instead of saying that two people were "going together" or "dating," as we might now, they would say that they were "courting." In a sense the terms "courtship" and "going together" or "dating" (or any of a number of other terms) are really just synonyms. The expression "courtship" has fallen into disuse over the past century as have many other terms. This happens in all cultures as words are dropped or change in meaning. For example, the word "prevent," at the time 1 Thessalonians was first translated into English meant, "to go before" or to "precede." It now carries the meaning of "to stop" in general usage.

In the recent revival of the word in Christian culture, courtship now carries an entirely different nuance than in its original usage. Now courtship is used to describe a parentally authorized and supervised relationship with the opposite sex that is a preparation for marriage. Variations can include everything from an old-fashioned fiddler-on-the-roof type arranged marriage to simply dating with the parent's consent. Indeed, a detailed study could be made of all the different versions of courtship that are being advocated today.

We will, however, focus on courtship as Bill Gothard is advocating it. As far as we are aware, Gothard was the first major proponent of "courtship" within the last ten or twenty years. The success of IBLP has been the primary springboard for the courtship movement as it now exists. The ideas are part of the ATI material and are effectively communicated to his committed followers.

Leaky Umbrellas?

To understand Gothard's teaching on courtship it is necessary to realize that this, too, is intrinsically linked to his general teaching about family relationships and his mechanistic prescriptions for life. In short, according to Gothard, all human relationships are governed by a chain of command similar to that in the military. It is *only* when we find our place in God's chain of command and get under our proper authority that God will be able to protect us.

Once we get under proper authority and implement the proper amount and types of mechanical steps and principles that Gothard prescribes, we ensure God's blessing in our life and family.

But there is always a danger of losing God's blessing. Remember that in Gothardspeak, authority is like an "umbrella of protection," and if and when we get out from under it we expose ourselves to unnecessary temptations which are too strong for us to overcome.[3]

The other danger is that the authority-umbrella will "leak," leading to real trouble for those huddled beneath it.

> Satan cannot get through to some sons and daughters unless there is a leak in the father's umbrella.[4]

Gothard writes that these truths about authority and chain of command form "The Basis of Achieving Great Faith." Says Gothard, "The size of our God is greatly determined by our ability to see how He is able to work through those in authority over us...."[5] In his booklets about authority one cannot avoid the impression that Gothard is trying to "sell" his idea to the reader. He begins by listing fifteen rewards that come to all who get under the proper authority, which include "You will have a long life.... You will avoid fear of condemnation.... You will receive the glory of God.... You will not blaspheme God or His Word.... You will be given clear direction.... You will be protected from evil people.... You will receive God's praise...."[6]

Gothard especially emphasizes this principle in family relationships. If the father's authority is not properly recognized, then everything else will fall out of place. For example, Gothard teaches wives that rebellious children are the direct result of their own failure to fully submit to their own husbands. Gothard, by implication, suggests that rebellion in children will vanish if the wife gets in line. Hence, everything in a family stands or falls on this issue of authority and submission. This applies no matter how ungodly and wicked — or abusive — the person in authority may actually be.

What Gothard actually means by authority and submission

extends far beyond the scriptural bounds, as the husband and father is to be treated as an autocrat with practically unlimited control. Gothard is preoccupied with an authoritarian pattern of human relationships that is not balanced sufficiently with love as a model. It seems that Gothard fails to adequately present the need for loving relationships with children, positing only the proper role and proper discipline necessary to implement the mechanistic steps that are guaranteed to bring about the desired response from children. The preoccupation is with control, pre-dictability, and proper behavior - instead of the need for nurturing relationships in which learned behavior and attitudes come from *models, not coercive manipulation.*"[7]

As a child matures into adulthood, Gothard teaches that "he passes from chain of command to chain of counsel." Yet, as other critics of Gothard have pointed out, in practice there is no discernable difference between Gothard's teaching on chain of command and chain of counsel—he believes no one should ever go against parental counsel, no matter how old the "child" is or how ungodly the parents may be. (The only exception he recognizes is if the parent commands something that is a direct and obvious violation of Scripture.) Gothard applies this principle to such an extreme that he even "suggests that, unless they have parental consent, adult single children should remain at home. Moreover, even marriage does not break this cycle of excessive dependence upon parental counsel, even if the parents are unsaved—in spite of Psalm 1."[8] The parental chain of command/counsel ends only if the parent delegates the authority to someone else.

In short, Gothard teaches that young people must allow *their authorities* to determine whom they will marry, and that *God can bless no marriage if it goes against parental counsel.*

Courtship Defined

Gothard's booklet *Establishing Biblical Standards of Courtship* opens with a picture of a handsome couple riding bicycles together. Beneath the picture are the following words:

Is this couple dating, or courting? The answer will have an important effect upon their lives, the lives of their families, and (if they marry) the lives of those in every generation which follows. There is a definite and vital difference between courtship and dating. Unless this difference is understood and the principles of courtship are applied, defrauding and hurts can result, as well as lasting physical, mental, and spiritual consequences.[9]

Gothard must view dating as an abominable sin if it can have consequences "in every generation which follows!" In fact, the evil of dating is a major reason why God had to destroy the ancient world. When the Lord, back in the pre-flood era, saw "that every intent of the thoughts of [man's] heart was only evil continually," (Genesis 6:5) Gothard teaches that "these thoughts were being cultivated through dating-type relationships which were common in that society...."[10] This is a shocking statement to a student of Scripture; there is nothing implicit or explicit in the text to validate this claim. But as we have pointed out, context is not a consideration for Bill Gothard. An out-of-context verse or portion of a verse will suffice if it can be bent to support the point he is attempting to make.

Definitions are very important in order to understand what someone is attempting to communicate. So we do well to ask, how Gothard defined the horrible sin of dating, which has "lasting physical, mental, and spiritual consequences" for those "in every generation which follows" and which led to the great Flood in the book of Genesis. Gothard defines dating simply as:

> ...having a special interest in a person of the opposite gender and cultivating that interest through thoughts, looks, notes, talks, or events... [Rather] than building mutual commitment toward the potential of marriage, the goal of dating is personal pleasure."[11]

Courtship, on the other hand, "is a father's agreeing to work with a qualified young man to win his daughter for marriage..."[12] "the Lord has warned us not to follow our natural inclinations but to receive His precise guidelines for carrying out a Godly courtship."[13]

In defining dating and courting so tightly and then juxtaposing them, Gothard creates a false dilemma by asserting that all who date do so for their own personal pleasure rather than with the motive of forming a mutual commitment, leading potentially to marriage. Why must Gothard's idea of "courtship," which is, in effect, arranged marriage, be the only alternative to casual dating, rather than serious, conscientious dating? In creating this false dilemma he has set up his followers to accept the idea that there is only one divinely inspired, God-ordained method of finding a spouse. Any other way is sure to bring God's cataclysmic judgement on the couple and their descendants for generations.

We find Gothard's courtship teaching to be unbiblical, unfair, unreasonable, unworkable and, ultimately, unwise.

Unbiblical

Gothard seems to be opposed to dating because of the assumption that the individual chooses his or her own partner, rather than simply submitting to his or her parent's choice. He sees this as opposing the biblical "model" of courtship and marriage. Gothard cites Solomon, David, and Samson as examples that "Those who were the most qualified to choose their own life partners brought sorrow into their lives when they tried to do so."[14] This is fallacious because it assumes that making wrong choices makes *choosing* wrong! Though all of us make choices every day, some good and some bad, the answer is not totalitarianism, but employing godly thinking and good sense in decision making. As a matter of fact, the narratives of David and Samson both show that there were problems in their character *before* the introduction of the foreign women. These character flaws influenced their personal decisions and led them to make errors that came back to haunt them. Welcome to the scary world of *free will*.

Another consideration is this — in Bible times, most people had arranged marriages, yet these unions were far from perfect. David's marriage to Michal was arranged by her father, Saul, yet the Bible does not portray this union as a roaring success. Arranged marriages, even today, can be either successful or unhappy. It is not that we are opposed to arranged marriage *per se*, but we do not believe that such a method is necessarily "God's way."

Also, Gothard's view assumes that since the majority of biblical characters, who were products of their times and culture, had arranged marriages, that the narrative text is communicating the correct, and godly, way to do courtship — the model we all must follow. The fact that the Bible *mentions* how people in those days prepared for marriage does not constitute *command for* us to do it that way. Was polygamy God's plan for marriage, since so many biblical marriages are portrayed as polygamous?

One of the reasons Gothard gives to ban dating is that "through the deception of dating, Satan is able to reduce the fruitfulness of one's ministry both in singleness and in marriage".[15] He reasons that single people spend too much time pairing off and enjoying companionship with members of the opposite sex. Hence, when they marry, they may soon get bored and "neglect the responsibilities of marriage to enjoy the benefits of singleness."[16]

Gothard argues that when a single person feels the need to have companionship, he or she is not being content with the Lord and "...unless we are content with the Lord in singleness, we will not be content with another person in marriage."[18] In other words, feelings of loneliness indicate a spiritual problem.

> When we experience loneliness, this often indicates to us that we are allowing the longings of our souls to dominate our lives, rather than enjoying the ever-present fellowship of God's Spirit with *our* spirits.... As the Lord brings us through difficult times and we begin to feel lonely, we can accept this as His signal to us that at the very same moment, He is experiencing the same anguish toward us and wants us to make *Him* our basic delight.[19]

This raises a question about God's competence regarding

Adam. God Himself said, "It is not good for man to be alone; I will make a helper suitable for him." (Genesis 2:18). This was prior to the Fall. There is no indication that Adam was not content with the Lord, yet he needed Eve. God doesn't seem to have taken this need as a personal slight, but generously provided the answer to that need: a human companion. It would seem that the need for human companionship doesn't necessarily indicate a lack of contentment in the Lord. In our fallen world, unmet needs can draw us closer to God, no question, but that does not make the need itself bad in any way. Loneliness is no more wrong than hunger or thirst. We are, however, obligated to meet our needs in legitimate ways. Eating is legit; stealing to eat is not. Marriage is legit; fornication is not.

In addition, suggests Gothard, there are too many things for single people to do for them to have any excuse for feeling lonely. Before beginning courtship, young people should develop basic skills in as many areas as possible, and in the areas necessary to reinforce what he sees as the five aspects of a dynamic home. Every home, according to Gothard, should be:

1. A worship center
2. A learning center
3. A hospitality center
4. A health center
5. A craft center.

Unfair

The exciting aspect about the way God designed the family, says Gothard, is that these skills can be learned while single by apprenticing to parents and applying them in the home. Young people should have plenty of time to do this, since Gothard discourages marriage before the age of thirty.[19] In addition, according to his *Seven Phases of a Godly Courtship*[20] the suitor should be financially well off. When a young man is old enough for marriage, sufficiently mature, has amassed monetary wealth, and has acquired the necessary skills for marriage (i.e., is capable of implementing these five aspects of a "dynamic home"), the Lord will indicate the woman he is to court through those who are in authority over him.

> When a young man has deepened his fellowship with the Lord, the means God will use to confirm direction toward a particular young lady will be through the authorities He has established.... Once the young woman's father has given the young man freedom to focus on winning her heart, the couple enters into courtship.[21]

It must be emphasized that under *no* possible circumstances is a courtship to be entered into without the consent of the parents. In his seminar Gothard says, "I'm firmly convinced that God never intended girls to turn down dates. He intended for their father's [*sic*] to." This principle applies equally to marriage. In Gothard's booklet *Establishing Biblical Standards of Courtship* there is a page for sons and daughters to cut out which is a covenant they sign with their fathers to "...demonstrate your commitment to God's plan for courtship instead of man's philosophy of dating...."[22]

The young person must say to his or her father, "I will wait for your full release before entering into marriage." The father, in turn, tells his daughter that "I will protect you from unqualified men." To his son the father says, "I will protect you from strange women." This covenant is "between a father and a son as witnessed by the Lord Jesus Christ" and must be signed by the child, the father, and the family's pastor.

In commenting on Gothard's Scripture-twisting misuse of the Book of Ruth for his *Seven Phases of a Godly Courtship*, Dr. Ronald B. Allen writes:

> ...Gothard is in serious error when he makes wealth a spiritual requirement for any man who is contemplating marriage. If Gothard's principles were applied consistently, the poor workers in the employ of Boaz could not have married, poor people in Jerusalem could not have married,

indeed, even Joseph could not have married Mary because he was a poor man.

How anyone could read the Book of Ruth and conclude that a man's wealth is a divine prerequisite for marriage is a mystery.[23]

In our opinion, and as we have shown throughout this book, mysterious and mystical Bible interpretation is a specialty of Bill Gothard.

Make Haste

Gothard teaches that once the actual period of courtship begins it should be as short as possible. This comes from Gothard's interpretation of 1 Corinthians 7:32-34, where Paul says that a single person should focus on pleasing the Lord while a married person focuses on pleasing one's spouse.

> While single, both the man and the lady are free to concentrate on pleasing the Lord, whereas one who is married is required by God to see how he can please his partner...
>
> During the time of courtship, however, neither one is able to focus full attention on either of these goals. The lady, in particular, may desire to please the Lord, but her attention and affections will be directed to the young man who is doing all he can to win her heart. In a short period of courtship, the focus is for the couple to see how they can please their parents. David's courtship of Michal, for example, involved King Saul's requirement that David slay one hundred Philistines, However, with the special motivation of a young man anticipating marriage, David killed *two* hundred Philistines.[24]

Based on these Scriptures, ripped from their context, Gothard concludes that we ought to work on "keeping courtship as short as possible."[25] This raises a practical problem: how are two people who are to be married supposed to get to know each other in such a brief period of time? Gothard's answer is that they get to know each other primarily through getting to know the parents!

> The proper way to get to know the young lady is by build-ing a relationship with her father.... In the biblical exam-ple of Isaac and Rebecca, Abraham clearly instructed that Isaac's wife was to be of his own kindred. This indicates that Isaac and Rebecca would have known each other through their fathers, and this explains why Rebecca did not hesitate to go with Abraham's servant and marry one whom she did not know personally....
>
> Dating is based on what is presently known about each other. However, God designed courtship to lead to a marriage covenant based on what *He* knows about each partner....[26]

Since "the proper way to get to know the young lady is by building a relationship with her father" it follows that a private *personal* relationship is not necessary for two people who are courting. As Howard Grant, one of Gothard's followers, said of his 28-year-old daughter's courtship,

> In a sense, the whole courtship hinged on this principle — a full agreement that there must not be a "private" rela-tionship built up. Without such an understanding, it's not a true courtship. That's why an understanding about letters and phone calls is so important, because for most people these things become key building blocks toward privacy.[27]

Another teacher Gothard shares an affinity for, Jonathan Lindvall, similarly tells about a man who gained permission to court a lady with the intention of marriage before they had any social interaction, and so, says Lindvall, "Essentially he was pro-posing to the father."[29]

The flaw here is that while a young man may learn *facts* about a girl from the girl's parents, he can only truly *know* her through a relationship with her personally. We cannot assume the principle of "like father like son," since there may be a world of difference between parents and their offspring

Walk in the Counsel of the Ungodly

A question which naturally arises in response to Gothard's teaching on courtship is this: What is the procedure when the parents are not Christians? Are young people in such situations expected to walk in the counsel of the ungodly? Gothard's answer is that it makes no difference how ungodly your parents may be, for whether they are Christians or unbelievers you still must not marry without their full consent or you are acting in rebellion and *will* have marriage problems.

To support this idea Gothard quotes Proverbs 6:20-21: "My son, keep thy father's commandment, and forsake not the law of thy mother: Bind them continually upon thine heart, *and* tie them about thy neck." Gothard makes the comment, "Notice that the spiritual condition of the parents is not listed as a factor in obeying these clear commands." Since this verse says to keep your father's command, and gives no qualifications or exceptions, Gothard concludes that we must obey our parent's no matter how wicked they may be and even when they tell us to perform actions we believe to be contrary to God's will. Yet the 'commands' and 'law' that this verse refers to are clearly a reference to the laws of Moses, using language very similar to Deuteronomy 6. Neither passage is addressing the situation of ungodly parents. In Deuteronomy 6, Moses was speaking to God's people Israel to instruct "God's people" on how to teach, focus on, and be fully permeated with the Mosaic Law. The Nation agreed to keep these Laws for their blessing (Exodus 24:3). In Proverbs 6:20-35 Solomon is warning against committing adultery. There is nothing in these passages, which give even a hint of submitting to and walking in the counsel of the ungodly.

As has been pointed out numerous times, this kind of Scripture twisting is typical of Gothard who has a habit of extracting single verses from their immediate context as well as the general teaching of the whole Bible, and then forming an absurd theology based on them. Yet, often, single verses cannot be interpreted in isolation, since other Scriptures qualify them. For example, this proverb which tells us to keep our father's commands must be understood alongside Psalm 1, where we read: "Blessed *is* the man that walketh not in the counsel of the ungodly." (Psalms 1:1; Proverbs 4:14; 1 Peter 1:18) So clearly if our parents are giving ungodly commands and telling us to do things which we believe to be contrary to God's will for our lives, we must not walk in their counsel. Obviously, if such a situation occurs it should be treated seriously by the young man or woman, and whatever is done should be done in a spirit of humility. Gothard allows for exceptions to his strict interpretation of Proverbs 6:20-21 only when parents require something that is against the direct command of God. If a parent told a child to directly violate a biblical command (to murder someone, for example), then Gothard would allow for an exception.

In Dr. Ronald B. Allen's excellent critique of Gothard's *Seven Phases of a Godly Courtship* he points out:

> Gothard seems obsessed with finding sequential, mechanical outlines of principles in the biblical narrative, even when these outlines of principles are not evident at all in the passage he uses.[29]

Returning from one of Gothard's seminars, Wilfred Bockelman reported on a testimony Gothard cites about two dedicated Christians who believed God wanted them to marry. They prayed about their relationship and decided to get married, convinced that their plans had God's blessing. But the parents of the girl, who were not Christians themselves, objected. What should she do? No matter how rational an argument you can give that she should go ahead and get married, the fact is that according to Gothard, this is not God's way; she must be obedient *always* to her parents.[31] We are not told any of the background of that situation; it may be that the non-Christian parents were wise and saw problems of which this young lady was not aware. But that is not the point. The point is that Gothard is attempting to establish a divinely inspired rule to which young people are expected to conform in every situation regardless of the background and particularities of individual circumstances, and regardless of personal convictions and spiritual leading.

But Gothard doesn't just stop there. He also argues that no romantic interest occur prior to its authorization in courtship.

> Being a "one-woman man" or a "one-man woman" means that we have accepted the *lifelong* commitment of marriage. The wisdom of proverbs praises the one who does the partner good *all* the days of his life (including *before* marriage). (See Proverbs 31:12.)
>
> We do this by remaining morally pure in our thoughts and actions for the one we will one day marry. Because this commitment to reserve ourselves for one individual, every person is like a "strange-man" or a "strange woman" to us except the one God directs to marry through the confirmation of parental authority and the love He places in our own hearts.[31]

According to this logic, each person really has only one chance to make a good match. What if one learns while "courting" that the relationship is not going to work out — that there are serious flaws in the other person or perhaps severe differences in outlook or personality that seem likely to doom the union? Must he or she go ahead and marry the person anyway, since a second courtship would be inevitably stained by the first?

Unreasonable

A favorite strategy of Gothard's is to cite all the references in the Old Testament where parents arranged their children's marriages, together with unrelated passages that he somehow manages to turn into mandates for courtship, and then overwhelm his listeners with the sheer volume of *apparent* support for his view. The manner in which he delivers his teaching allows no time to consider the hermeneutic and cultural issues necessary to understand the matter or place it in its proper context.

In the Jewish culture, the father or a representative of the father often selected partners, so of course Gothard can find examples of this happening in the Bible. This custom wasn't unique to the Jews, however, but was practiced by the surrounding cultures at large and is still practiced in parts of the east today.[32] The bride had to be "bought," if you will, by the bridegroom's father, either by money or service offered in exchange for the bride's father parting with her, while the bride herself received no dowry. It was not uncommon for the bride and bridegroom to be left out of the loop regarding a match, and they were often expected to marry partners they had never even met, as in the case of Isaac and Rebecca. One man could also have multiple wives (polygamy). In that culture marriage was often treated more like a contract or property sale than a relationship. Again, as Dr. Ronald B. Allen asks:

> If the Book of Ruth were to be read as the divine mandate for courtship and marriage, then what shall we do with the heavy overlay of ancient cultural elements?
>
> - Are brides still to be purchased along with property rights?
>
> - Are bridal purchases still to be made in the presence of the elders who sit in the city gates?
>
> - Are other claimants to the bride's favor still to be rebuked in public when they find they are unable to pay the full price?
>
> - Are widows really supposed to be under the authority of their mothers-in-law, as Gothard states (p.3)? As a matter of fact, the biblical text suggests the natural, cultural thing was for the widow to return to the protection of her parents, not to stay with the parents of her deceased husband.

The point is this: Gothard picks and chooses the elements that fit his point of view. He conveniently ignores others. Then he audaciously says he has discovered God's plan for courtship.[33]

While much more could be said about these cultural traditions, the point is that it is foolish for Gothard to pick just one aspect out of this entire cultural context and then argue for its application today. He does so without appreciating the overall mindset by which these people operated, which involved far more than merely that element to which Gothard would have us return. The fact that God gave Moses laws to show people how to behave in an already existing culture with its own traditions and practices does not mean that those traditions and practices set a divine precedent. God does not command everything He permits. Although Gothard argues otherwise, he does so only selectively and refrains from strictly applying customs that would be absurd in our culture, such as polygamy (as practiced by Isaac, Solomon and others), slavery, sowing diverse seed in the field, wearing only one type of fabric, etc.

Why the Popularity?

The popularity of courtship a la Gothard has received arises not as a result of it being scriptural, but as a reaction against the trends of lawlessness and unaccountability that plague contemporary society. It is not really surprising to see courtship raising interest as parents and young people are desperate to find *something* that works. Insofar as courtship is seen to be "unworldly," it is therefore assumed to be holy and therefore right. It may be little more than a radical pendulum swing in response to the current license.

Historically, the swing of the pendulum into licentiousness causes people to look to legalism for the answer. But in reacting against the improper latitude in modern relationships, let us not go into another equally undesirable ditch whereby we put young people into straightjackets with unnecessary rules and limitations. "As the bankruptcy of the modern dating system becomes increasingly obvious, the temptation to react will be present with us on every side. But reactionary behavior is always destructive, and this does not even include the calamities brought on by overreaction."[34] We would like to now consider some specific ways that "courtship" in its current incarnation can be destructive.

It is always destructive when the will of God is usurped and put into the hands of human control and administration. Gothard, and those who follow his ideas, assume that a young person who would object to this proposal must have bad character. This sets the stage for false guilt and manipulation. Thus, a humanly staged formula becomes equivalent to the Word of God and allows no room for the possibility that God's will may be something entirely different for an individual couple.

Unworkable

This is the basic principle on which Bill Gothard's courtship hinges: one fallible human decides the will of God and imposes it upon another. It isn't the man or woman who is getting married but additional mediators between them and God. There is a certain formula or method which, if implemented, *must* work in a cause/effect mechanistic progression. It is sort of a McDonald's approach to the Christian life: Follow each step precisely and the French fries, Big Macs, etc. will come out identical all over the world. But what works in burger land does not necessarily work for human beings. We're not all potatoes, and you cannot make a French fry out of a carrot.

The basic assumption that the parents — who serve as mediators between God and their offspring, will correctly perceive the Lord's will on the matter of whom their son or daughter should marry, just does not hold water. Since the courtship must be brought to an end if there is no consensus among the parents involved, you must assume *a priori* that you are dealing with flawless parents — or at least parents who will be infallible on the question of their children's marriages, even if they are unbelievers. But life is just not like that. While parents may often offer wise counsel, we should never think of them as we would a divinely inspired prophet guaranteed to always produce the right

answers and automatically hear correctly what the Lord is decree-
ing. Nor do we have any grounds for assuming that this is God's
only or even ideal way of revealing His will.

Even if the father is godly, he may form a misimpression of a
young man for any number of reasons. Considering the extreme
bias of most parents towards their offspring, they may not be
capable of true objectivity. It is difficult to disengage one's own
desires and preferences from what one believes the Lord is
revealing. This is true no matter how honest and upright the
father, or whoever else occupies the position of authority, may
be. Is anyone truly "good enough" to measure up to son John or
daughter Sue in the eyes of most parents you know? Yet it is the
son or daughter who is marrying and must live with this person,
not the parents! We do not dispute that it is possible for God to
give wisdom and illumination to parents (or friends, siblings, or
others) concerning a young person's boy or girl friend, before a
significant relationship has been established. Our dispute is with
the assumption that God *always* works this way, or that another
person's input can be certified as coming from God and therefore must *always* be heeded. It seems to us a good rule for life to
take the advice of others into consideration when making life's
major decisions, especially the advice of someone that we know
to be wise and concerned for our best interests. But not all parents are wise, and advice cannot carry the same weight as decree,
else the God-given free will of the individual will be seriously
compromised. We must leave room for the Holy Spirit's role in
leading the individual as he or she makes decisions in life.

In the long run (and marriage *is* a long run), it would be
counterproductive for a marriage to be based on a parents' decision alone. When the going gets rough and troubles arise, a couple should ideally be able to look back on the fact that the decision to marry was based on their *own* desire to be married, their
love for each other, and the mutual belief that it was God's will
for them to marry — a belief which is not taken on the authority
of someone else, but is reached directly by the two people as they
seek the Lord individually.

We suggest that any parents who truly love their son or daughter would want their child to marry the person whom their heart truly desires and with whom they would be happiest, even if the parents would not choose to spend their lives with that person. Children are not just young copies of their parents; they are their own persons. People are different and have different tastes and differing levels of tolerance/intolerance for certain personal traits. When wise parents realize this they are in a position to offer advice, not issue orders. Rather than saying things like "You should submit to my authority by marrying the person of my choice," they will say, "I don't think you will be happy with this person" or "I think you may be mistaking true love with what is simply a passing infatuation." When there is the understanding that the parents are not trying to push their own agenda but are trying to help their child marry well while leaving the decision to the young person, most sons or daughters will welcome input if they have a good relationship with their parents.

But the goal of parent should not be to foster their son's or daughter's lifelong dependence upon *them*, but to teach dependence on God while growing their child toward increasing *independence* from them. This is not easy to do. But, the Scriptures teach that a man "shall leave his father and mother and cleave to his wife." When the day comes that your son or daughter comes home and says, "Mom, Dad, I've met someone...," the parents' reaction will fundamentally be based on two things. The first is how much they trust God with their son's or daughter's ultimate welfare; the second is how well they feel they equipped him or her to make godly decisions as the child was growing up to prepare him or her for this day.

Gothard would object on the basis of his idea of authority, which stipulates that the authority of parents applies whether a son or daughter is 5 or 35. In fact, we know of cases where 30-year-olds are still living at home because they haven't been given permission to leave home or marry. But again we must ask, what is the purpose of parents expecting obedience from their children? Is it not that the child may learn right from wrong and grow to the point where he is capable of making choices *for himself* and of moving away from being dependent on the parents to being "independently dependent" on God? As Christian author and home school advocate Charlotte Mason puts it,

> ...the authority of parents.... is itself a provisional function, and is only successful as it encourages the *autonomy*, if we may call it so, of the child....
>
> Further, though the emancipation of the children is gradual, they are acquiring day by day more of the art and science of self-government, yet there comes a day when the parents' right to rule is over; there is nothing left for them but to abdicate gracefully, and leave their grown-up sons and daughters free agents, even though these still live at home and although, in the eyes of their parents, they are not fit to be trusted with the ordering of themselves.... it is too late now to keep them in training fit or unfit, they must hold the rudder for themselves.[35]

But when does the point arrive at which the son or daughter must, as Mason puts it, "hold the rudder for themselves?" This should be a gradual process and a goal to which the parents always strive, as the child will approach in gradations the point where his or her conscience has matured to being a faculty that is not dependent on the parents. Of this maturing toward autonomy Ranald Maccaulay and Jerram Barrs write,

> Genesis 2:24 speaks of a man leaving his father and mother when he gets married. But this does not mean that marriage should be considered the moment of independence. The independence of the child should be a goal to which the parents aim. And it should be fostered deliberately so that with each succeeding year quietly and perhaps imperceptibly because of its gradualness, the child moves from being under the parents to being alongside them. The Bible gives no age at which this is to be achieved, but it is clearly the whole intention of the parent/child relationship. The parents are to view

themselves only as *in loco parentis*, that is, in the place of the parenthood of God. This is what should be uppermost in their minds. In the sense of having their children dependent on them, they are parents for only a short period. God alone is the child's permanent parent. Therefore, they are to aim at withdrawing gradually from their position of authority.[36]

Once parents relinquish their authority over their offspring, although they may remain outspoken in the counsel they offer a son or daughter, they no longer have a right to *require* obedience; their son or daughter now bears the ultimate responsibility before God for his or her own decisions. This is evident from Paul's discussion of authority in 1 Corinthians, in which he writes, "the head of every man is Christ" (1 Corinthians 11:3). He didn't say the head of every man is the family patriarch and the head of the patriarch is Christ, as Gothard implies.

This aspect of a young man or woman's personal dependence on the authority of Christ alone is crucial where the marital decision is concerned. When a man decides to marry a woman, he is making a decision that will affect him for the rest of his life, long after his parents are dead. As he is the one who will live with the consequences of the decision, whether good or bad, it is he who must be responsible for making the decision. "In any event," write McCallum and DeLashmutt:

> ...whatever obedience may be due to parents by adult Christians is not unconditional but contingent on other factors, as with all obedience to human authority. (Compare Romans 13:1 with Acts 5:29.) Some atheistic or Muslim parents, for example, would never consent to a Christian marriage. Gaining the approval of parents for marriage plans is a value that we should pursue but is not necessarily a prerequisite for marriage.[37]

If a young man or woman has not reached the point where he or she is capable of making his or her own decisions about life but is still looking to parents to be in the driver's seat, that person is obviously not yet ready to be married. As the Clinebells point out,

> Young couples who have not completed the central task of adolescence — achieving a sense of identity — have a difficult time. They both desire and fear intimacy. It is difficult for them to let go of their dependency on parents and the wider peer group. They fear change and therefore hold on to old sources of satisfaction rather than taking the risk of discovering whether marriage can become their chief resource. Because of this, in-law problems often are acute. Since parents naturally have mixed feelings about losing their offspring's dependency, they may foster this unwittingly, not recognizing that it is hurting the marriage.[38]

Parents who prolong their control and do not raise their sons and daughters with the view of encouraging the child's eventual independence run the risk of making the child ill-equipped for marriage, for, as James Dobson and Norman Wright point out:

> A frequent source of conflict is the continuation of parental dependency in one or both partners.... Parental overprotection can be a marriage killer if not recognized and handled properly.[39]

However much restriction operates in a young person's life, it is impossible, under any system, to completely achieve the ends for which Gothard aims. Consider, for example, his teaching that single people are sinning if they feel a need for companionship. That flies in the face of the Apostle Paul's teaching throughout 1 Corinthians chapter 7. Nowhere does he state that the desires are sinful; rather, he teaches that one ought to marry before natural God-given desires lead to sin. We reiterate: Was God wrong when He said of Adam, "It is not good that the man should be alone."[40] If feeling the need for companionship is sin, then God created Adam with sin or a less-than-perfect creation in the beginning.

Unwise

What about the implication that being a "one-woman-man'"means no romantic emotions towards anyone other than the person you will marry? One gets the impression from Gothard's teachings that in order to please God we must behave like emotionless robots rather than human beings. How it is possible to remain emotionally sterile until authorization, and then as a sheer act of the will become emotionally fertile, is a process he has yet to explain.

What Gothard apparently fails to realize is that the romantic feelings, crushes, and infatuations young people experience are things that, to a large extent, cannot be controlled by the will. What can be controlled is how the person *responds* to these feelings, which can come and go like the wind. To try to tamper with the emotions themselves, however, is bound to be unproductive or even counterproductive. Yet Gothard assumes that attraction is something we can control and dictate – that two people can choose not to feel attracted to each other until God's will has been revealed. The only way to prevent such "unauthorized" emotions from happening would surely be to build monasteries and nunneries to house our youth – a solution that Gothard might endorse.

Gothard questions whether this age of fervor and intensity is really a necessary passage at all. In his view, adolescent emotional tempests are simply the result of cultural pressures. The trick to avoiding negative or potentially harmful (spiritually or otherwise) emotional states is to avoid emotions and emotional attachments altogether! They are to be considered inherently sinful in and of themselves. We do not agree with this concept at all. Emotions are God-given – gaining adult control over them is a normal part of the spiritual and emotional growth process. A broken heart of the sort that has a teenager sobbing into his or her pillow one day but heals into hope the next is a natural phase of life – adolescents could use adult help to learn how to cope with this developmental process – not misguided pressure to deny what they are feeling.

Often the broken heart is a private affair — we secretly like a boy or girl but never tell anyone, least of all the person in question! — but our heart skips a beat when we pass them and we dream all day about that person. Then the person leaves the neighborhood and our world comes crashing down. Or we "fall in love" with a wonderful person in a film or book and at the end of the story the beauty of it breaks our hearts, leaving us to cry ourselves to sleep, hardly knowing why. Such are the experiences of most young people: crushes, fantasies, dreams, and feelings which are very real to us at the time.

In time, however, such feelings fade, and we grow to see things more objectively. But if, at the time, scorn or ridicule had been meted out to us, we might, out of pain and hurt, close up our hearts, and determine to always keep our thoughts and feelings to ourselves. If we were brought up to feel there was something wrong with these experiences, something of which our parents disapproved, then we might have hardened ourselves emotionally and formed a crust around our hearts out of a desperation to be "correct." Others, unable to do this, may live in a perpetually guilt-ridden state, too ashamed to share their "sinful feelings" with anyone.

A broken heart may indeed be part of the Lord's plan in a person's life, to help mature that person, to teach them valuable lessons about themselves and others, and to draw that person closer to His heart. If, however, parents simply assume that broken hearts must be prevented at all costs and that it is always contrary to God's will when a person goes through a "tragic" relationship, then they are in danger of standing in the way of God's plan for that young person's life.

Parents who adopt Gothard's destructive view of normal adolescence may prevent guilt-prone youths from falling into the "sin" of having a crush on someone (or of admitting it if they do), but they will also prevent that child from experiencing the natural healing of that broken heart. The parent who is trying to tie up their youth's emotions is not at the same time able to help that youth come to terms with those feelings, to face them, accept them, grow from them, and grow out of them.

We are not saying that having a broken heart is an inherently good thing simply because we can grow from it, or that we should *try* to get our hearts broken in order to learn lessons. This is actually true of any kind of suffering. Although we should not go out of our way to experience suffering, neither should we go to extraordinary lengths to prevent it, and in the process unwittingly bring long-term harm to the very person we wish to protect for the moment.

It is the job of a parent to help young people grow through broken hearts rather than to lock them into emotionless closets to prevent any possibility of broken hearts. All parents desire to protect their children from pain of all kinds, but we all know that this is an absolute impossibility. It is a far better and attainable goal to be there for them and with them in their pain and to give them the tools necessary to deal with the various pains that life *inevitably* brings. In order to keep the child from ever committing the "sin" of having a broken heart you would need to train the child to have a heart that cannot be broken. A heart that cannot love is tragic indeed. C.S. Lewis puts this well:

> I believe that the most lawless and inordinate loves are less contrary to God's will than a self-invited and self-protective lovelessness.... We shall draw nearer to God, not by trying to avoid the sufferings inherent in all loves, but by accepting them and offering them to Him; throwing away all defensive armor. If our hearts need to be broken, and if He chooses this as the way in which they should break, so be it.[41]

An unattainable quest for an emotion-free, pain-free life has nothing to do with the true gospel, which produces a lightness and freedom and trust in God. There is no freedom in Gothard's brand of "Christianity," certainly no lightness. To place so much responsibility on a person to get every detail right one hundred percent of the time with complete emotional control is bondage of the worst sort. The emphasis is placed on *our* control, not God's.

Could it be that severe problems naturally arise among those who have been instructed to repress this side of our humanity? Is it possible that this mentality heavily contributed to the huge sex scandal that rocked Gothard's ministry in 1980 (see chapter 1)?

By repression we mean something very different than the control a mature person exercises over his or her natural passions and instincts. We mean the attempt, not to control but to *eradicate* such instincts, treating them — whether consciously or unconsciously — as things that are sinful, to try to bury them in a dark closet and hope they reemerge as infrequently as possible. Emotional castration *does not work*. Most often, the thing we try not to think about is the very thing that becomes the focus of our attention and overcomes us with a vengeance. There are examples in history which show this at work. Isabel Tang provides an account of one of the monasteries in Egypt, which had been founded by Pachomius (290-347). Central to these monk's asceticism was a pervasive sense of spiritual danger attached to anything remotely sexual. The rules the monks observed to reduce the temptation involved everything from rules against tucking their tunics up too high when washing clothes, to having their knees uncovered when sitting together, to prohibitions on being alone together in the dark. In the end, the extreme repression of sexuality led to an obsession with sexuality. In an attempt to prevent the temptations of sex, the whole organization of their life revolved around one thing — sex.[42] In this way, intense concentration on an object of paranoia can easily become a displaced outlet for that very thing through a kind of reverse fixation. The Apostle Paul shows this well in Romans chapter 7.

In addition to these observations, this sort of mentality tends towards a dichotomy between the things of the spirit and normal emotions. In this environment, young people have no idea how to give the Lord control of these areas because they have been taught to expect Him to take them away. In exactly the same way that Gothard teaches that loneliness is sin that must be repented of, emotions, which are a normal aspect of our humanity, are portrayed as "unspiritual." Romance and passion

are not viewed as something in which our whole person partici-
pates, but treated instead almost like a "thing" external to us that
we take on and off. It is always dangerous when life is divided
into compartments like this, for "the Lord made the whole of life,
and He has a place and a plan for each part."[43]

Can young people who grow up under such systems ever feel
fully comfortable about their own emotions and sexuality even
when enjoyed in the arms of a spouse? The liberation that love
should bring means that there need not be lasting jealousy over
the other's past boyfriends or girlfriends, as if this posed a lasting injury to the marriage. On the contrary, when a man or
woman who are right for each other fall in love and get married,
each is able to find healing from past mistakes through the love
of their spouse. Each is able to find in the other the fulfillment
of all their earlier dreams and romantic aspirations.

Consequently, the idea that a person will do damage to their
future marriage if they "release their heart" before first finding
out from God who they are to marry, is a fear indicating a totally false understanding of marriage. The idea that romantic relationships, emotions, or thoughts prior to marriage with anyone
other than one's future spouse leaves "less" of oneself to give in
marriage is a groundless fear. Emotions are not a limited quanti-
ty of something which is spent once and gone. Rather they have
the capacity for renewal. We see this in 1 Peter 4:8 where the
apostle writes, "And above all things have fervent charity among
yourselves: for charity shall cover the multitude of sins." The
word translated "fervent" has the idea of "stretched out" or
"expanded" and results in a covering over. Where love is true,
unconditional, and exclusive in a marriage, it overcomes any feelings of jealousy over past relationships through the solid reassur-
ance it provides.

While it is possible for past relationships to permanently
harm a present marriage, the problem probably lies with the
current relationship between husband and wife, not with past
relationships.

In all of Gothard's writing and teaching on the subject of

courtship and marriage, there is a complete absence of any under-standing of this special kind of intimacy between a man and a woman that cements a marriage together. In Gothard's booklet *Understanding the Biblical Foundations of Marriage*, no mention is made of anything even relating to intimate love. When Gothard does mention love, it is cold and clinical. Although Gothard's teaching on courtship does not explicitly *forbid* romantic love, one gets the impression that if it happens it's a bonus, not an essential ingredient for marriage. Safety is what matters, and giv-ing one's heart can truly be scary in an insecure world. However, the words of C.S. Lewis should be carefully considered:

> There is no safe investment. To love at all is to be vul-nerable. Love anything and your heart will certainly be wrung and possibly be broken. If you want to make sure of keeping it intact, you must give your heart to no one, not even to an animal. Wrap it carefully round with hob-bies and little luxuries; avoid all entanglements; lock it up safe in the casket or coffin of your selfishness. But in that casket — safe, dark, motionless, airless — it will change. It will not be broken; it will become unbreakable, impene-trable, irredeemable. The alternative to tragedy, or at least the risk of tragedy, is damnation. The only place out-side Heaven where you can be perfectly safe from all the dangers and perturbations of love is Hell.[44]

Chapter 10

Bill Gothard — Medicine Man

H ealth and well being have been a concern and interest through much of human history. From a Christian worldview we realize that sickness, disease, aging, and a whole host of suffering and maladies are the result of the Fall. The Apostle Paul wrote:

> And if Christ be in you, the body is dead because of sin; but the Spirit is life because of righteousness. But if the Spirit of him that raised up Jesus from the dead dwell in you, he that raised up Christ from the dead shall also quicken your mortal bodies by his Spirit that dwelleth in you.[1]

In addition to the stress of physical suffering there is sometimes mental anguish that accompanies the question, "Why me, Lord?"

In the desire to eliminate pain and suffering and bring about healing, medical science has made great strides, particularly over the last century, in understanding the human body and the nature of physical sickness and disease. Medicine has come a long way from the days when "bleeding" a patient to eliminate sickness was common practice. To be sure, medical science and doctors have made mistakes along the way and will continue to do so for the foreseeable future.

The average lay person often finds himself unsure of who or what to believe. In general, the public has come to regard family doctors and specialists as the experts in giving sound medical advice, while recognizing that doctors are fallible human beings who can and do make mistakes in their diagnoses. But another movement is afoot in the land, the alternative medicine show, which demonizes the medical establishment and offers its own cures for what ails us. Some of their advice is good common sense, but much of it is based upon junk science and/or New Age mysticism. Bill Gothard's medical advice which is disseminated from his Medical Training Institute of America closely resembles the latter.

William Dabney, M.D., who has been involved with Bill Gothard for some time, states,

> I have been increasingly alarmed since our association with Mr. Gothard over the last ten years, and over the last eight years as part of his home-school program, that he has overstepped his bounds in medicine. My daughter spent two and a half years in the midwifery training program, and finally I took her out of it because of a lack of clinical experience and clinical training. They emphasized a lot of the spiritual side of medicine. They emphasized Scripture memory and doing analogies on every illness or disease as being perhaps caused by a spiritual illness.[2]
>
> [Gothard's] *Basic Care Bulletins* under the MTIA are somewhat misleading and many times mix a great deal of homeopathic medicine with allopathic and they rely upon marginal references, many of them from Eastern Religion concepts that I feel are very unfounded. He does cause his followers to be very fearful of medical doctors and puts them at a bad light.[3]

As you find with all natural methods or homeopathic

treatment, it works for some but not for all, and much of it is not really not much more than witchcraft. [4]

The Medical Training Institute of America

In an effort to guide his followers in all areas of life, Bill Gothard started the Medical Training Institute of America. MTIA has produced a number of booklets and other information intended to assist followers in assessing and guiding their medical health decisions. The booklets cover a variety of topics including, *How to Make Wise Medical Decisions*, *How to Greatly Reduce the Risk of Common Diseases*, *The Vital Role of the Church in Wise Medical Decisions*, fasting, gallstones, immunizations, adoption, and much more. Unfortunately, in addition to much of what might be construed as practical, educational medical advice, Bill Gothard also presents diagnoses and cures for medical problems, which in some cases could possibly cause serious harm.

Where would one begin in evaluating Bill Gothard's medical advice? We started with *Basic Care Booklet 1*, *How to Make Wise Medical Decisions*. In the introduction we find the first of many assaults on the reader through the Scripture twisting and mystical medical style of Mr. Gothard. We read:

> God will hold us personally responsible for what we do to our bodies or allow to be done to them. *[God] will render to every man according to his deeds (Romans 2:6.)*.[5]

Of course, Romans 2:6 has nothing to do with medical decisions but rather is Paul's condemnation of the moralist, the man who judges others for what he himself practices. The Apostle Paul's point in this section is that people are responsible to God for the light He has given to them regarding their *spiritual* condition. As Dr. Earl Radmacher writes,

> God holds humanity responsible for this light of revelation through their conscience because they "show the work of the law written in their hearts, their conscience also bearing witness, and between themselves their

thoughts accusing or else excusing them" (2:15).[6]

Bill Gothard then strikes the chord that seems to be his favorite theme song — encouraging fear and distrust of doctors, stating in the manual that many of them "make extremely unwise and very damaging medical decisions."[7] Bill Gothard has produced these booklets to, as he puts it, "provide clear scriptural direction and wise medical knowledge which will allow God's people to make the wisest possible medical decisions regarding their health care."[8]

This introduction creates the first dilemma for readers. First they are told, and rightly so, that *they* are responsible for any medical decisions they make. This makes for a convenient disclaimer, limiting Gothard's responsibility if anyone should get sicker or even die while following his medical prescriptions. Yet on the other hand, Gothard tells them that God expects them to follow certain principles in health issues, which of course just happen to be the very principles that Gothard so neatly lays out for them. While we agree that adult human beings are ultimately responsible for decisions they make, Gothardites have been conditioned over time to uncritically accept all of Gothard's "advice" as from the Lord, which greatly hurts their ability to freely choose to disagree with MTIA material. After being warned not to trust doctors, readers are told that the purpose of this information is to give "clear scriptural direction." So, it follows that if one doubts what is contained in the booklets and other MTIA information, the conclusion can only be that they are fighting/doubting/rejecting Scripture. This material is not by any means being set forth as simply Bill Gothard's *opinions*. By implication, those rejecting these works are rejecting God's will for their lives.

What's in a Name?

Let's jump right in, then, and see what "Scripture" has to say about medical issues. According to Doctor Bill, where should you begin if you have a health problem, or just want to improve your health in general? Well, in MTIA *Booklet 1*, Bill Gothard would have you start by writing your name down in the booklet,[9] then writing the meaning of your name,[10] and then writing down what your "name related to good health would be."[11] He gives the following example:

> My name is Bill.
> My name means "protector."
> My name, related to good health, means:

> "*I am to protect my own health and the health of others.*"[12]

This is absurd. What if your name has nothing to do with good health? What if no matter what ridiculous lengths you go to in order to somehow make it *appear* related, such as Bill's "protector" example, you know it really doesn't work? Does that mean you are destined to a life of chronic sickness unless you change your name to Penicillin or Preparation H? The medical mysticism promoted by Bill Gothard begins here. For those who need to know the curative power inherent in a name, they are referred to his *Life Notebook* and *ATI Wisdom Booklet 17*.

We do know that biblical names have meanings which correspond to characteristics of specific ancient individuals or particular events in their lives. For example, Jacob means "following after" or "supplanter" and was given him after his curious birth because "his hand took hold on Esau's heel" (Genesis 25:26). Jacob's name was later changed to Israel, which means "ruling with God" (Genesis 32:28). The occasion for the name change was his wrestling match with God. Up to that point Jacob had lived a life of deception, including deceiving his father when he brought stew and pretended to be Esau. Jacob's father asked, "Who *art* thou, my son?" and Jacob lied in order to receive the blessing (Genesis 27:18). In Genesis 32 Jacob again asked for a blessing and God asked, "What is thy name?" This time Jacob answered honestly. We see from the context of the accounts that his name didn't *cause* his behavior — his behavioral change brought about the name change. We see this process numerous times in Scripture. Bill Gothard makes a mistake in promoting a mechanistic cause-and-effect relationship between someone's name and life circumstance. It is a sort of mystical determinism. The idea that there is a mystical power in someone's name which causes certain behaviors and events in his or her life is closer to occultism than to biblical Christianity.

In *ATI Wisdom Booklet 17* under the heading Medical Resource, we are told the story of a woman named Maria. In a conversation, Maria was asked about the meaning of her name:

> "Did you know that the basic meaning from which your name comes is *myrrh*, like the myrrh that the wise men brought as one of the three precious gifts to Christ? The myrrh is a bitter plant..."
>
> Maria interrupted her, "O yes, my husband always tells me that I'm bitter."
>
> The director's wife picked up on this statement. "Maria, did you know that the Bible says that bitterness will poison your body and the lives of those around you and can even cause you to have cancer of the bone marrow?"
>
> "O yes," said Maria. "The doctors told me last week that I have cancer."[13]

Is it truly Gothard's belief that Maria's name somehow caused her bitterness that caused her cancer? The thought boggles the mind. Even aside from the name business, does the Bible anywhere teach that bitterness causes "cancer of the bone marrow?" Where is the Scripture that states this? If Maria changes her name, will that change her character and effect a cure? Do all people named Maria ultimately get bone cancer? Are they all bitter people? Maria became a Christian, and we are moved on to another anecdotal report, but we are never told how Maria overcame the mystical power of her name.

But so far, in the introduction to the MTIA booklet and this additional information the reader is put in fear of doctors and brought into mysticism, under the guise of receiving the "scriptural" teaching on medicine.

Preparing to Meet the Doctor

On page five of *Basic Care Booklet 1* there is a recitation of the gospel with a place to record the date and place where you became a Christian. On page 6, you are required to enter the date and place when "I dedicated myself to God...." Then at the bottom of the page are "Questions to ask when consulting a doctor." The questions are:

1. What experience and results have you had in treating my condition?

2. Would you allow me to talk to a former patient who had my condition?

3. Will you honor present X-rays that I have (to avoid unnecessary rads)?

4. What are your charges for a consultation only with no tests?

    • Any test should be explained on a consent form before approval is given.

    • Do as much research as possible on your condition before your visit to the doctor.

    • A wise and trusted person should accompany you on every doctor visit.[14]

How could a physician answer question 1 until he knows what your condition *is?* An examination would have to be performed, symptoms discussed, and a diagnosis made *before* he would even know what condition he was dealing with. If the physician is unfamiliar with the condition or recognizes that it is outside of his or her realm of experience, the normal practice in 21st century America is to recommend a specialist. In cases of major, or potentially life-threatening illness, it is always advisable to get a second opinion if that is possible. But that is just common sense, not a moral or spiritual issue.

The second question is more problematic. You would have to

find an unethical physician who would be willing to violate doctor-patient confidentiality by putting you in touch with his former patients. In addition, it is also necessary to find a doctor who is unprofessional enough to accept obsolete X-rays that may tell him nothing about conditions that have developed since they were originally taken. To further instill fear of physicians, the reader is told that a "wise and trusted person should accompany you on every doctor visit."

Page 7 gives two things you must do to prepare for the visit to the doctor. Under the section titled, "Help your doctor to listen," Bill Gothard provides the reader with a homey little anecdote about a mother who had a boy with severe asthma, compounded by problems with kidney stones and bedwetting. The latest doctor the parents had taken the boy to wanted to see his medical records, but the mother preferred to just explain the problem to the doctor. This resulted in an accurate diagnosis and treatment. It's a great story — and perhaps useful, especially for people who are going to see doctors about medical problems with long histories, although it would seem wise for the doctor to look at the patient's records as well as listen to his story. It is true that doctors are not all-knowing, and the more information they have the better diagnosis they are likely to make. But of course it would not affect people who are dealing with new problems for which there is no history. Medical records may provide a link to the current ailment or eliminate connections to past ailments. The story does, however, tend to further undermine confidence in doctors as medical professionals.

Personal Assessment

The next subsection tells people to "Learn to be medically alert."[15] Bill Gothard explains that the next few pages are "designed to increase your alertness to what is actually happening to you during an illness and also what has happened to you and your family in the past."[16] By filling it out you will be able to assist your healthcare provider to make an accurate diagnosis. Pages 8-12 contain a list of questions with appropriate blanks for you to fill in:

1. What is my Chief Complaint (C.C.)?

2. When did my problem begin?

3. How did my problem begin?

4. Where does it hurt?

5. How does it hurt?

6. How often does it hurt?

7. How long does it hurt?

8. When does it hurt?

9. How does the pain affect other functions, or how is the pain affected by other functions?

10. What makes it feel better?

11. What makes it feel worse?

12. Have I ever felt these symptoms before?

13. If so, what treatment was I given for them?

14. Were these treatments successful?

15. Is constipation a problem?

Examples are then given as to how the patient might answer the question. We noted that "example answers" seem designed to lead in a certain direction. For instance, the example for question 3, "How did my problem begin?" is, "We went out to eat as a family and I noticed some pain about two hours after I ate French fries." The example for question 8 is similar: "The pain usually occurs two hours after eating fatty foods." And for question 11, you read, "Eating fatty foods makes it feel worse." And you think to yourself, "Okay! Okay! I get the picture! Cut out fatty foods!"

The Great Constipational Crisis

The last question asks, "Is constipation a problem?" Bill Gothard places great emphasis on the problem of constipation and devotes an entire page to the subject, in which the reader is asked detailed questions about the frequency of bowel movements and the size, consistency, and buoyancy of his stool. Gothard calls constipation the "most neglected sign and cause of illness."

Then on page 14 we find that there are still "further steps to take." The first step is to pray for wisdom."[17] Certainly prayer for wisdom should be a part of our daily walk with Christ. Many seem to live with the philosophy, "Why pray when you can worry?" So reminding people to pray about their health problems is certainly sound advice, and we have no quarrel with it. The next section, though, swerves off the track into medical mysticism.

Step two is to "Complete a spiritual examination." It is first flatly stated that a "majority of illnesses can be traced to spiritual problems," citing 1 Corinthians 11:28-30 to prove this point.[18] This is just another example of Gothard's propensity to misuse Scripture to back his own biased and, in this case, highly judgmental opinion. The passage states that *many* in the Corinthian congregation were sick because they took communion in an unworthy manner, but it does not say at all that a *majority* of illnesses stem from this source. This loads unnecessary and probably unfair guilt onto a person who is ill. Serious illnesses strike the elderly in far greater proportion than they do the younger among us...are the elderly greater sinners than the rest? And what about innocent babies? It reminds one of the disciple's ignorant question when they came upon the man blind from birth,: And his disciples asked him, saying, Master who did sin, this man or his parents, that he was born blind? (John 9:1-2) It is true, as the apostle Paul said, that some illness might result from taking communion without proper introspection. But we are instructed to examine *ourselves*; we are never told to examine our every illness and look for evidence of possible divine punishment in every one.

There is a major contradiction in Bill's thinking in the matter of illness. If it is true, as he says, that the majority of illnesses are caused by spiritual problems, what is the point of worrying about getting enough fiber in your diet to eliminate constipation? Will God's judgment be thwarted by a regular helping of shredded wheat every morning?

Demonic Birthing Rooms

There is a proper fear of God that can help us avoid being casual about committing sin, but Bill Gothard would have us not just fear God and act righteously, but to actually fear dolls! For example, his MTIA literature gives Cabbage Patch dolls the ability to cause mothers who had come full term in their pregnancies to be unable to deliver until the homes were cleansed "from evil influences."

> At one birth, the mom had been in labor for two or three days with no signs of problems for the mother or baby, but no progress. This was baby number five. The Lord prompted me to ask them about any items in their home through which Satan could gain entrance to interfere. There was a Cabbage Patch doll in their home. They threw it outside and agreed to burn it when they could get a fire going. Within two hours, this mom had a beautiful son.
>
> In the home of another born-again Christian couple, there was a similar situation, only with a rebellious daughter and lots of trolls in addition. This mom was not dilating well. Again, the Lord burdened me to approach this couple about what they had in their home that might allow demonic influence. I had seen one troll doll in their bathroom. They agreed to get rid of any they had — the dad collected a grocery bag full! Out went the trolls. This family had their first successful home birth that morning after having attempted one years before.[19]

One wonders, if the midwife had not disposed of the offending Cabbage Patch and troll dolls, would the babies still be in the womb? Is this type of "medical advice" really any different than shamans who convince their people that thunder is the result of making the gods angry?

Connecting disease to root spiritual causes

In Bill Gothard's year 2000 invitation to *The Minister's and Christian Leader's Seminar*, he writes that:

> Osteoporosis is a disease that causes the bones to deteriorate. Scripture states that, "envy is the rottenness of the bones." Scripture also says that a wife that shames her husband "is as rottenness of the bones."[20]

Does the Bible really teach that osteoporosis is caused by envy or a disrespectful wife? Absolutely not. Here again, we see Bill Gothard's penchant for reading into the text something that is not there. Neither passage cited is a medical diagnosis nor a predictor of medical conditions based on spiritual issues. These are metaphors, literary devices used to illustrate deeper truths. Envy and a wife who shames her husband have a similar effect spiritually and emotionally to that which "rottenness of the bones" has on physical well being. Proverbs is made up of wise statements to assist us in understanding spiritual and emotional issues. But, as we have pointed out throughout this book, Bill Gothard sacrifices the "meat" of a passage on the altar of proof-texting. The result is the elevation of his personal opinion to the level of inspired truth.

It doesn't end there. In the same document he writes:

> A discerning pastor in Georgia has traced eighty diseases to their spiritual causes. He is getting a 90 percent success rate in helping people clear up diseases such as rheumatoid arthritis, allergies, asthma, bulimia, Crohn's disease, heart disease, scoliosis, ulcerated colitis, osteoporosis, Parkinson's disease, and certain types of cancer.[21]

The "discerning pastor" is Pastor Henry Wright of Thomaston, Georgia. He claims in his book that women develop breast cancer because they hate their mothers[22] and that lupus is caused by self-hatred.[23] Demons, in Wright's view, are passed on genetically, and when the demon is cast out there are "genetic code changes."[24] Multiple sclerosis is the result of "deep, deep self-hatred, and guilt."[25] According to Wright, colon cancer is the result of how you treat others:

> There are a lot of strange things happening between the lips and the anus, and in between all kinds of things can go wrong for many spiritual reasons. If you poop on enough people, it comes back to you.[26]

That Bill Gothard considers such a man to be a "discerning pastor" is a scandal in its own right, and the fact that he advocates such horrific teaching should alarm us greatly.

The "Fast" Way to Health

According to Bill Gothard, Isaiah 58:8 promises that fasting will produce an "immediate improvement in health."[27] But if you read Isaiah 58:8 in the context of the chapter, you will see that it is not *physical* fasting that will bring about the promised benefits, but a "spiritual fast" of living righteously — caring for the poor, freeing the oppressed, etc. God *specifically rejects* the physical fasting that the people were performing in order to secure His blessing and personal well-being. He says that this is not the fast He seeks. As Charles C. Ryrie points out in his study Bible, God through Isaiah is showing "The Contrast between Right and Wrong Worship."[28] The prophet was addressing a spiritual problem which, if corrected, would bring about spiritual healing. Physical health is not the promise of this passage. Yet Gothard, true to form, does not let these facts get in the way of a good story. Gothard's use of this passage is simply another in a long string of out-of-context quotations which do not support the point claimed for them.

Fasting is certainly a practice found in the pages of Scripture. It may have some physical benefits as well as spiritual ones, but whatever medical benefits may accrue as a result of fasting were *never* the focus of Scripture. Scriptural fasting was a denial of self, not a means of self-enrichment. And what benefits may arise from the practice, it should be recognized that fasting is potentially dangerous. The Arthritis Foundation points out:

> The dangers of fasting far outweigh its benefits. Fasting without medical supervision is dangerous for anyone, but especially for people with arthritis. For one thing, fasting can cause a loss of muscle. Because people with inflammatory diseases like rheumatoid arthritis often have low muscle to begin with, fasting may be especially dangerous to them.

Yet Bill Gothard, through one of his myriad anecdotal stories, claims that fasting can *relieve* arthritis, thus encouraging arthritic people to engage in something potentially quite injurious to them. The following is the story of an arthritic woman who, along with her husband, fasted for the spiritual benefit of one of her children.

> Throughout the fast we drank only purchased distilled water...on the fifth day, I decided to try to bend the first joints of my ring fingers, as they had been "frozen" by arthritis for years. *Praise the Lord!* They both bent! I was thrilled and have kept them mobile ever since.[29]

According to Gothard, a person is to discern ahead of time the proper type and correct length of the fast. They might go on a total fast (no food or water), a normal fast (water but no food), or a partial fast of limiting their choices of food. They might fast for only one meal, or one day, for two or three days, or for longer periods. He offers us the example of Christ to illustrate this last type, "Who went without food for forty days."[30]

Gothard does not discourage people from long fasts, although he does acknowledge they can be dangerous and recommends doctor involvement. In fact, he greatly encourages them with these words;

> In the Basic Care Program, we have a significant

opportunity to carry out our research in the area of fasting which will make a valuable contribution to the field of health care. Fasts of between twenty and forty days will be of great significance for purposes of medical research; however, this goal should not override God's leading in your particular case.[31]

The key to safety in fasting, as in all of life, is to make sure you are under the protection of your God-given authority:

In every area of our lives, the Lord Jesus Christ must be our teacher and our example. In the matter of fasting, we can draw clear guidelines from His way of life and His experience during an extended fast. Before Jesus undertook an extended fast at the age of thirty, He was in subjection to the authority of His parents.[32]

Just as Jesus did nothing of His own will but did only the will of His Heavenly Father, so we must be sure that our fast is directed by the Lord. God directs us through the counsel of His Word, through the promptings of the Holy Spirit, and through the counsel of God-given authorities.[33]

Please note that Gothard places the advice of your human "authorities" right up there with the Bible and the Holy Spirit! Presumably, your proper "authorities" would be schooled in Gothard-think, and so would be very open to the idea of a seemingly healthy and well-nourished individual (as people allegedly will be if they follow Gothard's rules on eating) fasting for a dangerously long period of time.

Interestingly, though, after all Gothard's talk of parental authority even extending into adulthood, he does seem to make an exception here to following parental wisdom. Why do you suppose that is? It may be because many or most parents would balk at the idea of their child doing something so dangerous, even parents whose minds have been conditioned to knee-jerk reactions with the ideas of Bill Gothard!

The cautions that parents will normally have for a son or

daughter who wants to engage in a longer fast will not necessarily be God's direction not to do it.[34]

G. Richard Fisher, commenting on fasting in general and extended fasting in particular, in an article about *Dake's Annotated Reference Bible*, states;

> Jews in Christ's time usually fasted once a week. The Pharisee's claim to fame in Luke 18:12 was that he "fasted twice in the week." As well the Jewish fast was never total but only cutting down of quantities of food.
>
> In *The Land and the Book*, William Thompson said of fasting: "You may take this as a general canon of interpretation, that any amount much less than usual means nothing in their dialect; and if you understand more by it, you are misled. In fact, their ordinary fasting is only abstaining from certain kinds of food, not from all, nor does the word convey any other idea to them."
>
> Dake's suggestion of a 40-day fast would be a disaster if anyone tried to take him seriously. Yes, Jesus did it, but Jesus was Jesus! Except in rare cases, the fasts recorded in the Bible were one-day affairs. Only five fast days were commanded in the Old Testament (Leviticus 23 and Zechariah 8). There were occasional spontaneous one-time fasts for various reasons. The Pharisees piled on more fast days than required by God through their traditions. Colossians teaches that no man can require or command a Christian to fast. But to even suggest we could do it for 40 days, with benefit no less, is foolish and dangerous.[35]

Gothard does suggest that if one has certain serious health conditions, such as heart or kidney disease that require medication, he should get encouragement and supervision from his physician. But if one has learned anything from the *Bulletins* so far, it is that physicians cannot be trusted, and our spiritual authorities' advice counts for more than that of supposed worldly men.

Does Gothard know that he is asking people to do something potentially very harmful to their health? Yes he does:

There are also, however, physical symptoms which should indicate when it is time to end a fast. These would include unusual heart palpitation, prolonged headaches, extreme weakness, or other symptoms that would indicate the need for food. In any case, a person on a prolonged fast should be under medical observation.[36]

Confusion reigns, however, as to who might be responsible if you are indeed hurt seriously by an extended fast:

It was the Holy Spirit who led Jesus to fast for forty days, and afterward he was fed by the angels. It could be the evil one who prompts us to fast for eighty days, and afterward we are reproved with sickness and death.

Let's see — Doctors are bad, Fasting is good. Fasting can cure many diseases and conditions and is hugely beneficial physically and spiritually. The Bible and the Holy Spirit and your "authorities," except perhaps your fear-mongering parents, will tell you when and how long to fast, but if you fast *too* long and get very sick or even die, that counsel may have come from the devil. Of course! That wily old devil!

More questionable advice

Potentially more dangerous advice is given to parents of small children regarding whether to have their children immunized from childhood diseases. As usual, the scare is on:

Likewise, as side effects and consequences of the vaccines become more apparent, it may prove true that the disease is less threatening than the vaccine itself.[37]

Some estimate that 6,500 children experience temporary convulsions, and as many as fifty children a year suffer permanent brain damage. Others, however, estimate that eleven to twelve thousand children a year suffer sufficient brain damage to be labeled "learning disabled." [38]

Perhaps the link between the pertussis vaccine and

Sudden Infant Death Syndrome (SIDS) is the most frightening.... Today, there are nearly 10,000 SIDS deaths a year in the United States. Of these deaths, a significant number may be, at least, triggered by the pertussis vaccine.[39]

Let's see: "it may prove true" and "perhaps" are the scriptural reasons to avoid vaccines at all costs? Here is an area where Doctor Bill is less than reliable. As Dr. William Dabney comments:

A physician assistant living in Colorado and I were asked to review the Basic Care Bulletin "Vaccinations and Immunizations," we basically tore it apart and rewrote most of it. I am not sure if it was ever published again, but there was a great deal of anecdotal stories used as fact, and it promoted a great deal of misinformation and fear. This is in a day when we saw a tremendous outbreak in diphtheria in the Soviet Union following a change in government because of the lack of immunization programs and had over a millions deaths worldwide annually from measles. The question about the need for immunizations is really not a problem anywhere except the United States. People all over the world are crying for immunizations. My conclusion of course, is that we have been sated with good health for years...[40]

The Same Old New Approach

Earlier Bill Gothard discredited medical records as having any value in favor of "helping the doctor to listen." But now item 4 in this section is *Document Your Own Medical History*. By creating your own medical history "you will communicate to your doctor that you have assumed personal responsibility for your health-care decisions."[41] The history you create is to be used for "Vital medical research."[42] Writes Gothard:

Through the Basic CARE Program, we have an opportunity to research a "new" approach to medicine. This approach is based on the universal, non-optional principles of God's Word.

A careful examination of the material shows that there is really nothing "new" here. It is so far simply the same old alternative healthcare that you can find in any bookstore these days, *ad nauseum*. Many of these alternative medical books instill the same fear and distrust of the medical establishment as Gothard does. Every doctor is assumed to be part of the problem and is only seeking after his or her own personal enrichment. One way that the medical establishment allegedly soaks you is through the use of tests.

> ...about two-thirds of all tests are of no benefit to the patient. Among the reasons motivating tests are: the inexperience of the medical staff, the fear of malpractice, the overuse of consultants, the "hunt-and peck" method of diagnosis, and business connections with laboratories and expensive equipment.[43]

Take Two Elders and Call Me in the Morning

Gothard, of course, has a solution to this problem — call for the elders.

> Anyone who puts himself in the hands of doctors for major medical care before calling for the elders of the church is making an unwise decision.[44]

Let's consider this advice. How would it work out in the real world? Let's just say you are experiencing severe chest pain and realize that you are having a heart attack. A major medical decision is required here — a very quick decision at that. Should you a) call for the elders or b) call an ambulance? Bill Gothard has told us that any course of action besides first calling the elders is "an unwise decision." We disagree. In this life-threatening situation minutes and sometimes seconds will mean the difference between life and death. Should the elders, church family, and immediate family be called and have them pray? Absolutely! But someone else should call them *while you are on your way to the hospital!* This is just common sense. But Gothard would have you meticulously follow his alleged "biblical" steps to handle the crisis.

- I am to initiate the call to the elders.

- I am to confess my faults to the Lord and to them.

- I am to be anointed with oil.

- I am to exercise the prayer of faith.[45]

You have to be the initiator of the call to the elders. Sure, your lips are turning blue and the pain is increasing exponentially, but can you really afford to break God's supposed rule for making major medical decisions? This mandatory biblical principle is so important that MTIA has devoted Booklet 3 to this topic. What about confessing your sins to the elders? How much precious time will that require? All of this must be done before you can call the doctor? It sounds like a prescription for disaster.

Anti-Science

We don't know exactly where to place Gothard on the spectrum of alternative medical philosophies. But one thing is clear: he is anti-science.

As we page along in Booklet 1, we come to page 24, which is entitled, "Know what to do if hospital care is required." Here Gothard argues that 15 to 25 per cent of all surgeries are unnecessary that medications are over prescribed or incorrectly prescribed. Then, on pages 25-27, Gothard provides an extensive form to use in the event that a family member is ever hospitalized. It is entitled, "Daily Log of Visits by Hospital Personnel." It's actually rather simple, with columns for dates and times, the name and title of the person making the visit, what procedures were performed, and any comments. It's like a patient chart, except that the patient is the one keeping it (or a family member keeping it for him, assuming they're there around the clock). This, of course, is in addition to the chart the hospital keeps for the patient.

This personal chart-keeping is in step with the general atmosphere of mistrust and fear of physicians that Gothard's MTIA series encourages from the beginning. But now Gothard's antipathy comes right out in the open with a four-page (28-31) diatribe against medical science entitled, "Understand the Limitations of 'Modern Medicine.'"

In these pages Gothard comes out against the inductive method, calling it "dangerous." This is ironic, if not bizarre, since the very form that Gothard prescribes on pages 25-27 is a model of the inductive method, providing detailed information in chronological order regarding every step of a patient's treatment. Yet Gothard demonizes this same method on pages 28-31, even going so far as to claim that Francis Bacon (1561-1626) "rejected the truth of Scripture" — which, as anyone who has ever actually read Bacon's writings knows, is completely false.[46]

Man's Quest for White Bread

The love of white bread is seemingly the root of all evil. In *Basic Care Bulletin 2* we are told that most bad health is a result of rejecting God-given, home-made whole-grain bread and eating sinful man's store-bought white bread. According to MTIA, Jesus Himself confirmed this in John 6:35.[47] Here again we have a mixture of what may be some very good and useful information interspersed with Scripture-twisting to make it seem "spiritual." It is generally held to be true that whole-grain breads are more healthy than white bread. However, even a cursory reading of John 6 shows that Jesus was not speaking about nutrition.

Did you know there is a "spiritual" method of bread-baking? In the *Basic Care Bulletin 2*, 26-31, we are taught to bake a spiritually perfect loaf of bread. This includes how to properly knead it (by hand, no machines) and the role of yeast. But then, after all of that, we find out on page 30 that even if we bake God's bread God's way it may not be nutritious if we are not obedient to God's Word.

Following All The Rules In Bread-Making Is Still Ineffective Without Obedience To God's Word. Complete mixing, thorough kneading, patient rising, and exact baking may produce a perfect loaf of bread, but it will not furnish perfect nutrition. Jesus made it very clear that "...man shall not live by bread alone, but by every word that proceedeth out of the mouth of God" (Matthew 4:1-4)!

The Church and Health Care

MTIA's *Basic Care Bulletin 3*, which is titled, *The Vital Role of the Church in Wise Medical Decisions*, continues the trend of demonizing medical science. According to the introduction, "doctors, hospitals and insurance companies"[48] are all vying for control in medical decisions. They are leaving out the church and the patient in their drive for power and money. According to MTIA this has brought about an unprecedented medical crisis!

> This contest of control has both caused and contributed to the malpractice crisis of our day. Malpractice suits, in turn, have caused further detriment to the patient.[49]

Doctors certainly are prescribing more tests these days, but are they doing so purely for greed or inordinate control? We don't think so. Doctors do tend to do more testing these days, possibly in part to protect themselves from lawsuits, which have indeed reached epic proportions. Perhaps they are also trying to give their patients the very best in medical care, and so prescribe tests that were unavailable in past generations in order to make better diagnoses.

Bill Gothard admits that there may be a time to consult doctors but says:

> When we are seriously ill, God wants our first thought to be that of calling for the elders rather than calling a doctor.[50]

Again, we do believe that the elders, church family, immediate family, friends, and even total strangers can lift up those who are ill in prayer. God is the God of miracles and may choose to miraculously heal. We do not want in any way to diminish the role of believers in this or any area of life. However, is this really the divinely inspired, non-optional order of steps in medical care?

Gothard uses the biblical story of King Asa to engender more fear of doctors among his followers:

> "...we must be very sure that we are not following the tragic example of King Asa in putting our confidence in man rather than God for our healing. When King Asa, *"...in his disease...sought not the Lord, but to the physicians..."* God judged him with death. (See 2 Chronicles 16:12-13.)[51]

What a scare tactic this is! Watch out, people — consulting doctors before calling your elders may just bring down God's judgement upon you and kill you! But of course, that is not the point of the passage Gothard cites. Asa was not judged with death because he called the doctor before he called his elders, flaunting some divinely inspired order of steps in medical care. King Asa, once a godly king, had for a period of some years ignored God and relied upon men to save his hide. Consequently, Hanani had rebuked him (2 Chronicles 16:7-9). King Asa, in his rebellion, imprisoned Hanani and oppressed others. God allowed Asa's disease in order to get his attention, to turn his heart back to the Lord. Asa, however, refused to turn to God even in his distress.

J. Vernon McGee comments:

> God struck him with a disease which was serious and then became critical. He turned to the physicians. There is nothing wrong in that. The point is that he didn't turn to God in all of this. It is just as important for a believer to go to God when he gets sick as it is to call the doctor. When you get sick, there are two things you ought to do: you should

call the doctor and you should call upon God. [52]

Additionally, some theologians question what type of "doctors" Asa turned to. According to Dr. Charles C. Ryrie, the "physicians" he turned to were likely not medical doctors but occultists. As Dr. Charles C. Ryrie points out:

> These doubtless used more magic than medicine. Again, Asa failed to seek the Lord regarding his problem.[53]

In other words, King Asa had turned from God and may have consulted shamans, the "alternative healing practitioners" of that day. Of course, as Christians we are not to ignore God, as Asa did, but to rely upon Him. He is our ultimate source of healing and even life itself. But we need not fear going to doctors and receiving treatment from them, while recognizing that they are mere men who do not have the ultimate power of life and death.

Jesus did not spend much time bashing physicians or warning people about the dangers of soliciting their services. He drew an analogy between physical sickness and spiritual sickness. In Mark 2:17 He said, "They that that are whole have no need of the physician, but they that are sick: I came not to call the righteous, but sinners to repentance." Far from discouraging people from seeing physicians, Jesus affirmed that the sick have need of doctors, just as sinners need a Savior.

Anecdotal Stories to the Rescue!

Anecdotal stories can be utilized to "prove" almost anything. Gothard uses them copiously. Page 4 begins with the story of Pastor Wayne and Beverly Van Gelderen whose son, it is claimed, had an inoperable brain tumor. God intervened and brought about a miraculous healing. While this touching story may show that the God of miracles is still in the business of performing miracles, it does not validate the five non-optional principles that follow. In other words, Bill Gothard often takes the general biblical teaching (in this case that God heals) and attempts to validate his personal opinion on the subject (God heals through the five non-optional principles or steps). While the general is true, his personal opinion may, in fact, be false. With Gothard, the examples he employs usually do not prove the principle at all. His first principle, for instance, is to "Be Under the Spiritual Protection of a Local Church."[54] The example given? Job! What local church was Job under the spiritual protection of? None! Whose prayers were preserving him? Bill Gothard admits they were Job's own prayers!

> God was able to place that hedge of protection around Job and his family because of the faithful, persevering prayers of righteous Job.[55]

So, the example used proves the very opposite of the point which Bill Gothard is attempting to make. God is interested in a relationship with *individuals.* Individuals go to God in prayer and enjoy a relationship with Him, rather than mechanistically following a set of principles. Job wasn't healed because he was under the "spiritual protection of a local church," nor because he followed the five non-optional steps. He had a personal relationship with the living God Who created everything and is able to heal if He so chooses.

Another anecdote about an unidentified 1,400-member church in Texas is given. According to MTIA, when the elders began praying regularly for the church families, "Accidents and sickness were drastically reduced. Unemployment was decreased, and rebellion within families was greatly diminished."[56] The credit is given to the fact that the congregation got under authority, rather than crediting the prayer itself! Although we wouldn't necessarily agree with Abraham Maslow on many things the following quote seems fitting here: "If the only tool you have is a hammer, you tend to see every problem as a nail." This is true of Bill Gothard. Every benefit received is the result of "getting under God-given authority," and anything painful is a result of rebelling and getting out from under "God-given authority."

Principle two is titled, "Call for the Elders of the Church." We are told, "It is significant that the elders are not to initiate the action of this passage."[57] If the elders are unaware of someone's illness, contacting them is a good thing to do. But should James's statement be construed to mean that if the sick person does not initiate the call, the elders are not to contact and pray for him? According to Bill Gothard, they "are not to initiate." Why is that? According to Bill Gothard, by initiating the call the sick person will:

> ...confirm that he is looking to God as his primary healer and that he is willing to follow God's instruction regarding the steps he should take for his type of illness.[58]

What are the elders to do when they arrive? According to page 7, the elders are to determine the source of the illness, which is why they should be called before any medical treatment is given. But, "What if the elders are unqualified?"[59] In our view, this is a very good question. The answer? "Call for them anyway."[60] Since doctors can't be trusted and are to be feared, the elders will supposedly provide supernatural protection. However, the ill person should not feel too secure — we soon find out that the protective umbrella may have holes in it.

More Leaky Umbrellas

Page 9 tells the story of a sick young girl who God was unable to heal until her father confessed a hidden sin. After his confession, the girl was immediately delivered. We are also informed that if the elders don't confess their sins, there may be a hole in their umbrella of protection.

> Another important reason for elders to make sure that their lives are cleansed of sin is that if they have a hole in their umbrella of spiritual protection, Satan is given freedom to bring destruction to those under their care.[61]

Here is the Catch-22. If you trust your doctors and are not properly submitted to the local church, God may let you die. But even if you are properly submitted, you may be destroyed if your authority has sin in his life. This is not very comforting for the thinking person. The all-important "umbrella of protection" which is supposed to protect from sickness, unemployment, and emotional and spiritual problems might, in fact, *be the cause of these problems* if your authority is a leaky umbrella!

Adoption and Generational Curses

In *Basic Care Booklet* 5, pages 28-36, we are treated to the biblical understanding on how supposed "generational sins" are passed down genetically. Gothard writes:

> Medical researchers have discovered that because of the way our DNA "ladders" are constructed and the way our cells divide, we are literally a physical part of our forefathers. Thus, we were in "Adam" and a physical part of him when he sinned.
>
> It is vital that we understand the scriptural principles related to the sins of the forefathers and the practical implications that they have for us in dealing with temptation.[62]

The "discerning pastor from Georgia" who Bill Gothard formerly recommended weighs in on this as well. Pastor Henry Wright writes:

> If we want to do something for our children, let's go before God and get our lives straightened out, so that we can break the power of sin, so that genetically inherited diseases no longer exist. In our ministry, nationally, we have documented evidence of genetic code changes.[63]

> If God created an X chromosome perfect from the foundation of the world and if the devil, because of the generations of sin, mixed up the amino acid base that changed the genetics, God can change it back the way it was. *The devil is not more powerful that God is.* If Satan can mess up genetics, Who do you think can fix it? Would we dare believe that? I'm willing to give it a shot. I think we should say, "God, change the genetics," and expect Him

to do it.[64]

This is the breaking of inherited genetic curses. This is breaking inherited familiar spirits from your family trees, the rollovers, specifically meaning spiritually, psychologically and biologically inherited diseases.[65]

The Sins of the Fathers

Bill Gothard and MTIA use, as you might guess, more anecdotal evidence in an attempt to strengthen their point on generational sins and curses. These stories are purely subjective and prove very little. The entire premise, however, is built on very faulty reasoning and Scripture twisting. The belief is based on a partial reading of Exodus 20:5 and similar passages. The portion of the verse which is favored is, "I the Lord thy God, *am* a jealous God, visiting the iniquity of the fathers upon the children, unto the third and fourth *generation*...."

As a stand-alone quotation this partial verse would seem to support Bill Gothard's view. Of course, that is what he intends. However, when we look at the context we find that, as has so often been the case, it does not support Bill Gothard's contentions at all. In the context, God is telling His people not to worship other gods or idols (Exodus 20:3-4). He then says:

> Thou shalt not bow down thyself to them, nor serve them: for I the Lord thy God *am* a jealous God, visiting the iniquity of the fathers upon the children unto the third and fourth *generation* of them that hate me; and shewing mercy unto thousands of them that love me, and keep my commandments.[66]

God here commands the chosen people not worship or serve false gods or idols. The reason He gives is that He is a jealous God. The true God who created all things and by whose hand they are held together will not share His glory or His people's devotion with false gods and idols. As John D. Grassmick points out:

> He is zealous that devotion be given to exclusively to

Him. His uniqueness (Exodus 20:3) requires unique devotion. Absence of such dedication is sin and has its effect on future generations. Those who thus are influenced to **hate** God will be punished by Him. By contrast He is loyal (**showing** *hesed*, "loyal **love**") to those who **love** Him and who show that love by their obedience (cf. I John 5:3).[67]

In the context then, the "iniquity of the father" is idol worship. Notice that there are two groups being described in this passage. The first group is made up of "those who hate Me." These are the ones who reject the true God in favor of following false gods and idols. Their descendants will continue in this rebellion.

Group two is comprised of "those who love Me." That group is promised God's lovingkindness. To reiterate, the context of the passage is about false gods and idols. The "those who hate Me" group would be the ones who are rejecting what God has said here and are worshipping false gods and idols. The "those who love Me" group are those who are worshiping the true God. This theme follows through the other passages which Bill Gothard and MTIA use to try to validate their teaching.

A similar statement is made in Exodus 34:6-7 which came as a result of Aaron making a golden calf for the people to worship in Exodus 32. The "those who hate Me" group received this judgement. The "those who love Me" group are cautioned again not to worship other gods (Exodus 34:14).

The same is true of Leviticus 26:39-41. Leviticus 26:1 begins with these words:

> Ye shall make you no idols, nor graven image neither rear you up a standing image, neither shall ye set up *any* image of stone in your land: for I *am* the Lord your God.

The judgment of Leviticus 26:39-41 is a result of the nation turning from the worship of the one true God and following His statutes to follow false gods. We find the same type of message in Jeremiah 3:12-15. Charles H. Dyer comments:

Jeremiah paused in his condemnation of sin to offer a **message** of repentance and hope to the Northern Kingdom. If **Israel** would **return** to her God (cf. 7:3; 26:13), He would **frown on** her **no longer** and extend His mercy. But the people needed to **acknowledge** their **guilt** of rebellion and idolatry.[68]

One wonders why Bill Gothard misapplies these passages. It is clear that believers do not fall in the classification of "those who hate Me." The separation and alienation that exists between non-believers and God is removed upon redemption. As Earl Radmacher writes:

> Reconciliation means the removal of alienation between God and humankind. The Greek word for "reconcile" (*katallasso*) means to exchange enmity for friendship, hostility for peace.[69]

Once we are in Christ, believers are delivered from the previous judgement resulting from being at enmity with God. By avoiding the context and immediate interpretation, Bill Gothard and MTIA apply the judgement of non-believers to believers. This annuls the grace of Christ and the freedom we have in Jesus Christ and instead drags followers back into a legalistic and condemning system of Bill Gothard's own invention.

Doctors as Satan's Agents

In *Basic Care Bulletin* 7 warns about the satanic origins of a cesarean section. Doctors and other medical professionals are painted as the unwitting dupes of Satan in order to "destroy the Godly seed."

> Those who are trained in assisting women in childbirth are often unaware that their training is built on presuppositions that are damaging to women. In reality, a war is being waged against women and children. Indeed, from the beginning of time, Satan's agenda has been to destroy the Godly seed.[70]

In *Basic Care Bulletin 8 - How to Understand and Treat Morning Sickness*, MTIA writes:

> Christian women who are committed to Godly standards often have greater difficulties during pregnancy and child-birth than other women.[71]

The assertion is made with no statistics or scientific data. He simply states that this is true and moves on to build a case for why this is necessary:

> Because God's whole program depends upon raising up sons and daughters who are mighty in spirit, it would be expected that Satan will do all he can to oppose and destroy the Godly seed.[72]

Biblically, God is not dependent on us for anything. We are dependent on Him for everything! Colossians 1:17 declares: "And He [Christ] is before all things, and by him all things consist." Hebrews 1:3 reiterates this view: "Who being the brightness of His glory, and the express image of His person, and upholding all things by the word of His power."

In order to assist Gothard's dependent God, we must make sure to recite the "correct" prayers to ensure a healthy baby. The "correct" prayers are given us on pages 8 and 9 of this booklet. What sort of guilt will a mother and father suffer if their child is born with some physical defect? Did they miss one of the non-optional steps, principles, or prescribed prayers? The idea that these types of life circumstances are God's judgement on those who violate Gothard's "non-optional" principles has been a theme up to this point. It is further explained in the next booklet, *How to Understand the Causes and the Management of Miscarriages.* In the section "How robbing God can be related to miscarriages" we read:

> When a couple does not render to the Lord the percentage due Him — a simple token that all they possess belongs to Him — He warns that the "devourer" will be permitted to take from them things that they may hold dear.[73]

So, if God doesn't get his percentage He may cause physical impairment or even the death of the child. This sounds more like *The Godfather* than it does like God the Father!

Should we be praying for the unborn during pregnancy? Absolutely! Should we honor God in our giving? Again, absolutely! Does Bill Gothard's mechanistic approach guarantee physical, emotional, and spiritual health? No, it does not. He has successfully caused his followers to fear doctors, to reject medical science, and to greatly fear stepping out of line. As researcher Marty Butz wrote,

> As a result of Bill Gothard's misuse and misapplication of the Scripture, it cannot be accurately maintained that the *Bulletins'* foundation is the Bible. Though it can probably be accurately asserted that there is much practical information in the *Bulletins*, the mixture of truth and error contained therein disqualifies them as reliable guides. One cannot be sure that the medical information offered is any more trustworthy than the misapplied Scriptures used to support Mr. Gothard's prescriptions for health care and medical guidance. There is, for example, no supporting documentation or specific citation offered in the bulletins/booklets to support Bill Gothard's claim that, "*Christian Women who are committed to Godly standards often have greater difficulties during pregnancy and childbirth than other women.*" Nor is there any support for his assertion that, "*uncircumcised men have, as a group, been more promiscuous than circumcised men.*"
>
> Anyone who checks out the advice of the *Basic Care Bulletins* on medical issues would be wise to follow the well-known medical directive – get a second opinion![74]

It would indeed be a good idea to get a second opinion before following Gothard's advice, much of which is based upon alternative medical practices and ideas that are questionable at best, and potentially dangerous at worst. After scaring his followers away from medical doctors and telling them that he was offering them *God's way* to achieve good health, Gothard makes anyone who orders his medical publications and their spouse sign this disclaimer:

> I accept full responsibility for the medical decisions I make and understand that the *Basic CARE Bulletins* provide information only — not medical advice — for my consideration when making those decisions.[75]

This is nothing but double-talk. If you follow Gothard's medical advice — which is not really medical advice at all — and you or your loved ones happen to get sick or die as a result, don't come crying to Bill.

Epilogue

Fear of Flying

"I think a person who has never lived in a dictatorship can't understand the power of propaganda. If you just hear always the same...if you always read the same...and if you have very few possibilities of other information, then you become very impressed by the things you are told, and it is very difficult to make up your own mind and be critical."

Ewald von Kleist[1]

The Power of Propaganda

It is very difficult for people to leave authoritarian religious groups. Those who have never been in such a group often wonder why this is so. They can't imagine themselves tolerating the kind of mistreatment people suffer in such groups for one minute, much less imagine experiencing any crisis of conscience over making a quick getaway. "So what's the problem?" many think; "Just walk away!"

Well, it isn't quite that easy. If it were, we wouldn't have felt the need to include this section.

"Flying" from an abusive group is similar to fear of flying on an airplane. We can take the time to show the facts, safety measures, and percentage of successful flights, but for some the fear is so paralyzing that they cannot bring themselves to board the plane. In a similar way, even when members are made aware of very damning facts about their group they are seemingly unable to act on that information. Even more mystifying can be the loyalty they exhibit toward their group long after they've left on their own or been kicked out. People who have been horrendously treated by their former "friends" in the group still exhibit immense residual allegiance to them, becoming angry and springing to the defense of their former associates if someone correctly labels them as a cult or abusive religious group.

The suburban Chicago *Daily Herald* of April 6, 1997 ran an Associated Press article about a former member of Heaven's Gate, Lorraine Wilbur, whose own daughter was one of those who died in the mass suicide of that group. In the article Wilbur, who claims to be a founder of the group, defends not only her daughter's suicide, but also cult leader Marshall Applewhite, who led followers to their deaths through imaginative teachings he claimed to have channeled from beings from the "level above" human. The article states that Wilbur "dislikes the term cult," preferring to call the group "the fellowship." About Marshall Applewhite himself, she complains of media distortion and insists that he was "a kind and wonderful man."

Most people cannot understand her attitude, especially in light of the fact that she lost a daughter she loved. But anyone familiar with the mindset of former members of abusive religious groups who have not yet come to grips with their past will recognize this as a very typical reaction to criticism of their former group. She cannot now accept that she had so disastrously misjudged Applewhite, who was *not* a "kind and wonderful man" but a very dangerous religious con man who only *appeared to her* to be wonderful. We as human beings are very confident we can judge character and truth by outward appearance, but over and over we prove we are not good at doing so. Once we buy into their propaganda we give up our ability to really question or make criticisms of the group. Wilbur's "loyalty" to Applewhite was based upon her trust in her own ability to judge people as well as her belief in his propaganda, and was likely compounded by her own responsibility in her daughter's death. *If* she were to accept that her judgment had failed her — that what he taught was in fact, false — she would have to recognize and take responsibility for her own part in her daughter's suicide.

This indeed is a powerful tool which entraps many people into a number of groups. Their primary source of what they consider to be "reliable" information comes from the group itself. This is no less true with Bill Gothard and his IBLP than it is with Jehovah's Witnesses or was with Heaven's Gate. The world out there is chaotic and scary, but inside the group there is order and safety. Depending on the individual group, outsiders are viewed as downright evil, "worldly," or, at the least, far less spiritual than those inside. As Al Menconi pointedly confessed:

> Like many of [Gothard's] devotees, I became quite adept at applying his teaching and principles to my life. It wasn't very long before I became quite adept at applying his teaching to other people's lives as well. I was convinced that living according to these "life principles" would make me more spiritual than those who failed to apply them. I was quite the legal beagle. It began to make sense to me that if I could be more spiritual by keeping these commandments, then the one who was teaching them would be the most spiritual of all. I began to strive to imitate Bill Gothard.[2]

People who find themselves in this deep become afraid to point out even serious problems they finds along the way. If they recognize some signs of spiritual abuse, hypocrisy, or oppression, their minds tend to reject this input out of fear of reprisal or condemnation for presuming to judge the leader or leaders supposedly appointed or specially anointed by God. They will blame the victim; indeed, they will blame *themselves* before they will dare to find fault with such a "godly" man as the leader or leaders. This is very common among authoritarian groups. Leaders like Bill

Gothard take the view that a good offense is the best defense, and people quickly learn that "fault-finders" find themselves under siege, accused of some spiritual problem or other. Critical questions are not answered in a reasoned fashion. Rather, the response is crafted in such a way as to suggest that questioning itself indicates a rebellious spirit. To question "God's appointed man" is tantamount to questioning God. This mindset is very difficult to overcome. Even when one finds the courage to leave the group, one may have difficulty trusting that their decision was the right one. Feelings like those seen in the following story are common.

Some time after leaving IBLP Rachel Stevens[3] confessed, "Some days in my long journey away from Gothardism, I have wondered if I was all wrong. I've wondered if they were right. Maybe I was falling away from God. Maybe the principles were Bible-based after all."

After several years of struggling towards freedom and helping others whose lives had been devastated by their involvement with IBLP, Bill Gothard resurfaced in her life on April 11, 2001. He attempted to coerce her, through guilt and intimidation, to remove her web site,[4] which criticized both him and of IBLP. She was dismayed to find that he had somehow obtained her private email address and sent her an email requesting that she call him right away or send him her phone number so he could call her. He indicated that the Institute had formulated a response to her web site which he would like to discuss with her prior to posting. She responded that he should just proceed to post it and she would reply to the charges (whatever they might be) on her own site. Gothard's next email was intended to induce her through guilt to accede to his wishes, saying that, in the interests of Christian unity, he really didn't want to post their response and was hoping that she would change her site to "be in harmony with Christ's prayer of John 17:21." He subsequently forwarded her the information he intended to put on his web-site. She told us that what she read was primarily a fabrication of her childhood in IBLP that could be easily refuted, and the attempted intimidation had the unintended consequence of strengthening her resolve to oppose Gothard and his system. The lies and slander against her only served to remind her of Gothard's utter disregard for the truth and reconfirmed her original convictions. Says Rachel, "Mr. Gothard's behavior towards me and towards MCO[5] and PFO[6] has really reinforced for me that I was right. I'm not losing my mind! Bill does not live what he preaches."

Supremely Invested

As every serious Wall Street investor who's been trading for a while knows, the time inevitably comes when one must "cut one's losses," so to speak, and dump a tanking stock. The higher the cost of the original investment, the more painful this will be. Some find it so excruciating that they can't bear to bite the bullet, and they end up losing even more in the process. Perhaps they hold on in the vain hope that the share price will at least climb high enough to allow them to break even. They know that once they sell and take their losses, their wounded pride will compound the pain of the financial setback. These same dynamics are at work in the lives of those who find it difficult to leave cults and often continue even after they've left.

Many will remember the interview on CBS's *60 Minutes* of two former members of Heaven's Gate. The interviewers seemed incredulous to learn that both men still believed that Applewhite was right and their former associates were at that very moment speeding through space aboard a spaceship hidden behind the Hale-Bopp comet. One man's wife was "aboard the craft," in his view, and he regretted that he didn't go with her. Why would he persist in this belief when there was no rational reason for it? The fact is, of course, that there is a very rational explanation for the loyalty he showed, as his responses in the interview made plain. The man told of how he and his wife became involved with the group — how after they had attended just one meeting they came home and gave their daughter away so they could join up with the separatist group.

Now, ask yourself a question: How easy would it be to admit to yourself that you, a supposedly rational human being, had *given your daughter away* and run off with a flimflam man who captivated you *in a matter of hours* with a fantastic yarn? Having invested everything, it is much easier to keep right on believing a spectacular falsehood than to face yourself with that awful truth. Human beings are driven by pride to a high degree, and to recognize that one has been deceived to that extent would be a tremendous blow to one's ego. Considering how difficult it can be for human beings to admit to having made a poor restaurant choice or to have taken a wrong turn on the highway, imagine the devastating embarrassment and shame of admitting to an error of judgment of this magnitude. The consequences of his choice were so *horrendous* — his child abandoned by her parents and his wife now dead — that Applewhite's Hale-Bopp theory just *had* to be true for this man to live with himself. The level of loyalty one exhibits towards his former associates is often directly tied to the magnitude of the sacrifices made — sacrifices which would now appear very foolish indeed if they turned out to be *needless sacrifices* after all.

Such sacrifices are not always matters of life and death as this man's were, but they can still be compelling reasons to refuse to accept the truth about whatever group one happens to be involved with. For example, imagine that you have given up years of your life peddling "God's magazines" from door to door for a Brooklyn publishing concern which claims to be God's only channel on earth, as many Jehovah's Witnesses have done. You've given up holidays and birthday celebrations, and you have deprived your children of not only these things, but also such normal childhood activities as sports involvement or perhaps higher education. You have sacrificed your right to vote or hold public office and have even agreed not to *think independently* or to disagree with the leadership in any detail. And those are the *small* sacrifices! The big sacrifices have involved giving up family members or good friends who disapproved of your involvement or who tried to talk you out of joining. How easy would it be to admit that you had been deceived? How foolish would you feel to accept it, no matter what confirming evidence you were shown that the Watchtower Society, though seemingly mainstream, is a destructive cult, whose policies have caused the death of many more innocent people than Jonestown and Waco put together?

It is just as difficult for some to walk away from Gothardism, possibly for some of the same reasons. As we recounted in chapter 7, Sally's parents still believe in Gothard — they hold no ill will towards him and remain committed to the belief that he is a good and humble man. They have persuaded themselves that the problem lies with the employees, who they see as irresponsible and unqualified. After having given their daughter to Gothard as "Hanna had given Samuel" and subsequently witnessing the torment she suffered while in his "care," it would be very difficult to admit they were wrong about him and are thus responsible for putting their child in harm's way. They find themselves in too deep to get out now — their emotional "investment" is just too great.

Other Gothardites have different reasons to remain invested — some, through their staunch advocacy of Gothard's teachings within their churches, have caused great dissension among Christian brothers or have instigated church splits. Pastors have been removed from their pulpits or not considered for a particular pastorate because they reject Gothard's teachings. Numerous churches have contacted Midwest Christian Outreach and Personal Freedom Outreach for help as factions of Gothardites were striving to remove pastors who were not supportive of Gothard. For those who have inflicted this kind of disunity and damage in the body of Christ, the emotional cost of being so wrong is too high to allow them to recognize that their champion is greatly in error. He must be as great as they perceive him to be or they will have to admit their own gross error in supporting him at the expense of other innocent people and the welfare of the body of Christ.

Facing the Music

Fear of ridicule is another thing that keeps people bound up with their former cult or authoritarian group. They fear family members or "worldly" friends (friends outside the group) will crow "I told you so" or laugh at their error. Consider this Associated Press interview with the head of the Unarius Academy of Science, another UFO cult. "In a small town outside San Diego, 76 year old Charles Spiegel eagerly awaits the 1,000 aliens who will descend from 'Myton' around 2001.... He shrugs off the skeptics who note that the Unarius spaceships failed to show up for their last appointment with Earth in 1976. 'We will have the last laugh,' Spiegel said." He believes (and is probably correct) that he and his fellow cultists have been *laughed at*, so he desperately *wills* his religion to be true, against all evidence to the contrary, in order to be vindicated and get the last laugh! That's very sad but supremely human. Most of us seem more willing to endure the rack than to be laughed at by our peers. How many Jehovah's Witnesses remain in that group despite the many false prophecies and despite seeing so many doctrinal flip-flops because they have been ridiculed and their wounded pride stubbornly refuses to give up the hope they will have the last laugh after all? How many of us can claim to handle humbling experiences without employing similar defensive strategies?

We have had more than one discussion with Gothard followers who, despite having no biblical defense to offer for his positions, remain adamant that his teachings simply *must* be true. One such incident was at a large church in the northwest suburbs of Chicago. Don Veinot was teaching a mid-week series on basic apologetics. A young man approached him at the end of the first session and said he had really enjoyed the teaching. He informed Don that he receives and loves the ministry's *Journal* and agrees that the church needs to better equip their people, but he maintained that we need to repent of "attacking" God's man, Bill Gothard. This young man and Don talked about the issues involved, and he even agreed that there are "some problems" with Gothard's teachings, but he would not agree that there were serious, fundamental problems in Gothard's teaching. Why?

According to him, "If Bill is wrong I have wasted my life since I was a kid. Those whom I have tried to get to go to the Basic Seminar would think I was foolish." Fears of ridicule or wounded pride can function as powerful blindfolds indeed.

Paralyzing Fear

Fear of making a *deadly* mistake is yet another reason people stay in abusive religious groups. One woman who called the Midwest Christian Outreach help-line had been a Jehovah's Witness for 25 years. She was very unhappy as a Witness, but she was scared to death to leave. You see, a Jehovah's Witness is taught that everyone outside of that organization is soon to be destroyed by God at Armageddon. This fear draws many into the group in the first place, and this same fear keeps many of them there even when they want so badly to breathe free. The woman had quit going to meetings, she said, but she lived in fear — not merely for herself, which she could tolerate, but the fear that she would be responsible for the destruction of her family who quit going when she did. We are happy to report that she listened to what we had to say and courageously left that organization. She accepted Christ and started attending a church, yet it took a long time to completely eradicate the fear of Armageddon that had been drummed into her. Having realized she had been so terribly deceived by them, she had a hard time trusting that she had made the correct judgment *this* time.

It is really no different in IBLP. The Gothardites' fear is not that of being destroyed at Armageddon but that their lives and their families will be destroyed, and God will reject them and punish them for leaving. After all, God has given Gothard all of the principles that, if followed obediently, protect families from divorce, teen rebellion, grave illness, financial loss, and other horrors. They've been persuaded that God works and blesses only through Gothard's chain of authority — there's no telling what catastrophic events might befall them if they get out from under this umbrella. These are issues which pastors and church leaders need to understand in order to be prepared to minister to such individuals. Many fine Christians have unwittingly switched their loyalties from God to Gothard and are very afraid to go against his teachings. In their minds, to do so might mean loss of family unity and God's blessing. These individuals need Christian love and compassion to unwind and let go of their fears. For years, the Bible has meant what *Gothard* says that it means. It is important to go over Scripture with them, asking them to look closely at the text. This will help them greatly to see that often the text itself teaches the very opposite of what Gothard has taught. Once they begin to grasp the significance of this, their fear will dissipate as their devotion is turned away from Gothard and back to God where it belongs.

Only the Gullible?

Another stumbling block is the terrible difficulty human beings have accepting that the highly intelligent people whom they know within the group can be deceived. Brother so-and-so is a rocket scientist, and *he* believes all of this teaching, therefore it *must* be true! People instinctively but wrongly assume that only stupid or highly gullible people would wind up believing and accepting false things, but *nothing could be further from the truth!* Our Jehovah's Witness and Mormon friends are highly intelligent people. Intelligence alone has nothing to do with deception! Look how many brilliant people have bought into what evolutionist Denton calls a "fairy tale for adults" — evolution. How many evangelicals believed Mike Warnke in the 1970s when he claimed to have been a former highly placed Satanist, without ever checking out his story? How many good people of normal or above-average intelligence believe that Benny Hinn truly heals people, or that the Holy Spirit has an interest in pinning people to the floor or throwing them into uncontrollable fits of laughter? The fact is that even Christians (of whatever intelligence) are not immune to deception, which is why the Bible warns us time and time again *not to be deceived.* If we could not be deceived, why the warnings (e.g., Matthew 24:4, Colossians 2:4, 8)?

But They're So Nice!

Similar is this objection concerning the leaders or group members: "But they're such nice people! Isn't that a sign that they're on the right track?" No. Anyone, no matter how nice, no matter what age or level of education, can be deceived. If you don't believe *you* can be deceived, you're deceiving yourself!

Joy Veinot had dialog online with an agnostic who was ridiculing Christians for their gullibility in believing fantastic conspiracy theories and such nonsensical rumors as Procter and Gamble secretly putting a satanic symbol on their products some years back. She had to agree with him because he was right, and we know Christians can be deceived just like others. It is part of the human condition. But she cautioned him that skeptics can also be deceived, which was hilariously confirmed when he informed us of a "Christian fundamentalist plot" against atheist Madalyn Murray O'Hair. Joy was *keenly interested* to learn who was involved in this secret conspiracy, but unfortunately our skeptic could provide us with no evidence or even the most rudimentary details of the supposed dark plot.

The Prospect of Great Loss

Even though every human being can be deceived, and it is not easy for *anyone* to admit it and change course, the *consequences* of changing course for the adherents of totalitarian religious groups are often far more devastating on a personal level than for the average person. We may be embarrassed to admit we have been fooled, but we won't be shunned as a result. But personal rejection and loss of friends and family members is not an unusual price to pay for making the break from such a group. Almost all of them shun former members and consider them not merely misguided but *evil*. Rachel Stevens is still trying to establish a relationship with her parents, who have cut her off and are shunning her. They are so completely invested in IBLP and ATI that they *must* believe that the problem lies completely with her and that she is rebellious and condemned.

Most people cannot imagine the courage that it takes to do the right thing in the face of this type of rejection. We don't relish being rejected by *strangers* much less being considered an ungodly or evil person by someone we love, and treated accordingly. Many disillusioned members try to just drop out of the group quietly to avoid the personal loss, and for some that works, at least for a time. Yet eventually most have to decide whether it is more important to tell the truth to those they love within the group and risk losing them or watch their loved ones continue in their deception.

Loss of God

The former member, once out, has still another obstacle to overcome. They have been heavily indoctrinated to believe that there are no true Christians outside of their group. A common cult belief is that all of Christendom was "paganized" in some early century, and that the "nominal" church of our present day is full of ungodly people who are Christian in name only. The people in the group are the white hats, devoted to God and full of integrity and righteousness, as opposed to all those phonies in the churches. Thus poisoned, they often become spiritually empty "loners," no longer able to believe what they once did, but *sure* that there is nowhere else to go.

Gothardites do not necessarily believe that all outsiders are unbelievers, but they certainly have been led to believe that those within IBLP are a spiritually cut above outsiders. If Gothard is shown to be wrong, where can they go? By God's grace, many former members find that the true God is not tied to a self-appointed religious guru. Sadly, however, there are many burned-out people out there who, after trying so hard to please God in their own strength by law-keeping, leave God altogether, exhausted and convinced that the Christian life is impossible to live.

It is absolutely true that to successfully live the Christian life by law and principles as Gothard promotes it, is quite impossible. It will not work. The flesh will win out, and the law-keeper will be defeated time and time again, no matter how hard he or she tries to "do better." We can't reform the flesh; we must accept God's grace — a grace that is not limited to getting us started on the Christian journey, but one that will carry us through.

Grace That Is Greater Than All My Sin

In the American business world there are two ways of declaring bankruptcy. You can declare temporary bankruptcy, or you can declare permanent bankruptcy. As Jerry Bridges puts it, the only way to enter the Christian life is by declaring permanent spiritual bankruptcy before God:

> So what kind of bankruptcy did we declare? To use the business analogy, did we file under Chapter 7 or Chapter 11? Was it permanent or temporary? I suspect most of us would say we declared permanent bankruptcy. Having trusted in Jesus Christ alone for our salvation, we realized we could not add any measure of good works to what He has already done. We believe He completely paid our debt of sin and secured for us the gift of eternal life. There is nothing more we can do to earn our salvation, so using the business analogy, we would say we filed permanent bankruptcy.[7]

And of course, the Bible amply testifies to the truthfulness of this. The basic requirement for salvation is simple to understand: one must believe the gospel, that forgiveness of sins and eternal life is a completely free gift of God that must be accepted by faith. In Romans 10:9-10 the Apostle Paul writes:

> That if thou shalt confess with thy mouth the Lord Jesus, and shall believe in thine heart that God hath raised him from the dead, thou shalt be saved. For with the heart man believeth unto righteousness and with the mouth confession is made unto salvation.

We come with empty hands, with no righteousness of our own to offer God in order to earn His approval. As Ephesians 2:8-9 emphatically states,

For by grace ye are saved through faith; and that not of yourselves: *it is* the gift of God: not of works, lest any man should boast.

Many, if not most, of those who are involved in IBLP were already believers who accepted the biblical teaching on salvation prior to attending a seminar. But even before they attended they may have already bought into a rather common error that compromises the true grace of salvation. Bridges writes:

However, I think most of us actually declared temporary bankruptcy. Having trusted in Christ alone for our salvation, we have subtly and unconsciously reverted to a works relationship with God in our Christian lives. We recognize that even our best efforts cannot get us to Heaven, but we do think they earn God's blessings in our daily lives.

After we become Christians we begin to put away our more obvious sins. We also start attending church, put money in the offering plate, and maybe join a small group Bible study. We see some positive change in our lifestyle, and we begin to feel pretty good about ourselves. We are now ready to emerge from bankruptcy and pay our own way in the Christian life.[8]

So how does this attitude manifest itself in the Christian life? Well, to begin with, we start measuring our spiritual progress — and thus our relationship with God — by how well we conform to whatever set of rules and regulations we're introduced to at the beginning of our Christian walk.

Are we consistent in our church attendance? Are we faithful in our daily devotions? Do we witness to non-Christians on a regular basis?

But soon enough these measuring sticks begin to seem inadequate. It's not long before we replace them with more difficult ones to measure up to. Are we *fully committed* as much as we can be at our local church? Isn't there some project we can help out with? Some committee we can join?

Do we faithfully get up *before sunrise* to have devotions and make sure that we pray for *at least one hour* in the process? Do we read through the *entire Bible* in a year, while simultaneously studying *every verse deeply* and meditating on it for the rest of the day?

Have we not only witnessed, but *have we led anyone to Christ* in the past year? In the past six months? In the past several weeks? Fairly soon, the Pharisees may have nothing on us when it comes to meticulously attempting to follow man-made traditions. And like the Pharisees, comparing our righteousness to that of others becomes standard practice to determine how well we're doing in this God-pleasing business. Cleaning up the outside person may seem easy enough at first, but the old nature within cannot be squelched by any amount of will power.

After a while the pressure from this works-oriented, performance-based approach to the Christian life starts building within. Honest people who examine the thoughts and motivations of their hearts will clearly see that they are not measuring up to the spiritual standard they are committed to, while other people (whose interior struggles they are unfamiliar with) seem to be way ahead of them in the spiritual game. And then, as if the ongoing failure to measure up were not bad enough, the unthinkable happens:

> Then the day comes when we fall on our face spiritually. We lapse back into an old sin, or we fail to do what we should have done. Because we think we are now on our own, paying our own way, we assume we have forfeited all blessings from God for some undetermined period of time. Our expectation of God's blessing depends on how well we feel we are living the Christian life. We declared temporary bankruptcy to get into His Kingdom, so now we think we can and must pay our own way with God. We were saved by grace, but we are living by performance.[9]

But more often than not, we don't see it. And in many Christian circles, and in many churches, we're not encouraged to see it. Instead, we've been beaten over the head about how we can't afford to blemish our testimony before a watching world, and how God's blessing in our lives depends on our performance and whether we faithfully and consistently do this, that, and the other thing. As Bridges writes:

> If you think I am overstating the case, try this test. Think of a time recently when you really fell on your face spiritually. Then imagine that immediately afterward you encountered a terrific opportunity to share Christ with a non-Christian friend. Could you have done it with complete confidence in God's help?[10]

In the beginning believers are wonderfully attracted to God by the love of Christ. Later we strive upward toward doing the things we think God desires from us out of a sincere wish to please Him. But unless we remain mindful that our standing before God is *forever* based upon His lovingkindness, eventually we will fall from grace as Paul expresses it in Galatians 5:5. We will find ourselves slogging uphill, exhausted, weary, so heavy-laden with guilt over our poor performance that we almost forget what attracted us in the first place: the utterly merciful love of Christ. It is somewhere along this continuum that many Christians discover Bill Gothard and IBLP and become seduced by his promise to make them more successful performers.

Christ's Higher Standard

Many go to IBLP in search of answers to life's problems and are taught the seven non-optional principles which, if followed correctly, will solve these problems. Gothard's "prescription" for higher performance seems simple enough — first, the Christian must stop sinning. He points out that the apostle Paul in Romans chapter 6 tells the believer not to heedlessly continue in sin, with a view to increasing God's grace. We concur with Paul but disagree with Gothard about how this life change is accomplished. According to Gothard, our sanctification is achieved by pursuing "a higher standard of Godly living than is generally accepted by

Christians in our day."[11] And according to Gothard, the Christian's standard for living is contained in the Sermon on the Mount. He writes:

> The phrase "the apostles" doctrine is used only once in the New Testament. It defines the teaching that the apostles gave to the multitudes of new believers after the Day of Pentecost.... It is obvious that the teaching which the apostles gave came from the three years of training they had just received from the Lord Jesus Christ.... What then was the basic content of the teachings of Jesus, also referred to in Scripture as the doctrine of Christ? "Whosoever transgresseth, and abideth not in the doctrine of Christ, hath not God. He that abideth in the doctrine of Christ, he hath both the Father and the Son." The teachings of Jesus are clearly stated in His Sermon on the Mount (Matthew 5-7).[12]

Here Gothard claims that "the apostles' doctrine" and the "doctrine of Christ" are none other than the teachings of the Sermon on the Mount. In our discussions with him, Gothard has stated that Christ *raised the standards* required by the Law. This misguided view, however, sorely misses the point of the Sermon on the Mount (and Romans chapter 6), thus bringing his followers into legalistic bondage. It also brings into question his understanding of the gospel. About his assertion that "the Apostles' Doctrine" and "the doctrine of Christ" are one in the same, Dr. Harry Adams asks:

> Does Gothard establish that the biblical references to "the Apostles' doctrine" and "the doctrine of Christ" are equivalent to the Sermon on the Mount? No, he does not.[13]

Dr. Adams goes on to examine the meaning of the phrase, "the Apostles' Doctrine" which occurs in Acts 2:42 and the meaning of "the doctrine of Christ" which occurs in 2 John 9. He shows that by studying the book of Acts, we can see that the

"Apostles doctrine" had to do with the fulfillment of the Old Testament promises by Jesus, proving Him to be the Jewish Messiah. It also included an explanation of what Jesus had accomplished on the cross and how one could be saved or born again. Dr. Adams points out:

> Thus, we see the preaching of the kingdom by the Apostles was not the retelling of the Sermon on the Mount, but the proclamation of the work of Christ.[14]

In other words, "the Apostles' doctrine" consisted of what the Apostles taught about Christ. It was certainly not merely a repetition of what Christ had taught. Dr. Adams explains further that 2 John 9, speaking of the "doctrine of Christ," has to do with the incarnation. It was written in response to the heresy of John's day that denied that Jesus Christ was a physical being and taught that He was just a spirit who appeared to be physical. Again, the "doctrine of Christ," like the apostles' doctrine, has to do with teachings *about* Christ, not things taught *by* Christ while on Earth. Are these somehow connected to the Sermon on the Mount, as Gothard asserts? Dr. Adams responds:

> So, the concern of John with respect to "*the doctrine of Christ*" had nothing to do with teaching the Sermon on the Mount. Once more, Mr. Gothard has demonstrated how he twists Scripture to prove his point.[15]

What about Gothard's claim that Christ was instituting a new standard, higher than the Law of Moses? The *Bible Knowledge Commentary* notes:

> This section presents the heart of Jesus' message, for it demonstrates His relationship to the Law of God. Jesus was not presenting a rival system to the Law of Moses and the words of the prophets, but a true fulfillment of the Law and the prophets — in contrast with the Pharisees' traditions... Jesus' fulfillment would extend to the smallest Hebrew letter, the "jot" (lit. *yod*), and even to the smallest stroke of a Hebrew letter, the "tittle."[16]

Jesus did put forth a much higher standard than the hypo-critical religious leaders of the day were keeping, which they sup-posed was making them righteous in the sight of God. How wrong they were. Jesus began by saying, "For I say unto you, that except your righteousness shall exceed *the righteousness* of the scribes and Pharisees, ye shall in no case enter into the kingdom of heaven" (Matthew 5:20). Jesus then went on to explain what he meant. The Pharisees had become expert at keeping the letter of the law while violating the spirit of the law in the inner man. While they did not physically commit adultery, thus *appearing* righteous concerning commandment number seven, they inward-ly lusted after women who were not their wives in the privacy of their hearts where others could not see. They did not commit mur-der, but their hearts were filled with hatred. Instead of recogniz-ing their utter inability to please a holy God, they saw themselves as holy men, fully deserving of His acceptance and blessing. Rather than mourn their spiritual poverty, they were puffed up with self-righteousness. Jesus was putting them on notice, telling them that God sees and judges the motives and thoughts of the heart — if one is unrighteous in his heart, he is unrighteous, peri-od. It would have been a fearful revelation, both to the Pharisees and the common man, since everyone knows his own heart, even if others do not. Jesus fully meant to bring them to their knees, revealing to them their own hopeless situation. They were bank-rupt, owing to God a great debt of holiness they could not possi-bly pay.

Jesus' point was not that we could live holy lives by striving to meet a higher standard of righteousness, but that we are in deep trouble and need a Savior. Until one recognizes one's ter-minal illness, he will not accept the only cure. Mankind lives in denial. The late Dr. J. Vernon McGee said it well:

> I hope you don't misinterpret what I am saying in this sec-tion which we call the Sermon on the Mount. I am not say-ing that we are free to break the Mosaic Law. The fact of the matter is that the Law is still a standard. It reveals to me that I cannot measure up to God's standard. This

drives me to the cross of Christ. The only way I can fulfill
the Law is by accepting the only One who could fulfill it –
Jesus Christ. It is very important to see His point right
here. The Pharisees had a high degree of righteousness
according to the Law, but that was not acceptable. How can
you and I surpass their righteousness? It is impossible in
our own efforts. We need Christ to do it for us.[17]

The Galatian Fallacy

Grace doesn't begin and end with salvation – grace is essential
to our sanctification also – the living of the Christian life suc-
ceeds only when it is pursued by faith. That was the error that
the church in Galatia had fallen into – Pied Pipers of the Law
came along, robbed them of their freedom in Christ, and stuck
them right back under the Law of Moses. Many, if not most,
Gothard followers have suffered a fate similar to that of the
church in Galatia. They at one time understood the gospel of the
grace of God. They began by faith, recognizing that they had
nothing in themselves to offer God with which to earn His favor.
Subsequently, however, they have been persuaded that God
requires them to keep the Law, packaged as non-optional "steps"
and "principles," in order to maintain His favor and blessing.
They have become convinced through Gothard's propaganda
that they have the ability, as well as the obligation, to live up to
the "higher standards" of holy living recorded in Matthew 5-7.
But as Dr. McGee affirmed, it is an impossible task. We need
Christ to do it for us. But sadly, Gothardites have completely lost
sight of the biblical teaching of sanctification by faith because of
the works mentality that has been drilled into them so effectively, accompanied by Scripture-twisting that makes the Bible
appear to teach the very opposite of what it teaches. This
includes, as we pointed out in chapter 4, a redefinition of "grace"
as something that one merits. Gothard writes:

> In the Old Testament, those who found grace possessed
> qualities that merited God's favor.[18]

The term *unmerited favor* would not apply to the favor that Noah received from the Lord, because that favor was based on his being a righteous man.[19]

Sanctification by Works

If grace is merited, then one must be sanctified by his own efforts. There are two potential problems that sprout from this teaching. The first is Phariseeism — some will actually believe they have attained sinless perfection in this life. They will play the comparison game and tend to focus on and magnify other people's sins, while downgrading their own to mere "mistakes." Arrogance and pride will be the result. Like the Pharisees, they will become blind to their own sin, withdrawing from other Christians, whom they see as spiritual "inferiors."

The second problem, which afflicts many more, is a downward spiral into hopelessness. Their own honest appraisal shows them that they are not making it — they see they are not living up to the "higher standard" that they believe they are mandated to perform. This is tragic, because Gothard lured so many of these people with the promise of "success" and then put them on a treadmill that constantly reminds them of their "failures." In his book *When Being Good Isn't Good Enough,* Steve Brown invites all his readers to jump off this kind of treadmill when he writes:

> You tried. You really tried, but in the end you failed. You really wanted to do better, but you only did worse and you didn't know how to fix it. Maybe you considered giving up completely. You said to yourself, "I'll never get it right. I'm probably not a Christian at all."
>
> Rules and regulations are Satan's way of reminding Christians that they have failed. But even worse, rules and regulations are the reason we do fail.
>
> Let me give you a wonderful secret, the basic secret of this entire book. In fact, if you understand this, you don't need to read any further: When success isn't the issue, success becomes reality.[20]

We Have Found the Enemy, and He Is Us

Like the Apostle Paul in Romans chapter 7, Christians find a battle going on within and are baffled and even repelled by it. Paul affirmed the righteousness of the Law and his own utter inability to keep it. He desired to do the right thing but found himself doing the opposite. He was filled with revulsion at his own failure to do right and to avoid wrong.

How can we, the saved, those declared righteous, find ourselves sinning? We *hate* sin and are convinced of its ugliness and destructive power. So how can we understand this conundrum? It is as though we were all born with spiritual cerebral palsy. Adam was created as a perfect specimen but contracted the disease when he sinned and he passed it down to the whole human race. Everyone is affected greatly but in varying degrees. An individual with physical cerebral palsy experiences a life of frustration. The disease doesn't really affect their thinking ability or desire to do certain things, but they cannot accomplish them since their body won't cooperate. According to Paul, we have the same spiritual problem. Spiritually, we cannot walk or even crawl without great difficulty, much less run a race, shoot a basket or hit a baseball.

Then the law comes on the scene and makes our situation *far worse*. Why worse? Because the law acts as a mirror in a gym. It exposes the fact that we are *not* running, *not* shooting baskets, and *not* batting well, if at all. We're not even in the game! As the authors of the Thirty-Nine Articles of the Church of England put it in 1563:

> ... man is very far gone from original righteousness, and is of his own nature inclined to evil, so that the flesh lusteth always contrary to the spirit; and therefore in every person born into this world, it deserveth God's wrath and damnation.[21]

It's not that we're just unrighteous on balance. We are "*very far gone* from [the] original righteousness" of our first parents. It's not just that we don't "bat 1,000" on the moral baseball diamond of life. The Law demonstrates that we're batting .000!

This is very bad news, indeed! Our situation appears to be hopeless. But fortunately for us, Jesus enters the scene. He is a perfect specimen, just like Adam originally was. He runs like a Gazelle, he makes the basket every time, and he bats 1,000 all of his life, and He is thus entitled to eternal life. Hurray for Jesus! Even better, though, He is not just a man, but God, so He is able to ransom us from the consequences of hell. He has run *for* us, shot *our* baskets, taken *our* turn at bat, and taken upon Himself the punishment for *our* lack of ability. All we must do is believe in Him. No strings attached. Believe on Christ — no hell to fear.

As Paul nears the end of Romans 7, the cry of this palsied man goes up: "O wretched man that I am! Who shall deliver me from the body of this death?" (Romans 7:24) In the previous chapters Paul has given us the remedy for eternal healing, but how do we live the rest of this life? Paul then turns our attention to the One who is able to resolve the dilemma. "I thank God through Christ Jesus our Lord. So then with my mind I myself will serve the law of God; but with the flesh the law of sin." (Romans 7:25).

We can live better — much better — right now. No more crawling, no more slamming into other people, no more pitiful attempts just to stand. As we give up on our own efforts, which are doomed to failure, Christ takes control. It is as though he straps Himself to our arms, hands, legs, and feet and miraculously we will be able to walk as He did. We will have His power in our lives to walk, run, play, and do all that is good and right and that we lost because of Adam. We still have the palsy, but as long as we rest in Him and He holds onto us, we can live the life that He did.

Gothard's system is simply a futile attempt to give people steps, principles, and rules to better control their palsied bodies. The Apostle's point is that it will never happen. It is our relationship with Christ, not our relationship with the rules, that makes the change.

A Son or a Slave?

The difference between cultic and authoritarian theology and true Christian theology is the difference between being a son or a slave, loved or owned. The slave's well-being is tied to his performance, the son's to his unalterable position in his father's heart. In Romans 8:15 Paul speaks of being released from the fearful insecurity of the slave as one receives the spirit of sonship, but this is a very difficult concept for a former member of an abusive group to grasp. They're used to filling out time cards, attending meetings, and sporting professional "Christian" attire and haircuts. They are "organization men and women," bound by rules, laws, and "non-optional principles." They know nothing of the freedom that we are called to in Christ (Galatians 5:1). Chuck Swindoll, in his excellent book, *The Grace Awakening*, writes:

> More and more Christians are realizing that the man-made restrictions and legalistic regulations which they have been living have not come from the God of grace, but have been enforced by people who do not want others to be free.[22]

When Bill Gothard states that "Christians can't handle freedom" it speaks volumes about his view and teachings. It also places him in the group of those "who do not want others to be free."

Paul, on the other hand, teaches that freedom is a good thing, that Christians should guard their freedom jealously and not allow others to steal it from them.

The Unmerited Favor of God

We did nothing to merit our earthly birth, and we can do nothing to merit our spiritual birth. We were born into "the Adam family" – born in sin, and under a curse – but we have been given the option through Christ's ransom to switch sides and be *born again* into Christ (Romans 5:12-19). It's a *free gift*, with no strings attached, and we receive it by faith in Christ alone

(Ephesians 2:8-9). This is indeed wonderful news, which is *why* it's called the gospel, which means good news. Peter said it this way: "…. In [God's] great *mercy* he has *given us* new birth into a living hope through the resurrection of Jesus Christ from the dead, and into an inheritance that can never perish, spoil or fade — kept in heaven for you, who *through faith* are shielded by God's power until the coming of salvation that is ready to be revealed in the last time" (1 Peter 1:3-5). Jesus Himself said in John 3:16 that "whoever *believes* in him shall not perish, but shall have eternal life."

To believe is to trust in, to have faith. And sadly, fear erects the final and perhaps most daunting barrier for the former members of cults and abusive religious groups. Having been deceived, they are fearful of ever trusting again. You may be able to show them that the Bible says that acceptance by God and adoption into His family is based solely upon grace through faith, but it sounds too good to be true to their battered souls, and they are *afraid* to believe it! If anyone reading this is in that position right now, we want you to know that fearlessness is *not* a requirement for salvation or sanctification. You can be scared and have faith at the same time. You may be terrified of flying in an airplane, but if you have enough faith to get aboard, that's *enough* faith! You needn't hold off boarding until you are convinced that you're *fearless.* The plane will fly whether you are scared or not! God knows your weakness. He is fully aware of what you've been through. He asks you to put your faith and trust in His Son. Just call upon Jesus. The Bible says you will not be disappointed (Romans 10:9-13 and 1 Corinthians 1:2). Your knees may be knocking, or your heart pounding, but get on that plane. He will deliver you safely home.

Endnotes

Prologue

1 The Institute in Basic Life Principles (IBLP) started out as The Institute in Basic Youth Conflicts (IBYC) and gradually made a name change in the mid 1980's. The Medical Training Institute (MTIA) and Advanced Training Institute (ATI) have also been added. As we quote from their material, it should be noted that IBLP, IBYC, MTIA, and ATI are the same parent organization functioning under different names.

2 *"Alumni"* is the term the Institute in Basic Life Principles uses when referring to those who have attended the Basic Seminars.

3 Available through www.impactapologetics.com

4 Helena Petrovna Blavatsky, *Studies in Occultism* (Pasadena, CA: Theosophical University Press, n.d.), p. 138 as quoted by Josh McDowell and Don Stewart, *Handbook of Today's Religions* (San Bernardino, Ca: Here's Life Publishers, Inc. for Campus Crusade for Christ, 1983), p. 86.

5 Joseph Smith, Jr. (introduction and notes by B.H. Roberts), *June 10, 1844*, History of the Church, vol. 6 (Salt Lake City, Utah: Deseret Book Co., 1978), p. 432. Mormon Founder Joseph Smith, as Mayor of Nauvoo, Illinois, ordered the *Nauvoo Expositor* to be destroyed. The newspaper had printed an affidavit that exposed Smith's "doctrine of a plurality of wives." Smith recorded: "I immediately ordered the Marshal to destroy it without delay."

6 Phillip Johnson, *The Wedge of Truth* (Downers Grove, IL: InterVarsity Press, 2000), p. 19. Johnson suggests Wentworth was probably only a Christian in a cultural sense with a belief that good works will merit God's blessing in this and the future life; whereas, as bad works will bring about God's judgement in this and the future life. This is a kind of "Jesus-plus" plan of salvation. Although Phillip Johnson may be right about Wentworth, it is very likely many true Christians were experiencing the same difficulty.

7 "Education/Timeline: History 101," *World Magazine* (May/June

2001), p. 13.

8 H.B. Brown, "Euthanasia," *Woodhull & Claflin's Weekly* (15 November 1873).

9 Steven W. Mosher, "The Repackaging of Margaret Sanger," *Wall Street Journal* (5 May 1997).

10 *Murray vs. Curlett*, 374 U.S. 203, 83 S. Ct. 1560 #119, p. 1. (Argued 27 February 1963, decided 7 June 1963. Justice Clark delivered the opinion of the Supreme Court.) The Supreme Court overturned a Maryland law (specifically, Art. 77, Sec. 202 of the Annotated Code of Maryland). According to the text: "The rule provided for the holding of opening exercises in the schools of the city, consisting primarily of the 'reading, without comment, of a chapter in the Holy Bible and/or the use of the Lord's Prayer.' "

11 It is difficult to pin down exactly when Bill Gothard's organization was "founded." Currently, it prefers to date itself back to Gothard's first seminar in 1964.

12 Wilfred Bockelman, *Gothard–The Man And His Ministry: An Evaluation* (Santa Barbara, CA: Quill Publications, 1976), p. 35.

13 *The Encyclopedia of the Jewish Religion*, eds. Werblowsky and Wigoder (New York, NY: Masada Press LTD, 1965), p. 373-374.

Chapter One—Citizen Kane and a History of Inconsistency

1 Pastor Donald A. Waite, *Bill Gothard's Sex Scandals: Watergate or Waterloo?* (Collingswood, NJ: The Bible for Today Ministries, 21 May 1982, photocopied), p. 1. (Note: This document was compiled with the aid of former staff members; and in our interviews with many of them, they referred us to this as the most accurate record of events. This is by no means an affirmation of other writings or positions of Pastor Waite or the ministry of The Bible for Today.)

2 Don Veinot, Joy Veinot, and Ron Henzel, *A Matter of Basic Principles: Bill Gothard and the Christian Life* (Springfield, MO: 21st Century Press, 2002), p. 41.

3 Samuel J. Schultz, notes from former board member S.J. Schultz which were read at board meeting of the Institute in Basic Youth

Conflicts [IBLP], Oakbrook, IL, 11 December 1980 (Collingswood, NJ: The Bible for Today Ministries, photocopy), p. 1.

4 The staffers we spoke with believe Steve was genuinely sorry for his actions. They assert that when Steve finally was confronted biblically with the Bible's teachings on repentance and restoration, he was truly broken and contrite. He moved, became involved in a local church (something which Bill Gothard strongly discouraged among staff members, according to several former staffers with whom we spoke), and eventually married.

5 Waite, *Bill Gothard's Sex Scandals...*, p. 44.

6 Waite, *Bill Gothard's Sex Scandals...*, p. 61. Dr. Edwin Brown was re-elected in November of 1980 for a short time and then removed by Bill Gothard and Dr. Hemwall. Bill Gothard gave three reasons for Brown's removal and upon being confronted by Dr. Brown, confessed to those he had given these false reasons that they were, in fact, untrue.

7 Tom Minnery, "Gothard Staffers Ask Hard Questions and Press for Reforms in Institute," News, *Christianity Today* (6 February 1981), p. 69.

8 Ibid.

9 Ibid.

10 Schultz, notes, p. 3.

11 Waite, *Bill Gothard's Sex Scandals...*, p. 53.

12 Ibid., p. 60.

13 Ibid.

14 "Bill Gothard Steps Down During Institute Shakeup," *Christianity Today* (8 August 1980), p. 46.

15 Ibid., p. 44.

16 Ibid.

17 Bill Gothard, confession at second staff meeting of the Institute in Basic Youth Conflicts [IBLP], Oakbrook, IL, 17 May 1980 as reproduced in Waite, *Bill Gothard's Sex Scandals...*, p. 44 and confirmed by former staff.

18 Ibid.

19 Ibid.

20 Waite, *Bill Gothard's Sex Scandals...*, p. 45.

21 Chuck Lynch, personal interview with Don Veinot, 2000. Lynch, who was third in command at the Institute in Basic Youth Conflicts during this time, said he and other former high-level staffers call the time after this revelation "the slaughter of '76." A number of high-level staffers left to "begin other ministries," take pastorates, and a number of other things. According to other former staffers, some of those who left were given two hours by Bill to vacate their offices. Steve, on the other hand, not only didn't lose any managerial responsibilities, but now was at the retreat center in Michigan with some of the secretaries there and more being sent up by Bill. In at least one case, a mother pleaded with Bill not to send her daughter to the Northwoods, but Bill's decision was made. The young lady also became sexually involved with Steve while at the Northwoods facility. While being secluded away developing the *"Character Booklets"* which are still being used today, the affairs continued and pornographic films were ordered and paid for with ministry funds.

22 Russell Chandler, "Moral, Morale Questions Rock Gothard Ministry," *Los Angeles Times* (5 April 1998).

23 Schultz, notes, p. 2.

24 Waite, *Bill Gothard's Sex Scandals...*, p. 46.

25 Ibid., p. 47.

26 Ibid., p. 49.

27 Schultz, notes, p. 5.

28 Waite, *Bill Gothard's Sex Scandals...*, p. 50.

29 This is yet another example of Gothard's employment of double standards in order to protect his interests. Although Tony's unmarried status was used to bar him from further information gathering, Bill Gothard's single status did not prevent *him* from meeting with the secretaries over the next several weeks.

30 Waite, *Bill Gothard's Sex Scandals...*, p. 52.

31 Schultz, notes, p. 4.

32 Waite, *Bill Gothard's Sex Scandals...*, p. 53.

33 Tony Guhr, during one of several interviews with Don Veinot, 2000. According to Guhr, Dr. Hemwall, one of the directors, backed up this version of events when asked.

34 Waite, *Bill Gothard's Sex Scandals...*, p. 53.

Chapter 2—The Unconfrontable Bill Gothard

1 Bill Gothard, *A Response to the Midwest Christian Journal* (Oak Brook, IL: Institute in Basic Life Principles, 2001, photocopy).

2 Ronald B. Allen (Th.D., Professor of Hebrew Scripture, Western Baptist Theological Seminary) *Issues of Concern–Bill Gothard and the Bible: A Report* (report, Western Baptist Theological Seminary, 30 May 1984), p. 1.

3 Ronald B. Allen, Th.D., a faxed open letter *There You Go Again, Bill Gothard and "The Facts," An Open Letter,* 7 November 1997, p. 3.

4 Ronald B. Allen, Th.D., *Issues of Concern...*, p. 2.

5 Ibid., p. 4.

6 Bill Gothard, letter to Dr. Earl Radmacher, 23 February 1990, p. 3.

7 Ibid., p. 4.

8 L.L.(Don) Veinot, Jr. and Ron Henzel, "Bill Gothard's Evangelical Talmud," *Midwest Christian Outreach, Inc. Journal,* vol. 3, no. 4 (September/October 1997), p. 9.

9 Bill Gothard, letter to Midwest Christian Outreach, Inc., 25 October 1997, p. 3.

10 Ronald B. Allen,Th.D., *There You Go Again...*, pp. 6 & 7.

11 Bill Gothard, letter to Ronald B. Allen, Th.D., 29 November 1997, p. 1.

12 Bill Gothard, *A Response to the Midwest Christian Journal* (Oak Brook, IL: Institute in Basic Life Principles, 2001, faxed to Midwest Christian Outreach, Inc. on 3/3/01), p. 1.

13 Ibid.

14 Bill Gothard, letter to Midwest Christian Outreach, Inc., 25 October 1997, p. 1.

15 Ibid., p. 3.

16 Midwest Christian Outreach, Inc., faxed letter to Bill Gothard, 4 December 1997, pp. 1-4.

17 [MTIA], *How to Make a Wise Decision on Circumcision*, Basic Care Bulletin 11 (1990; Oak Brook, IL: Medical Training Institute of America [IBLP], rev. 1992), p. 2.

18 [IBLP], *Instructions for our Most Important Battle* (Oak Brook, IL: Institute in Basic Life Principles, 1976, booklet), p. 27.

19 Ron Henzel, "Bill Gothard's Evangelical Talmud, Part 3: Gothard and the Law," *Midwest Christian Outreach, Inc. Journal*, vol. 3, no. 5 (July/August 1998), pp. 6-9.

20 Bill Gothard, faxed letter to Midwest Christian Outreach, Inc., 17 July 1998, p. 1.

21 Ibid.

22 Shingleton, Hugh and Heath, Clark, letter to Dr. Peter Rappo, 16 February 1996, concerning the position of the American Academy of Pediatrics on circumcision and the prevention of penile or cervical cancer.

23 Bill Gothard, letter to Dr. Norm Geisler, 2 March 2001.

24 Ibid.

Chapter 3—The Emerald City

1 Ronald B. Allen, Th.D., a faxed open letter *There You Go Again, Bill Gothard and "The Facts,"* An Open Letter, 7 November 1997, p. 1.

2 L.L.(Don) Veinot, Jr. and Ron Henzel, "Bill Gothard's Evangelical Talmud," *Midwest Christian Outreach, Inc. Journal*, vol. 3, no. 4 (September/October 1997), p. 9. These concerns were pointed out originally in this article. Attempts had been made to contact Mr. Gothard prior to writing or printing our research findings to no avail. Bill Gothard, called and then wrote in response to the article, 25 October 1997:

> A further note on accuracy should be stated about your comments on Dr. Allen, "When Dr. Allen attempted to arrange a

meeting with Gothard through his seminary president, Dr. Earl D. Radmacher, in order to discuss these problems, Gothard told Radmacher that 'he had no interest in meeting with me [Allen] to discuss these issues.' "

The facts are that I did meet with Dr. Allen and wrote a detailed response to each of his concerns and then asked for a further meeting with him.

When we contacted Dr. Allen for his comments and to confirm the accuracy or lack thereof in our article, he responded with a seven-page open letter ("There You Go Again, Bill Gothard and 'The Facts,' An Open Letter"). In this document, he declares such a meeting never occurred in spite of a 23-year attempt on his part to bring this about. In it, he stated that, at this point, the only thing he wishes to receive from Bill: "It is a brief, no-excuses, no-defenses, abject apology for your blatant, outrageous lies about me." This letter is reproduced in its entirety on our web site at www.midwest-outreach.org

3 Wilfred Bockelman, *Gothard–The Man and His Ministry: An Evaluation* (Santa Barbara, CA: Quill Publications, 1976), pp. 39-40.

4 Ibid., pp. 19-20.

5 Bill Gothard, letter to Midwest Christian Outreach, Inc., 28 November 1997. Gothard wrote in response to this statement: "The next presupposition in your second article is equally inaccurate. 'Gothard materials are difficult to track down these days, unless you actually know some "alumni" who will let you borrow their copies.' I am enclosing a publications order form which is distributed at our seminars and sent to anyone who requests information on books that are available to the public." Upon review of the catalog, it was noted the material in question is not available to the public (as we pointed out) and does not appear in the catalog. Unwittingly, Mr. Gothard confirmed our statement as accurate.

6 Bill Gothard (instructor), *Basic Seminar Textbook* (Printed in United States of America: Institute in Basic Youth Conflicts [IBLP], 1979), p. 3.

7 Ibid., p. 12.

8 Bill Gothard, letter to Midwest Christian Outreach, Inc., 28 November 1997. Gothard wrote in response to this statement: "It is quite an assumption for you to say positively what Jesus did not have in His mind when he spoke to the needs of the common people. And when by the Holy Spirit He guided Paul in writing that 'All Scripture is given by inspiration of God, and is profitable for doctrine, for reproof, for correction, for instruction in righteousness:' (2 Timothy 3:16)" While it is true we cannot know positively what Jesus had on His mind, it is equally true that neither can Mr. Gothard. We only have the text with which to deal, and this is a mystical understanding of the passage not based on any recognizable or commonly accepted hermeneutic.

9 Bill Gothard (instructor), *Basic Seminar Textbook*, p. 20.

10 Bill Gothard, *The Sevenfold Power of First-Century Churches and Homes* (Oak Brook, IL: Institute in Basic Life Principles, 2000), pp. 83-84.

11 Jay E. Adams, *The Christian's Guide to Guidance: How to Make Biblical Decisions* (Woodruff, SC: Timeless Texts, 1998), p. 41.

12 Dr. Harry Adams is a graduate of Dallas Theological Seminary and was in pastoral ministry for over 25 years. In late 1997, he was diagnosed with Lou Gehrig's disease which ended his pulpit ministry. He continues a writing ministry and is an occasional contributor to the *Midwest Christian Outreach, Inc. Journal*.

13 The practice of divination (which is prohibited in the Scriptures) using the Scriptures.

14 Dr. Thomas Howe is co-author (along with Dr. Norman L. Geisler) of *When Critics Ask* (Wheaton, IL: Victor Books, 1992) and is currently Professor of Biblical Languages at Southern Evangelical Seminary in Charlotte, NC.

15 These areas will be discussed in chapter ten, "Bill Gothard: Medicine Man"

16 Bill Gothard (instructor), *Basic Seminar Textbook*, p. 20.

17 Ibid.

18 Ibid.

19 Ibid.

20 [WTBTS], "Theocratic Organization with which to Move Forward Now," *The Watchtower* (15 December 1981), p. 754.

21 [WTBTS], "Move Ahead with Jehovah's Organization," *The Watchtower* (1 June 1967), p. 337. Emphasis in original.

22 [WTBTS], "Exposing the Devil's Subtle Designs," *The Watchtower* (15 January 1983), p. 22.

23 Ibid., p. 27.

24 Martin Luther, *The Bondage of the Will,* trans. J.I. Packer and O.R. Johnston (Old Tappan, NJ: Fleming H. Revell Company, 1957), p. 69.

25 James Sire, *Scripture Twisting: 20 Ways the Cults Misread the Bible* (Downers Grove, IL: InterVarsity Press, 1980), p. 41-42.

26 The *Midwest Christian Outreach, Inc. Journal* is a quarterly publication of Midwest Christian Outreach, Inc., Lombard, IL.

27 Bill Gothard, letter to Midwest Christian Outreach, Inc., 28 November 1997.

28 Last name withheld at their request.

29 According to Jack and Chris Schultz, this was partially the result of a family whom the pastor had attempted to assist in entering the Advanced Training Institute program a year earlier who were now considering leaving the church. They had begun asking the pastor pointed questions about concerns they had. The pastor assumed Chris had influenced the family to ask the questions, and questioning the pastor's authority is not allowed in IBLP teachings.

30 *Vine's Complete Expository Dictionary of Old and New Testament Words,* ed. W.E. Vine, Merrill F. Unger, William White, Jr. (Nashville, TN: Thomas Nelson Publishers, 1985), p. 438.

31 Ibid., p. 607.

Chapter 4—IBLP: Institute in Basic Legalistic Practices

1 Bill Gothard, letter to Midwest Christian Outreach, Inc., 25 October 1997.

2 Ibid.

3 For definitions from three evangelical writers: Erwin W. Lutzer, *How In This World Can I Be Holy?* (Chicago, IL: Moody Press, 1974), pp. 82-92; J.I. Packer, *Concise Theology* (Wheaton, IL: Tyndale House, 1993), pp. 175-77; Charles C. Ryrie, *The Grace of God* (Chicago, IL: Moody Press, 1963), pp. 73-84.

4 [IBYC], *Instructions for our Most Important Battle* (Oak Brook, IL: Institute in Basic Youth Conflicts [IBLP], 1976), p. 27.

5 [IBLP], *How to Respond to the Term Legalism* (Oak Brook, IL: Institute in Basic Life Principles, 1996, tract), p. 1.

6 The Federal Reserve Board Chairman heads the agency that controls the American money supply.

7 Philippians 3:4b-6 NIV. Emphasis added.

8 Erwin W. Lutzer, *How In This World Can I Be Holy?* (Chicago, IL: Moody Press, 1974), pp. 82-92.

9 Ibid., p. 83. Also J.I. Packer, *Keeping in Step With the Spirit* (Tarrytown, NY: Fleming H. Revell, 1984), p. 112; J.I. Packer, *Concise Theology* (Wheaton, IL: Tyndale House, 1993), p. 176.

10 Jerry Bridges, *Transforming Grace: Living Confidently in God's Unfailing Love* (Colorado Springs: CO: NavPress, 1991), pp. 122-124; Erwin W. Lutzer, *How In This World Can I Be Holy?* (Chicago, IL: Moody Press, 1974), pp. 83-84.

11 Millard J. Erickson, *The Evangelical Mind and Heart: Perspectives on Theological and Practical Issues* (Grand Rapids, MI: Baker Book House, 1993), p. 69; John Calvin (1509-1564), "2.7.16," *Institutes of the Christian Religion*, vol. 1, in the Library of Christian Classics, vol. XX, ed. John T. McNeill, trans. Ford Lewis Battles, (n.d.; reprint, Philadelphia, PA: The Westminster Press, 1960), p. 364; William Ames (1576-1633), "1.39.9," *The Marrow of Theology*, trans. John D. Eusden, (n.d.; reprint, Durham, NC: Labyrinth Press, 1968), p. 206. Westminster Confession of Faith, XX.I.

12 [IBLP], *How to Respond to the Term Legalism*, p. 1.

13 The *Mishnah*, tractate Aboth 1:1

14 Aboth 3:14.

15 Matthew 11:28-30 KJV.

16 *The Internet Encyclopedia of Philosophy*, gen. ed. James Fieser, Ph,.D. and asst. ed. Bradley Dowden, Ph.D., The term "supererogation" refers to good action beyond what is morally required. The expression has its roots in Christian Theology referring to good works done in a state of grace in excess of the strict requirements of the divine law, and constituting a store of merit which may be used for the benefit of souls in purgatory of other penitent persons. The Roman Catholic doctrine of supererogation rests upon a distinction between what is mandatory and what is merely advisory in the divine law. With reference to the latter, humans are free and may lay up a store of merit which under given circumstances may be applied to the benefit of others. The doctrine involves a point of radical difference between Catholic and Reformed Christian churches, the latter denying the validity of the distinction on which the doctrine of supererogation exists.

http://www.utm.edu/research/iep/s/superero.htm

17 Carl B. Hoch Jr., *All Things New* (Grand Rapids, MI: Baker Book House, 1995), p. 212.

18 Bill Gothard, *The Sevenfold Power of First-Century Churches and Homes* (Oak Brook, IL: Institute in Basic Life Principles, 2000), p. 88.

19 Walter Kaiser, "The Law as God's Guidance for the Promotion of Holiness," *The Law, the Gospel, and the Modern Christian* (Grand Rapids, MI: Zondervan, 1993), p. 198.

20 [MTIA], *The Unexpected Benefits of Periodic Abstinence In Marriage* (1991; Oak Brook, IL: Medical Training Institute of America [IBLP], rev. 1992), p. 5.

21 [MTIA], *How to Make a Wise Medical Decision on Circumcision* (1990; Oak Brook, IL: Medical Training Institute of America [IBLP], rev. 1992). The statement had to do with the general topic of circumcision.

22 Ibid., pp. 11-14.

23 Ibid., pp. 7-8.

24 Ibid., p. 2.

25 Robert J. Sheridan, "Bill Gothard and Dispensationalism" (term paper, Calvary Bible College, 1984), p. 20. In this paper, Sheridan

wrote, "...if there is a dispensational approach [in Gothard] it is inconsistent. However, I detect few, if any, dispensational tendencies in Gothard."

26 "Formula of Concord, Article VI," in Philip and David S. Schaff, eds., *The Creeds of Christendom*, 6th ed., rev. by David S. Schaff, vol 3 (1931; reprint, Grand Rapids, MI: Baker Book House, 1985), pp. 130-31.

27 [IBLP], "We Despised His Law," *The Power of the Living Church: A Biblical Strategy for Courageous Pastors and Congregations* (Oak Brook, IL: Institute in Basic Life Principles, n.d.), p. 24. See especially point 25.

28 Ibid.

29 [IBLP], *Be Alert to Spiritual Danger* (Oak Brook, IL: Institute in Basic Life Principles, 1980), p. 12.

30 S.I. McMillen, M.D, *None of These Diseases* (n.d.; reprint, Tarrytown, NY: Fleming H. Revell, 1963).

31 Ibid., pp. 17-22.

32 From the Greek word *apologia* meaning "a speech made in defense." *Vine's Complete Expository Dictionary of Old and New Testament Words*, ed. W.E. Vine, Merrill F. Unger, William White, Jr. (Nashville, TN: Thomas Nelson Publishers, 1985), p. 154.

33 Especially R.K. Harrison, *Introduction to the Old Testament* (Grand Rapids, MI: William B. Eerdmans Publishing Company, 1969), p. 605; and R. Laird Harris, "Leviticus," *Expositor's Bible Commentary*, vol. 2 (Grand Rapids, MI: Zondervan, 1990), pp. 529-30.

34 Gordon J. Wenham, "Leviticus," *New International Commentary on the Old Testament* (Grand Rapids, MI: William B. Eerdmans Publishing Company, 1979), pp. 167-168.

35 [MTIA], *How to Make a Wise Medical Decision on Circumcision*, p. 2.

36 Ibid., p. 5.

37 N.T. Wright, *The Climax of the Covenant: Christ and the Law in Pauline Theology* (Minneapolis, MN: Fortress Press, 1992), p. 241.

38 See also: R.Y.K. Fung, who further writes, "Paul does not mean that the law exerts a gradual, educative influence on people, either by inclining them toward good until they receive Christ or by

enabling them to realize their own sin, turn their backs on trusting their own merits, and desire the grace of Christ. ... Paul's primary concern in these verses (22-25) is not to describe the genesis of individual faith in terms of psychological development, but to sketch the progress of salvation history. His meaning is rather that the law brought mankind into, and kept mankind under, an objectively desperate situation, from which there was no escape until the revelation of faith as a new possibility." *Galatians* (Grand Rapids, MI: William B. Eerdmans Publishing Company, 1988), pp. 168-179. Thus, it is obvious that to say that the law still functions as a schoolmaster directly contradicts Paul's point. F.F. Bruce agrees, writing, "Paul does not ascribe an educative role to the law..." *Galatians* (Grand Rapids, MI: William B. Eerdmans Publishing Company, 1982), p. 182. NASB renders the verb (*ginomai* in the perfect tense) as "has become" which is an attempt to bring out the perfect tense but at the cost of introducing ambiguity. It is still not the same as "is." F.F. Bruce's use of "has been" is a better choice.

39 Ibid.

40 [MTIA], *The Unexpected Benefits of Periodic Abstinence in Marriage*, Basic Care Bulletin 12 (1991; Oak Brook, IL: Medical Training Institute of America [IBLP], rev. 1992), pp. 5 & 6.

41 Rev. James M. Freeman, A.M., *Manners and Customs of the Bible* (Plainfield, New Jersey: Logos International, 1972), p. 73. Rev. Freeman points out the prohibition in verse 19 is not against eating dairy and meat together, but rather it is a prohibition against a pagan sacrificial practice:

> XXIII, 19, Thou shalt not seethe a kid in his mother's milk.

> As this injunction is put in connection with sacrifices and festivals, it seems to have referred to some idolatrous practices of the heathen. Cudworth says, on the authority of an ancient Karaite Comment on the Pentateuch, that it was an ancient heathen custom to boil a kid in the dam's milk and then besprinkle with it all the trees, fields, gardens, and orchards.

This was done at the close of their harvests for the purpose of making trees and fields more fruitful the following year. It will be noticed that the injunction of the text is given in connection with the feast of harvest.

See also Joseph P. Free, Ph.D., *Archaeology and Bible History* (Wheaton, IL: Scripture Press Publications, Inc., 1974), p. 123

When Moses was giving certain restrictions and dietary law, he repeated a command which appeared two times earlier in the Pentateuch, "Thou shalt not seethe a kid in his mother's milk" (Ex. 23:19, 34:26; Deut. 14:21). Though commentators have sought the explanation of this rather strange command, it was not until the discovery of the Ras Shamra tablets that an adequate explanation was forthcoming. A similar rite is recorded on the Ras Shamra tablets, which indicates that if one wishes to gain favor with a deity, he should slay a kid in milk and present it to the deity. The discovery of this Ras Shamra text suggests why the Lord prohibited this rite before the children of Israel entered the Canaan. He was forewarning Israel of the pagan rites which she would be tempted to practice in imitation of her pagan neighbors in Canaan.

Chapter 5—Character First!

1 Bob Norman, "Little Soldiers in the Culture War: Evangelical Radical Bill Gothard's *Character First!* Curriculum Teaches Students in Fort Lauderdale to Obey His Will," *New Time Broward – Palm Beach Online* (http://www.newtimesbpb.com/issues/1999-02-18/feature.html/page1.html, 2/18/1999), pp. 1-2.

2 Ibid., p. 2.

3 Bill Gothard, *Definition of Grace* (Oak Brook, IL: Institute in Basic Life Principles, 2000), p. 3.

4 Ibid., p. 1.

5 Ibid.

6 The standard lexicon for New Testament Greek is: Walter Bauer, *A Greek-English Lexicon of the New Testament and Other Early Christian*

Literature, 2d ed., eds. William F. Arndt, F. Wilbur Gingrich and Frederick W. Danker (Chicago, IL: University of Chicago Press, 1979). The standard lexicon for biblical Hebrew and Aramaic is: Francis Brown, S.R. Driver, and Charles A. Briggs, *The Brown-Driver-Briggs Hebrew and English Lexicon* (1906; reprint, Peabody, MA: Hendrickson Publishers, 1996). These authorities do not support Bill Gothard's definition of grace.

7 About 84 percent of the time, *charis* is translated simply as "grace" in the KJV; and just short of four percent of the time, it uses the nearly synonymous "favour." Nearly eight percent of the time, the KJV renders *charis* with words relating to the concept of gratitude ("thank," "thanks," "thanked," and "thankworthy"), and twice it has "pleasure." All other KJV translations ("gracious," "liberality," "benefit," "gift," "joy," and "acceptable") occur only once each.

8 Gothard, *Definition of Grace,* p. 2.

9 Cf. *Theological Dictionary of the New Testament,* eds. Gerhard Kittel and Gerhard Friedrich (n.d.; abridged 10 vols. in one by trans. Geoffrey W. Bromiley, Grand Rapids, MI: William B. Eerdmans Publishing Company, 1985), p. 1306.

10 Gothard, *Definition of Grace,* p. 3.

11 For example, on page 3 of *Definition of Grace,* he uses 2 Corinthians 8:9 to demonstrate "Grace Enables Generosity," rather than it's actual meaning—our spiritual poverty (a euphemism for our sins) was imputed to Christ, while His spiritual wealth has been imputed to us.

12 Gothard, *Definition of Grace,* p. 3.

13 Ibid., p. 1.

14 Ibid., p. 3.

15 J.I. Packer, *Knowing God* (Downers Grove, IL: InterVarsity Press, 1973), p. 120.

16 "Grace in its fullest definition is God's unmerited favor in the gift of His Son..." Charles Caldwell Ryrie, "Grace" in C.F. Pfeiffer *Wycliffe Bible Encyclopedia,* eds. H.F. Vos, and J. Rea (n.d.; 2 vols. in one, Chicago, IL: Moody Press, 1975), p. 726. "God's 'grace' means his 'unmerited favor.' " Wayne Grudem, *Systematic Theology* (Grand

Rapids, MI: Zondervan Publishing House, 1994), p. 729. "...[grace's] meaning is that of undeserved blessing freely bestowed on man by God..." Philip Edgcumbe Hughes, "Grace," *Evangelical Dictionary of Theology*, ed. Walter Elwell (Grand Rapids, MI: Baker Book House, 1984), p. 479. Examples such as these could be multiplied *ad infinitum*.

17 J.I. Packer, *God's Words: Studies of Key Bible Themes* (Downers Grove, IL: InterVarsity Press, 1981), p. 96.

18 Gothard, *Definition of Grace*, p. 3.

19 Gothard, *Definition of Grace, p.* 3. At this point Gothard writes, "For example, Martin Luther was so committed to the fact that salvation is by grace alone that he did not know how to deal with the verse in James that states, 'faith without works is dead.' " But Luther's actual problem was interpreting verses like James 2:21, "Was not Abraham our father justified by works?" While Luther's rejection of James from the canon of Scripture was wrong, so also is Gothard's distortion of his reasons.

20 "The Canons and Decrees of the Council of Trent," Session VI, Chapter XVI, in Philip and David S. Schaff, eds., *The Creeds of Christendom*, 6th ed., rev. by David S. Schaff, vol. 2 (1931; reprint, Grand Rapids, MI: Baker Book House, 1985), p. 108.

21 See especially "The Canons and Decrees of the Council of Trent" Session VI, Chapter VIII, in Philip and David S. Schaff, eds., *The Creeds of Christendom*, 6th ed., rev. by David S. Schaff, vol. 2 (1931; reprint, Grand Rapids, MI: Baker Book House, 1985), p. 97. In this chapter, the Tridentine bishops reasoned, "...we are therefore said to be justified *freely*, because that none of those things which precede justification-whether faith or works-merit the grace of justification itself." However, in the context of Roman Catholic theology, this only applies to the initial stage of salvation (*regeneration*, which we call "justification," and which for Rome, comes at infant baptism). From that point on salvation is conditioned on our works. See also Norman L. Geisler and Ralph E. MacKenzie, "Justification," in *Roman Catholics and Evangelicals: Agreements and Differences* (Grand Rapids, MI: Baker Book House, 1995), pp. 221-248.

22 "The Canons and Decrees of the Council of Trent," Session VI,

Chapter VII, in Philip and David S. Schaff, eds., *The Creeds of Christendom*, 6th ed., rev. by David S. Schaff, vol. 2 (1931; reprint, Grand Rapids, MI: Baker Book House, 1985), p. 94.

23 [WTBTS], *Our Kingdom Ministry*, vol. 36, no. 12 [Brooklyn, NY: (Watch Tower Bible and Tract Society of Pennsylvania) Watchtower Bible and Tract Society of New York, Inc. and International Bible Students Association, 1993], p. 7.

24 Leupold wrote concerning the Hebrew word *tsaddîq* ("righteous"): "However, the term is basically forensic. Therefore, though there be divine approval, that does not imply perfection on Noah's part. It merely implies that those things that God sought in man were present in Noah. Primarily, God desired man to believe Him and His promise of help through the seed of the woman. This basic requirement Noah met, and his conduct showed it." Herbert Carl Leupold, *Exposition of Genesis*, vol. 1 (Grand Rapids, MI: Baker Book House, 1963), p. 265.

25 Gothard, *Definition of Grace*, p. 3.

26 Ibid.

27 Ibid.

28 Ibid., p. 4.

29 John A. Miller, *Bill Gothard: How His Teachings Will Put You into the Bondage of Legalism*, (essay, 24 July 1997).

30 John Calvin (1509-1564), *Institutes of the Christian Religion* vol. 1, in the Library of Christian Classics, vol. XX, ed. John T. McNeill, trans. Ford Lewis Battles (n.d.; reprint, Philadelphia, PA: The Westminster Press, 1960), p. 837.

31 Charles Hodge, *Systematic Theology*, vol. 2 (1871-1872; reprint, Grand Rapids, MI: William B. Eerdmans Publishing Company, 1982), pp. 517-518.

Chapter 6—A Black-and-White Gospel for a Color World

1 Jerry Bridges, *Transforming Grace: Living Confidently in God's Unfailing Love* (Colorado Springs, CO: NavPress, 1991), pp. 130-131.

2 Bill Gothard, A *Response to Antinomian Rationalism* (self-published paper, Oak Brook, IL: Institute in Basic Life Principles, n.d.), p. 1.

3 Bridges, *Transforming Grace...*, p. 130.

4 Gothard, *A Response to Antinomian Rationalism*, p. 2.

5 Ibid.

6 Ibid., p. 3.

7 Ibid.

8 Ibid., pp. 2-3. "The Test of Scripture," "The Test of the Holy Spirit," and "The Test of Faith and Genuine Love."

9 Bill Gothard, "A Note From Bill..." to "alumni" of his Basic Seminar (Oak Brook, IL: Institute in Basic Life Principles, n.d.), promotional literature. Based on its photograph of Gothard (find it posted on the web site at http://www.midwestoutreach.org/02-Information/02-OnlineReference/04-Etc/01-TheJournal/Volume3/No5-BillGothardsEvangelicalTalmudPt2.html) we estimate it was printed in the late 1970s or early 1980s. In it, Gothard wrote, "The message of the Basic Seminar is being looked to by a growing number of judges, mayors, governors, and international leaders as the only answer to youth crime and family breakdown." Especially notice that Gothard credits his seminar with being "the only answer" to this problem. In the next paragraph he wrote, " 'We have no answers,' these leaders say to us, 'but we see the results in your families and young people, and we will do whatever it takes to have the same results.' " Gothard does not cite his sources for these quotes.

10 Gothard, *A Response to Antinomian Rationalism*, p. 1.

11 Perhaps the most notorious such incident took place on April 20, 1999, at Columbine High School in Littleton, Colorado. Two students, Eric Harris and Dylan Klebold, armed with semi-automatic handguns, shotguns, and explosives conducted an assault there that left one teacher and 12 of their fellow students dead, 24 students hospitalized, and another 160 students who required treatment at the scene. The suspects killed themselves inside the school by means of self-inflicted gunshots.

12 At the time of this writing, the web site for the U.S. Department of Justice's Bureau of Justice Statistics was located at http://www.ojp.usdoj.gov/bjs/

13 Ibid. According to the spreadsheet data referred to in the next note, "Violent Index offenses include murder and non-negligent manslaughter, forcible rape, robbery, [and] aggravated assault."

14 This information was taken from spreadsheet data downloaded from the "Criminal Offenders Statistics" page of the U.S. Department of Justice's Bureau of Justice Statistics web site, which at the time of this writing was located at http://www.ojp.usdoj.gov/bjs/crimoff.htm The link to the spreadsheet file was found under the heading "Selected Statistics," where it describes it as, "The number of violent crime arrests of juveniles (under age 18) and adults (age 18 or older), 1970-99, 10/00 Spreadsheet (11K)." The data source indicated in the spreadsheet is "FBI, Uniform Crime Reports."

15 Ibid.

16 Gothard, A Response to Antinomian Rationalism, p. 1.

17 Ron Henzel, "Bill Gothard's Evangelical Talmud, Part 3: Gothard and the Law," Midwest Christian Outreach, Inc. Journal, vol. 4, no. 3 (July/August 1998), pp. 6-9.

18 Peter A. Angeles, Dictionary of Philosophy (New York, NY: Barnes and Noble Books/Harper and Row, Publishers, 1981), p. 236. See "rationalism."

19 Webster's New Collegiate Dictionary (Springfield, MA: G. & C. Merriam Co., 1977), p. 958. See "rationalism."

20 Francis A. Schaeffer, The Church at the End of the 20th Century (Downers Grove, IL: Inter-Varsity Press, 1971), p. 11.

21 Erwin W. Lutzer, How In This World Can I Be Holy? (Chicago, IL: Moody Press, 1974), p. 81.

22 "The History of the Creeds," Philip and David S. Schaff, eds., The Creeds of Christendom, 6th ed., rev. by David S. Schaff, vol. 1 (1931; reprint, Grand Rapids, MI: Baker Book House, 1985), pp. 278-279. Twentieth-century church historian Robert D. Linder concurs: "Agricola argued that people were sufficiently motivated by hearing of Christ's sacrifice for their sins that the preaching of the law was unnecessary and perhaps even harmful. Luther responded that although the severity of Christ's sacrifice indeed demonstrated the enormity of

human sin, the law still needed to be preached forcefully, and people still had to be convicted of their sin by the law." "Agricola, Johann," *Evangelical Dictionary of Theology*, ed. Walter A. Elwell (Grand Rapids, MI: Baker Book House, 1984), p. 25.

23 D. Martyn Lloyd-Jones, *Romans: An Exposition of Chapter 6, The New Man* (Grand Rapids, MI: Zondervan, 1973), pp. 9-10 as quoted in Steve Brown, *When Being Good Isn't Good Enough* (Nashville, TN: Thomas Nelson Publishers, 1990), pp. 102-103.

24 Ibid., pp. 71-72. Emphasis his.

25 Henny Youngman, *The Best Little Book of One-Liners* (Philadelphia, PA: Running Press, 1992). The pages in this tiny, hand-sized book are not numbered.

26 Gothard, *A Response to Antinomian Rationalism*, p. 4.

27 Henzel, "Bill Gothard's Evangelical Talmud, Part 3...," pp. 8-9.

28 Gothard, *A Response to Antinomian Rationalism*, p. 5.

29 Ibid., p. 1. At one point Gothard writes, "When I discovered that the chief writer of the article had never attended a Basic Seminar, we made an unprecedented attempt to accommodate his schedule by lending him a set of the Basic Seminar tapes for his private viewing. After several more months and additional articles, he still had not viewed the whole Seminar. Therefore, I began to realize that his issues of concern were different than what I had suspected." In reality, Henzel personally informed Gothard during a phone conversation that he had viewed "about 90 percent" of the taped Seminar, and needed more time to view the remainder. This was during a period in which Henzel was working on a master's degree, had just adopted an infant son with his wife, and was working a regular full-time job. Shortly after that conversation, Don Veinot granted an interview to a Christian radio station in Milwaukee, and the interviewer brought up the subject of Bill Gothard, so Veinot responded with his honest opinions. Immediately after that, members of Gothard's staff contacted Henzel demanding the return of the videos. In a private conversation with the IBLP staff member who came to retrieve the videos from Henzel, the staff member acknowledged it was Veinot's radio interview that provoked the demand that the tapes be returned.

30 Gothard, A *Response to Antinomian Rationalism*, p. 4.

31 Ibid., p. 6.

32 Ibid., p. 3.

33 Isaac Watts (1674-1748), *At The Cross*, first stanza.

34 Gothard, A *Response to Antinomian Rationalism*, p. 2.

35 The Greek in the last clause of Romans 14:1 is somewhat ambiguous. The phrase rendered in the KJV as "but not to doubtful disputations" can also be rendered as "without passing judgment on disputable matters"(as in the NIV) or "but not for the purpose of passing judgment on his opinions" (as in the NASB). However, the basic thought remains the same.

36 Gothard, A *Response to Antinomian Rationalism*, p. 3.

37 Rebecca Manley Pippert, *Out of the Saltshaker and Into the World* (Downers Grove, IL: InterVarsity Press, 1979) as quoted by Alice Gray, *More Stories for the Heart*, Alice Gray, comp. (Portland, OR: Multnomah Press, 1997), pp. 32-33.

Chapter 7—The Orwellian World of Bill Gothard

1 Mrs. Jenice Miller, "20 Years a Gothard Slave—Free At Last!!" B.F.T. #1953, A Critique of the Works of Bill Gothard (essay, North Chicago, IL: December 1989), p. 9.

2 *Stepford Wives*, produced by Edgar J. Scherick, directed by Bryan Forbes, 115 minutes, Anchor Bay, 1975. This reference comes from the film starring Katherine Ross, Paula Prentiss, and Peter Masterson, in which the men of the town of Stepford conspired together to replace their wives with automatons who were non-thinking, obedient women.

3 Melody Pake is the wife of Judge David Pake who is on the Board of Governors for IBLP's correspondence law school.

4 A totalistic group is one which portends to have all the answers to all of life's questions, discourages independent thinking, and requires total submission of all aspects of your life to their authority.

5 Pastor Keith Gibson, "When Gothard Comes to Church," *Midwest Christian Outreach, Inc. Journal*, vol. 6, no. 1 (Winter 2000), p. 4.

6 The *Watchtower* is one of the bi-weekly publications of the Watchtower Bible and Tract Society, more commonly known as Jehovah's Witnesses.

7 [WTBTS], "The Devil's Subtle Design," *The Watchtower* (15 January 1983), p. 22.

8 Mrs. Melody Pake, telephone conversation with Don Veinot, August 2000. Mrs. Pake pointed out that while at *Alert!*, her son's phone calls were monitored and all of his mail was opened and read prior to being given to him. (*Alert!* is a paramilitary training school for teenagers IBLP/ATI operates. It was in Watersmeet, MI, until it was recently moved to Big Sandy, TX.)

9 Gibson, "When Gothard Comes to Church," p 5.

10 Ibid.

11 Dr. James Alsdurf, who had been conducting research on abuse, said of Bill Gothard in an interview in Willmar Thorkelson, "Evangelical Pastors Alerted on Wife Abuse," *Washington Post* (13 April 1985), p. D12, "...the one-dimensional model of submission that flows from the Bill Gothard model can in many situations be ripe ground for both the psychological and physical victimization of women because it gives men implicit permission to mistreat women."

12 http://members.tripod.com/Glenwood37/homepage.htm

13 Carmen Langhofer, e-mail to Don Veinot, 11 September 1999. Don Veinot has had numerous telephone discussions with Carmen Langhofer over these issues as well.

14 As we discussed in chapter 2, according to Gothard a *rhema* conveys the idea that God gives additional special revelation. Thus, Gothard is essentially claiming to be a prophet. If the prophecy he had given regarding Pastor Johnny Jones being the man for whom he had prayed six years wasn't true, Gothard is a false prophet. On the other hand, if it was true, Gothard was now in rebellion to God.

15 Mail tampering is a Federal offense.

16 [IBLP], *Establishing Biblical Standards of Courtship* (Oak Brook, IL: Institute in Basic Life Principles, 1993), p. 6.

17 Ibid., pp. 6-7.

Chapter 8—Alpena Mountain Home

1 Steve Hamm's father was an orange grower.

2 Bill Gothard, letter to Steve Hamm, 22 November 1999.

3 James L. White, " 'Eagle Mountain' Looks at New Facility," *Times Viewer* (18-22 June 2000), p. 24. This article reiterates this.

4 Nancy Varvil, "Officials See Poor Rural Enforcement Of State Safety Codes," *Arkansas Democrat Gazette* (13 May 2001), p. 17.

5 James Hughes (Hughes Building Inspection), letter to Steve Hamm, 4 May 1996.

6 During typical construction, the area at the perimeter is excavated (dug down) to below the normal frostline to clay or some substantially solid surface. A concrete footing is installed upon which the foundation is then built.

7 James Hughes, (Hughes Building Inspection), letter to Donnie Barr (IBLP), 27 August 1996.

8 A large tractor-type machine with a shovel designed for digging foundations.

9 Roger Kobie, letter to Judge David and Melody Pake, 10 February 2000.

10 Rev. G. Richard Fisher is pastor of the Laurelton Park Baptist Church in Bricktown, NJ and researcher and writer for Personal Freedom Outreach.

11 A legal agreement which would protect the Hamm family and hold the Institute in Basic Life Principles solely responsible for any injury or property damage due to these unsafe conditions.

12 Steve Hamm, letter to Bill Gothard, 3 October 1999, p. 1.

13 Ibid., p. 2.

14 Deborah K. Sexton (Deborah Sexton Attorney at Law, representing Steve Hamm), letter to Steve Hamm, 12 October 1999.

15 Steve and Karen Hamm, letter to James Sammons (board member, IBLP), 22 October 1999.

16 Ibid., p. 3.

17 Robert J. Barth (General Counsel, IBLP), letter to Deborah K.

Sexton (Deborah Sexton Attorney at Law, representing Steve Hamm), 20 October 1999.

18 Ibid.

19 Deborah K. Sexton (Deborah Sexton Attorney at Law, representing Steve Hamm), letter to Robert J. Barth (General Counsel, IBLP), 27 October 1999, p. 1.

20 Ibid., p. 2.

21 Hamm family, letter to Bill Gothard and the IBLP board members, 19 November 1999, p. 1.

22 Ibid., p. 1 & 2.

23 Bill Gothard, letter to Steve Hamm, 22 November 1999, p. 1.

24 Ibid., p. 2.

25 Eagle Mountain West is a nearby property where IBLP had begun to focus its attentions earlier and completed a 12,000 square foot building by June of 2000.

26 Bill Gothard, letter to Steve Hamm, 22 November 1999, p. 2.

27 Bill Gothard, letter to Steve Hamm, 26 November 1999, p. 1.

28 Ibid.

29 Bill Gothard, letter to Steve and Karen Hamm, 10 December 1999, p. 2.

30 Hamm family, letter to Bill Gothard, 24 February 2000.

31 Bill Gothard, letter to Steve & Karen Hamm, 29 May 2000.

32 Ibid.

33 Ibid.

34 Bill Gothard, letter to Steve and Karen Hamm, 30 May 2000, p. 1.

35 Ibid., p. 2.

Chapter 9—The Courtship Game

1 Joshua Harris, "Searching For True Love Part 1: Beyond Formulas," *New Attitude: The Christian Magazine for Home School Teens*, vol. 3, no. 2 (summer 1995), p. 9.

2 Ronald Barclay Allen, *Gothard–Again* (Course: Old Testament

523-Exegesis in Wisdom Literature, Western Baptist Seminary, 1985), p. 2.

3 Bill Gothard (instructor), *Basic Seminar Textbook* (Printed in United States of America: Institute in Basic Youth Conflicts [IBLP], 1979), p. 20.

4 Bill Gothard, cited by Wilfred Bockelman, *Gothard–The Man And His Ministry: An Evaluation* (Santa Barbara, CA: Quill Publications, 1976), p. 73.

5 Bill Gothard (instructor), *Basic Seminar Textbook* (Printed in United States of America: Institute in Basic Youth Conflicts [IBLP], 1979), p. 19.

6 Institute in Basic Youth Conflicts, *How To Get Under God's Protection* (Oak Brook, IL: Institute in Basic Youth Conflicts [IBLP], 1987), pp. 3-4.

7 Bockelman, *Gothard–The Man and His Ministry: An Evaluation*, pp. 80 & 83. On page 82, Bockelman cites some interesting examples of what typically happens when these theories are put into practice. One person is cited as saying, " 'I used to have a good relationship with my boss. He was kind. I thought we worked together well. We respected each other. Then he went to an institute in Basic Youth Conflicts Seminar, and ever since then he has been much harder to work for. He now has the idea of authority, and we no longer have the spirit at work we used to have.' A friend told me, 'I have a sister and brother-in-law, who have just the greatest family. They have two children, both below 10. There is an excellent relationship between the parents and the children. The kids get along well with each other and with their parents. It's just the kind of ideal family I'd like to have. Then the father went to the Institute in Basic Youth Conflicts, and now everything is changed. He's an authoritarian tyrant The kids are getting nervous. Something happened.' "

8 Rev. G. Richard Fisher, "A Study in Evolving Fadism: The Cultic Leanings of Bill Gothard's Teachings," *The Quarterly Journal of Personal Freedom Outreach*, vol. 16, no. 2 (April-June 1996), p. 7.

9 [IBLP], *Establishing Biblical Standards of Courtship* (Oak Brook, IL: Institute in Basic Life Principles, 1993), p. 6.

10 Ibid., p. 6.

11 Ibid., pp. 6-7.

12 Ibid., p. 8.

13 Ibid., p. 7.

14 Ibid., p. 6.

15 Ibid., p. 9.

16 Ibid.

17 Ibid., p. 10.

18 Ibid., p. 11.

19 Jacob Prasch, "What the Holy Ghost Explicitly Says About The Last Days," MORIEL Prayer and Newsletter (December 1999/January 2000), the subtitle "Doctrines of Demons" begins on page 2 and the quote about Gothard is on page 3. Jacob Prasch writes, "Disturbing also is the anti-matrimonial bias of Bill Gothard and his youth seminars. The potential consequences of Gothard's bias can be devastating. He discourages marriage until the age of 30, the gynecological age where if a female has not already had a child she runs the risk statistically of infertility, miscarriage, and a host of possible congenital birth defects for her baby. Gothard is neither medically nor theologically qualified."

20 [IBYC], Seven Phases of a Godly Courtship, Advanced Training Seminar Manual (Oak Brook, IL: Institute in Basic Youth Conflicts [IBLP], 1984), pp. 157-164.

21 [IBLP], Establishing Biblical Standards of Courtship, p. 11.

22 Ibid., p. 16.

23 Allen, Gothard–Again, pp. 3-4.

24 [IBLP], Establishing Biblical Standards of Courtship, p. 8.

25 Ibid.

26 Ibid., p. 11.

27 Howard Grant, Best Friends for Life (Minneapolis, MN: Bethany House Publishers, 1997), p. 135.

28 Jonathan Lindvall, Training Godly Teens, (Springville, CA: Bold Christian Living, n.d.), audiocassette.

29 Allen, *Gothard–Again*, p. 2.

30 Bockelman, *Gothard–The Man and His Ministry: An Evaluation*, p. 74.

31 [IBLP], *Establishing Biblical Standards of Courtship*, p. 13. (Note: The idea of retroactive matrimony has more recently been popularized and elaborated on by Jonathan Lindvall. For a fuller elaboration on this, see Robin Phillips, "The Dating Game," *Midwest Christian Outreach, Inc. Journal*, vol. 6, no. 3 (Summer 2000.), pp. 4,5,10,11,12-14.

32 For example, we have friends who have moved here from India. After graduating college and beginning to work, each began to prepare for marriage. The father began looking at potential wives and chose their future spouses. They met a few days before the wedding.

33 Allen, *Gothard–Again*, p. 6.

34 Douglas Wilson, "Courtship Horror Stories," *Credenda Agenda*, vol. 9, no. 5 (1997), http://www.credenda.org/issues/9-5childer.php

35 Charlotte M. Mason, *Parents and Children*, Home Education Series, vol. 2 (London, England: Kegan, Paul, Trench, Trübner & Co., 1904), p. 17.

36 Ranald Macaulay and Jerram Barrs, *Christianity with a Human Face*, British Edition (Leicester, England: Inter-Varsity Press, 1979), p. 177.

37 Dennis McCallum and Gary DeLashmutt, *The Myth of Romance: Marriage Choices That Last A Lifetime* (Minneapolis, MN: Bethany House Publishers, 1996), p. 146.

38 Howard J. Clinebell, Jr., and Charlotte H Clinebell, *The Intimate Marriage* (New York, NY: Harper & Row Publishers, 1970), p. 113.

39 James Dobson, *Love For A Lifetime: Building A Marriage That Will Go The Distance* (Milton Keyenes, England: Word Publishing, 1987), p. 25.

40 Genesis 2:18 KJV.

41 C. S. Lewis, "The Four Loves" in *The Inspirational Writings of C. S. Lewis* (n.d.; compilation 4 books in one vol., New York, NY: Inspirational Press, 1960), p 279.

42 Isabel Tang, *Pornography: The Secret History of Civilization* (London: Channel 4 Books, an imprint of Macmillan Publishers, Ltd., 1999),

p. 46.

43 Susan Schaeffer Macaulay, *For the Family's Sake* (Wheaton, IL: Crossway Books, 1999), p. 34.

44 C. S. Lewis, "The Four Loves," pp. 278-9.

Chapter 10—Bill Gothard: Medicine Man

1 Romans 8:10-11 KJV.

2 William Dabney, M.D., letter to Don Veinot (Midwest Christian Outreach, Inc.), 12 April 2001, p. 1.

3 Ibid., p. 2.

4 Ibid., p. 3.

5 [MTIA], *How to Make Wise Medical Decisions*, Basic Care Booklet 1 (1990; Oak Brook, IL: Medical Training Institute of America [IBLP], rev. 1994), p. 2. "The Purpose of the Basic CARE Booklets." Emphasis in original.

6 Earl D. Radmacher, *Salvation*, Swindoll Leadership Library (Nashville, TN: Word Publishing, 2000), p. 82.

7 [MTIA], *How to Make Wise Medical Decisions*, p. 2.

8 Ibid.

9 Ibid.

10 Ibid.

11 Ibid.

12 Ibid.

13 [IBYC], Wisdom Booklet 17 – Preliminary Edition (1987; Printed in USA, Institute in Basic Youth Conflicts [IBLP], rev. 1988), p. 719.

14 [MTIA], *How to Make Wise Medical Decisions*, p. 6.

15 Ibid., p. 7.

16 Ibid.

17 Ibid., p. 14.

18 Ibid.

19 Carol Storm (Council Bluffs, IA), "How The Exit Of Trolls And

Dolls Was Followed By The Entrance Of Babies," *Basic Care Newsletter/ATIA Newsletter* (January 1996),p 3.

20 *Your Invitation to the Ministers' and Christian Leaders' Seminar*, IBLP advertisement, 2000, item 4.

21 Ibid.

22 Pastor Henry Wright, *A More Excellent Way: A Teaching on the Spiritual Roots of Disease* (Thomaston, GA: Pleasant Valley Publications, a division of Pleasant Valley Church, Inc., 1999), p. 94.

23 Ibid.

24 Ibid., pp. 12,43,57.

25 Ibid., p. 111.

26 Ibid., p. 122.

27 [MTIA], *How to Make Wise Medical Decisions*, p. 15.

28 Charles Caldwell Ryrie, Th.D., Ph.D., *The Ryrie Study Bible*, New American Standard Translation (1976; reprint, Chicago, IL: Moody Press, 1978), p. 1099.

29 [MTIA], *How to Discover the Rewards of Fasting*, Basic Care Bulletin 4 (1990; Oak Brook, IL: Medical Training Institute of America [IBLP], rev. 1991), p. 8.

30 [MTIA], *How to Make Wise Medical Decisions*, p. 15.

31 Ibid., p. 24.

32 [MTIA], *How to Discover the Rewards of Fasting*, p. 17.

33 Ibid., p. 24.

34 Ibid., p. 17.

35 Rev. G. Richard Fisher, "The Pentecostal Study Bible: Why Hasn't Anyone Said Anything About the Dangers of the Dake Bible?" *The Quarterly Journal of Personal Freedom Outreach*, vol. 12, no. 4 (October-December 1992), p. 8.

36 [MTIA], *How to Discover the Rewards of Fasting*, p. 18.

37 [MTIA], *How to Make Wise Decisions About Immunizations*, Basic Care Bulletin 17 (1990; Oak Brook, IL: Medical Training Institute of America [IBLP], rev. 1992), p. 26.

38 Ibid., p. 28.

39 Ibid.

40 William Dabney, op. cit., p. 2.

41 [MTIA], *How to Make Wise Medical Decisions*, Basic Care Booklet 1 (1990; Oak Brook, IL: Medical Training Institute of America [IBLP], rev. 1994), p. 16.

42 Ibid., p. 20.

43 Ibid., p. 21.

44 Ibid., p. 22.

45 Ibid.

46 e.g., see Francis Bacon, *The Essays*, (New York, Penguin Books, 1985). His essays make it clear that Bacon took great pains to base his worldview on Scripture.

47 [MTIA], *How to Greatly Reduce the Risk of Common Disease*, Basic Care Bulletin 2 (1990; Oak Brook, IL: Medical Training Institute of America [IBLP], rev. 1991), p. 21.

48 [MTIA], *The Vital Role of the Church in Wise Medical Decisions*, Basic Care Bulletin 3 (Oak Brook, IL: Medical Training Institute of America [IBLP], 1990), p. 2.

49 Ibid.

50 [MTIA], *The Vital Role of the Church in Wise Medical Decisions*, p. 2.

51 Ibid.

52 J. Vernon McGee, *Thru The Bible With J. Vernon McGee* (Nashville, TN: Thomas Nelson Publishers, 1983), p. 436.

53 Ryrie, *The Ryrie Study Bible*, p. 662.

54 [MTIA], *The Vital Role of the Church in Wise Medical Decisions*, p. 4.

55 Ibid., p. 5.

56 Ibid.

57 Ibid., p. 6.

58 Ibid., p. 7.

59 Ibid., p. 8.

60 Ibid.

61 Ibid., p. 9.

62 [MTIA], *How to Make Wise Decisions on Adoption*, Basic Care Booklet 5 (1990; Oak Brook, IL: Medical Training Institute of America [IBLP], rev. 1994), p. 28.

63 Pastor Henry Wright, *A More Excellent Way*, p. 12.

64 Ibid., p. 43. Italics in original.

65 Ibid., p. 57.

66 Exodus 20:5 & 6 KJV.

67 John D. Grassmick, "Mark," *The Bible Knowledge Commentary*, New Testament vol., eds. John F. Walvoord and Roy B. Zuck (Wheaton, IL: Victor Books, 1985), p. 138. Emphasis in original.

68 Charles H. Dyer, "Jeremiah," *The Bible Knowledge Commentary*, Old Testament vol., eds. John F. Walvoord and Roy B. Zuck (Wheaton, IL: Victor Books, 1985), p. 1134. Emphasis in original.

69 Earl D. Radmacher, *Salvation*, p. 60.

70 [MTIA], *How to Avoid Unnecessary Cesarean Section*, Basic Care Bulletin 7 (1990; Oak Brook, IL: Medical Training Institute of America [IBLP], rev. 1993), p. 2.

71 [MTIA], *How to Understand and Treat Morning Sickness*, Basic Care Bulletin 8 (Oak Brook, IL: Medical Training Institute of America [IBLP], 1990), p. 5.

72 Ibid., p. 6.

73. [MTIA], *How to Understand the Causes and the Management of Miscarriages*, Basic Care Bulletin 9 (1990; Oak Brook, IL: Medical Training Institute of America [IBLP], rev. 1991), p. 13.

74 Marty Butz, "Bill Gothard's Mystical Approach to Medical Issues," *Midwest Christian Outreach, Inc. Journal*, vol. 4, no. 4 (September/October 1998), p. 8.

75 IBLP publication order form.

Epilogue

1 Ewald von Kleist (German army officer and anti-Hitler conspirator) interviewed in the documentary TV series *The World at War*, series

produced by Jeremy Isaacs, segment producers: David Elstein, Peter Batty, Ted Childs, Martin Smith, Ben Shephard, John Pett, Phillip Whitehead, Michael Darlow, Hugh Raggett, and Jermome Kuehl, 26 one-hour segments, Thames Television, 1975.

2 Al Menconi, *Dear Mr. Gothard: A common sense response to criticisms of today's Christian music* (n.d.; reprint, San Marcos, CA: New Song Publishing, a division of Al Menconi Ministries, P.O. Box 5008, San Marcos, CA 92069-3621, 1995), p. 1.

3 Her story was told in chapter seven.

4 At the time of this writing, the web site was located at http://members.tripod.com/Glenwood37/homepage.htm.

5 Midwest Christian Outreach, Inc.

6 Personal Freedom Outreach.

7 Jerry Bridges, *Transforming Grace: Living Confidently in God's Unfailing Love* (Colorado Springs, CO: NavPress, 1991), pp. 16-17.

8 Ibid., p. 17.

9 Ibid.

10 Ibid.

11 Bill Gothard, letter to Midwest Christian Outreach, Inc., 25 October 1997, p. 1.

12 Bill Gothard, *The Sevenfold Power of First Century Churches and Homes* (Oak Brook, IL: Institute in Basic Life Principles, 2000), pp. 57-59.

13 Dr. Harry Adams, "Bill Gothard's Powerless Gospel," *Midwest Christian Outreach, Inc. Journal*, vol. 7, no. 1 (Winter 2001), p. 11.

14 Ibid.

15 Ibid.

16 Louis A. Barbieri, Jr., "Matthew," *The Bible Knowledge Commentary*, New Testament vol., eds. John F. Walvoord and Roy B. Zuck (Wheaton, IL: Victor Books, 1983), p. 30.

17 J. Vernon McGee, *Thru the Bible* (Nashville, TN: Thomas Nelson Publishers, 1983), p. 32.

18 Bill Gothard, *Definition of Grace* (Oak Brook, IL: Institute in Basic

Life Principles, 2000), p. 1.

19 Ibid., p. 3.

20 Steve Brown, *When Being Good Isn't Good Enough* (Nashville, TN: Thomas Nelson Publishers, 1990), pp. 26-27.

21 "The Thirty-Nine Articles of the Church of England, Article IX," with English style and spelling updated in the American Revision of 1801, in Philip and David S. Schaff, eds., *The Creeds of Christendom*, 6th ed., rev. by David S. Schaff, vol. 3 (1931; reprint, Grand Rapids, MI: Baker Book House, 1985), p. 493. The original was composed in Latin in 1563, with a now-archaic English translation following in 1571.

22 Chuck Swindoll, *The Grace Awakening* (Waco, TX: Word Publishing, 1990), p. xiii.

Scripture Index

Ministry Resources

Midwest Christian Outreach, Inc. (Main Office)
P. O. Box 455
Lombard, IL 60148-0455
Phone (630) 627-9028
E-Mail: info@midwestoutreach.org
Website: www.midwestoutreach.org

Midwest Christian Outreach, Inc. – Florida
3338 Landover Blvd.
Spring Hill, FL 34609-2619
Phone: (352) 684-4448
E-Mail: dgholson@atlantic.net

Midwest Christian Outreach, Inc. – North Carolina
1229 E. Council St
Salisbury, NC 28146
Phone: (704) 630-9379
E-Mail: gadfly7@aol.com

Midwest Christian Outreach, Inc. – Iowa
408 Main St.
Lohrville, IA 51453-1004
Phone: (712) 465-3010
E-Mail: mco@cal-net.net

Midwest Christian Outreach, Inc. – Kansas
P.O. Box 201
Scranton, KS 66537
Phone: (785) 793-2143
E-Mail: mcoscranton@usa.net

Personal Freedom Outreach
P.O. Box 26062
Saint Louis, MO. 63136
Phone: (314) 921-9800
Website: www.pfo.org

Personal Freedom Outreach – East
P.O. Box 514
Bricktown, NJ 08723-0514

Christian Research Institute
P.O. Box 7000
Rancho Santa Margarita, CA 92688-7000
Phone: (949) 858-6100
Website: www.equip.org

Watchman Fellowship – Texas
P.O. Box 13340
Arlington, TX 76094
Phone: (817) 277-0023
Website: www.watchman.org

Watchman Fellowship – Alabama
P.O. Box 530842
Birmingham, AL 35253-2858
Phone: (205) 871-2858

ARC
P.O. Box 531204
Birmingham, AL 35253
Phone: (205) 879-1616

MacGregor Ministries
P.O. Box 454
Metaline Falls, WA 99153-0454
Phone: (250) 352-5474
Website:

Reasoning From the Scriptures Ministries
P.O. Box 80087
Rancho Santa Margarita, CA 92688-0087
Phone: (949) 888-8848
Website: www.ronrhodes.org

Centers for Apologetics Research
P.O. Box 1196
San Juan Capistrano, CA 92693-1196
Phone: (949) 582-5890

Answers in Action
P.O. Box 2067
Costa Mesa, CA 92628-2067
(949) 646-9042
Website: http://answers.org

Wellspring
PO Box 67
Albany, OH 45710
Phone: 740/698-6277

National Association of Nouthetic Counselors
3600 W. 96th St
Indianapolis, IN 46268-2905
(317) 337-9100
Website: www.nanc.org